D1559842

THE WONDER CREW

THE
WONDER
CREW

*The Untold Story of a Coach,
Navy Rowing, and Olympic
Immortality*

SUSAN
SAINT SING

ST. MARTIN'S PRESS
NEW YORK

THE WONDER CREW. Copyright © 2008 by Susan Saint Sing. All rights reserved. Printed in the United States of America. For information, address St. Martin's Press, 175 Fifth Avenue, New York, N.Y. 10010.

www.stmartins.com

Library of Congress Cataloging-in-Publication Data

Saint Sing, Susan
    The wonder crew : the untold story of a coach, Navy rowing, and Olympic immortality / Susan Saint Sing.
        p.   cm.
    Includes bibliographical references.
    ISBN-13: 978-0-312-36703-9
    ISBN-10: 0-312-36703-1
    1. United States Naval Academy—Rowing—History.   2. Midshipmen—Maryland—Annapolis.   3. Glendon, Richard A., 1870–1956.   4. Rowing—Coaching.   5. Rowing—United States.   6. Olympic Games (7th : 1920 : Antwerp, Belgium)   I. Title.

GV796.S35   2008
797.12'3—dc22

                                                                    2008012728

First Edition: July 2008

10   9   8   7   6   5   4   3   2   1

To Bruce. Real love knows
no time, no distance, no circumstance.

CONTENTS

CONTENTS

ACKNOWLEDGMENTS

To the people who gave their time and effort and generosity of spirit and talent for this project, I am eternally grateful. To my agent, Joe Veltre, and to my editor, Marc Resnick, for believing in me and in this story.

To Murray Bodo, OFM, who helped me tirelessly with the writing, rewriting, and research for this book. To Duncan Glendon, grandson of Richard A. Glendon, who got the project started with his collection of memorabilia and photographs and who assisted throughout, and to all the descendants of the 1920 Olympic crews in England and the United States: Duncan and Eileen Glendon, Wayne Geehan and Sr. Mary of the Pure Heart, O. P. (Richard Glendon); David and Kevin Clark (Sherman Clark); Barbara and Bill Luscomb, Jon and Karen Luscomb, and Joe Milks (Vincent Gallagher); Oz, Ruth, and Josh Sanborn (Alden Sanborn); Mr. and Mrs. Michael Jordan, Michael and Christina Boldrich (Michael Jordan); Steve Woodall and Joe Carter (Donald Johnston); Tommy and Beverly Jacomini, Katherine Jacomini Master, and Janice Wichar (Victor Jacomini); Barbara Moore and Virginia (Edward Moore); Mr. and Mrs. David Swann, Peggy Swann, Sue Brock-Hollinshead (Sidney Swann). To John Melvin for Sherman Clark, and Jerry Denham and Alan Kirschbam for Clyde King. And Doug Hornsby for Eddie Graves.

To the folks at Leander Rowing Club: Caroline Mulcahy and Charles Barker; to U.S. rowing coaches Ted Nash, Bob Ernst, Mike Teti; boatbuilder Mike Vespoli; and Dwight Philips. To

Clete Graham, Commodore of the Schuylkill Navy; Hart Perry and the U.S. Rowing Museum at Mystic Seaport and Friends of Rowing History. To Michael Rowe of the River and Rowing Museum Henley-on-Thames; John Gartin—thanks for your understanding; Ginger Doyle; Bob Chambers, Commodore of the Annapolis Yacht Club, for allowing me to look at their archives; Lisa Teetor; researcher Stella Marinakos; Kyle and Rob Finley; Paula Hubby, my English connection in the States; and Officer Dennis Fritchie. To Kenny Dreyfus, U.S. National Rowing Team member and good friend. To Steve Murray for letting me view the "Glendon House," and to Betsy Evans for her help with Cape Cod.

To James Cheevers, Senior Curator of the U.S. Naval Academy Museum, for his wonderful input; Beverly Lyall of the Nimitz Library; Ric Clothier, Michael Hughes, Nicole Stimpson, Chris Allsop, and all the U.S. Naval Academy crew coaches; Gen. Terry Murray, U.S. Marine Corps; and Veronica Gibson and Donna Wickstrand of the Naval Academy Alumni Association, for your patience. To Capt. Bernard Warner and Officer Ned Tutton of RMS *QM2* for their accurate input on seamanship for the chapter "The Crossing."

To Deborah at the Maitland Public Library, William Fahthing at the Danville Public Library, Mrs. Rhinehardt and Lorna at the Grinnel Public Library, Dorrie La Londe at the Montezuma Public Library, and Michael at the University of Virginia Alumni Association. To Bill Mauro in Warrenton, Virginia, Matt at the Richardson Gaffney Funeral Home, Vicky Ginther, Reference Librarian at Faquier, Warrenton, Virginia, and Mark Mollan of the U.S. National Archives, Washington, D.C.

To professors: Bob Eckhardt, John Lucas, Betz Hanley, Nan Woodruff, and Scott Kretchmar for your patience with me during the initial research and doctoral examinations on this subject. And

ACKNOWLEDGMENTS

a special thanks to Greg Lauer, to Tom Moser for your generous help on the text, and to Michael Sipkoski for your skill at digital photography.

And to all the guys and women of my rowing crews over the years who gave me their personal experiences and trust to build upon. This is for you. . . .

AUTHOR'S NOTE

In trying to make the 1920 Olympics and the events surrounding it come alive, I have made every attempt to keep conversations true to the sport and the circumstances. If not actually said by a 1920 crew member, conversations are based on inferences and facts given to me by the descendants of the 1920 crews. When not cited, conversation is from actual rowers, rowing coaches, or rowing officials who shared their experiences and authenticity with me during my years of coaching and competition.

Susan Saint Sing, Ph.D.
1993 U.S. National Rowing Team

THE EIGHT-OARED SHELL

LENGTH — 58'   WEIGHT — 200 LBS.   TOP SPEED — 18 KNOTS   OARS AT THE FINISH

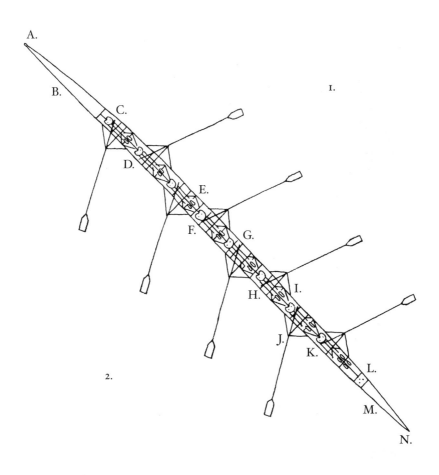

A. Bow Ball	H. Six Seat	1. Starboard
B. Bow Decking	I. Rigger	2. Port
C. Bow Seat	J. Seven's Oar	
D. Rigger	K. Stroke Seat	
E. Foot Stretcher	L. Coxswain Seat	
F. Four Seat	M. Stern Decking	
G. Gunwale	N. Rudder	

In the calm oily sea of a Chatham, Massachusetts, evening at low tide, 8 July 1956, Richard Alfred Glendon passed. Upon hearing the news, Admiral Chester Nimitz ordered that a message be sent out to the entire U.S. fleet throughout the globe that the greatest crew coach in the world had died. Nimitz ought to know: He was the stroke man for Glendon's 1904 crew.

THE WONDER CREW

INTRODUCTION

I have never heard anyone profess indifference to a boat race. Why should you row a boat race? Why endure long months of pain in preparation of a fierce half hour, or even six minutes, that will leave you all but dead? Does anyone ask the question? Is there anyone who would not go through all its costs, and more, for the moment when anguish breaks into triumph—or even for the glory of having nobly lost? Is life less than a boat race? If a man will give all the blood in his body to win the one, will he not spend all the might of his soul to prevail in the other?

—Justice Oliver Wendell Holmes, Jr.,
Yale University commencement, 1886

There were ten men on the Antwerp dock the day the Naval Academy won the 1920 Olympic gold medal. The coxswain, the stroke, and up through seats seven to bow—Gallagher, Johnston, Sanborn, Moore, Jordan, Graves, Jacomini—and, of course, their coach, Dick Glendon. What a moment it must have been as they laid hands on the hull and, at coxswain S. R. Clark's bark, lifted it, "Overhead, ready up!" And the Olympic shell rose even higher than its watery glory into the air, droplets streaming off, and then dropping down to the shoulders of the Olympians to be walked off, into the world away from Olympic records and cheering crowds. Their battle won, their point proven, the Naval Academy crew strode off the dock with Dick Glendon beaming with pride and clapping backs, shoulders, and the backs of heads in unabashed glee as his boys walked by. They had done it—beaten the unbeatable British—and they had done it together.

These young upstarts from Annapolis, not blue bloods from the great families of Harvard and Yale, but ordinary boys from across America, from Pasadena to Baltimore, groomed by a crusty old New England Salt named Richard Glendon, who was himself just the ordinary son of a fisherman, had dared to climb the sacred slopes of Mount Olympus to defeat its rowing god. The British had been rowing competitively since 1715, and the Americans defeated their composite Leander crew—considered the best crew Britain ever boated, meaning the best crew the world had seen in two hundred years—and they did it in world-record time in the Olympic Games.

While it would be improbable to claim that a single rowing coach created a style of rowing simply to influence nationalism, it would be feasible to say, based on historical evidence, that the performance of this one crew, this one event, affected nations. When the U.S. Naval Academy's eight-oared shell won the Olympic gold medal at Antwerp, Belgium, in 1920, rowing on two continents changed forever. Social prejudices were sliced through, class lines faltered, and the British were left to retreat—flattened back to the fluid surface like the tracings of blade puddles disappearing on still water.

One nation's pride swelled while the other nation grieved.[1] At 5:00 P.M. on 29 August 1920, in 6 minutes and 2 seconds (6:02), the

U.S. Naval Academy crew, racing in a unique style, exemplified a kinetic breakthrough, a startling new vision of human performance.[2] The 1920 Olympic victory of the Naval Academy seized the spirit of a sport traditionally attributed to the British, and stole it from the Empire by introducing a style of rowing uniquely American and uniquely Glendon.[3] Glendon's innovative style slashed race times and turned the heads of coaches all over the world.

Why? In our time this upset would be akin to the United States beating the Russian hockey team in the "Miracle on Ice." Or, because of the origins of the sport, the win is as unbelievable as Liechtenstein beating basketball's Dream Team. Basketball is an American invention, imitated worldwide with lineups and coaching staffs directly augmented with U.S. college coaches and players or those trained in U.S. methods. Similarly, rowing in 1920 was a British affair with racing shells, coaches, oars, and a stroke style "exported" directly or indirectly through British-trained protégés to colleges like Harvard and Yale. The rudiments of this story lie in the role played by the U.S. Naval Academy crew in severing sporting ties with the British rowing tradition, to produce an All-American Olympic team capable of beating the British in the premier sport of the day. No U.S. crew was strictly an American creation in boat, oars, and style until Glendon's came onto the scene. In the shadow of Harvard and Yale (using English-made boats and English-trained coaches who taught the English rowing style), Navy stalked their goal, a goal set in 1894 when a young Naval Academy midshipman, Capt. Winston Churchill (the American novelist of ironically the same name as the great English statesman), aspired to beat the British and urged the Academy

crews to master the art of rowing on a world scale.⁴ The mind-set
of the day was, if you wanted to excel and win, you had better be as
British as possible. That is, until the 1920 Naval Academy crew up-
ended the British in their own premier sport and in doing so, set
up a tour de force of the United States winning every Olympic
men's heavyweight eight race for the next forty years—the longest
streak. And the record still stands.

We tend to see the past through sepia-colored or black-and-
white prints, and we tend to think that the souls who peopled it
were that way, too; lacking. But it was as bright and gay and as
Technicolor as we are. Their story of the hunt for world supremacy
involves moxy with sweat and blistered hands, sunburned faces,
racing hearts, and toughness born in endless, cold, forlorn predawn
practices. It involves the intrigue of British rowing, the fledgling
Olympic Games, the blue-blood schools of Oxford and Cambridge, the famed Harvard and Yale race, early scullers and the issues of amateurism particularly as they pertained to American
sculler and fellow 1920 Olympian Jack Kelly (father of Princess
Grace of Monaco), British Royalty, and Hollywood. Their names
and accomplishments were heralded in ticker-tape parades in New
York City, their races attended by over 100,000 people were the
largest Olympic crowds to date, they were the guests of honor at a
dinner with the governor of New York at the Waldorf Astoria, they
headlined as "heroes" in the same sentence as Babe Ruth and Man
o' War.⁵ Glendon and his Wonder Crew altered the understanding,
the performance, the dynamics and forces of rowing forever. One
coach and nine men together advanced the sport of rowing into
the modern age of science over brawn. They began and paved the
way for the longest winning streak by any one nation in a single

event in the history of the Olympic Games and in doing so, advanced a nation.

AND IT ALL BEGAN ON THE SHORES OF A CONTInent that loved an underdog, rooted for the little guy, honored American initiative and Yankee ingenuity. It began when a young man named Glendon stepped off the decks of a mackerel schooner, walked away from the moors of Cape Cod and the cranberry bogs of his youth, and boarded the train for Boston. There he was to learn the ways of a poor Irish white kid filling in as a sparing partner to "Boston's Strong Boy," John L. Sullivan.[6] Through grit and fate he discovered he had a knack for coaching rowing, which he put to good use in Boston's upscale athletic clubs, and eventually to the graced lanes, wharfs, and mansard edifices of the "new" Naval Academy being constructed in Annapolis.

He arrived at the time when John Paul Jones's corpse, found in an unattended grave in a niche of a Paris cemetery in 1905, was exhumed and shipped in pomp and circumstance to eventually lie in state in a marble crypt beneath the New Chapel's dome, at a time when midshipmen saluted a nine-foot wooden statue of Tecumseh on a daily basis for the sake of tradition and duty and honor and glory; when the stars and stripes, battle plans, fate, and destiny were strategies to be learned and plotted on grids and maps, not accolades to be waited upon. It was a time and a place where presidents and dignitaries like Teddy Roosevelt and French ambassadors stepped out of newfangled automobiles with top hats and gold watch chains shining in the sun. It was a time and place to congratulate and educate and encourage bright young men like a shoeless Virginia lad named Edward Moore and a shoe-shine boy named Clyde King, both of whom would spit-shine themselves into dashing gentlemen and heroes. It was a time when admirals thanked rowing coaches for helping to win world wars.

The Academy, indeed the young country, went looking for its heroes and when they found them, loved them like gods—and it was a brief time in history when the likes of Richard Alfred Glendon and "his boys" walked among them. . . .

I. THE OLD MAN

Weakness? One's inability to succumb to passion. No one is willing to live or to die for a life of mediocrity.

—Patrick O'Dunne,
2007 Pan American Games rowing gold medalist

THE SEA. ALWAYS THE SEA. DICK GLENDON headed toward the smell of it, on this, his first night in Annapolis. As he walked along the harbor's pier at the end of Compromise Street, the cold damp January sleet coming off of it was no stranger to a Cape Codder like himself. It greeted him here on the west bank of the Chesapeake as it would welcome him home again when he returned to South Chatham, Massachusetts, when this—his first season as head coach of the U.S. Naval Academy crew—finished in June. The water, like cellophane folding in on itself, mirrored grays, violets, and blues in the fading light. He liked its mood. He felt he would come here often and think at the shore of the deep-water roots he learned his rowing craft from when just a boy. These would be his home waters now.

The wind sweeping in from the Atlantic—across the bay, past Thompson Point Shoal Light, up the Severn River and Spa Creek toward the boat sheds, across Franklin Street, to the Annapolitan Club, his home away from home—bit at his forehead, urging him to pull his round canvas cap down farther over his light brown hair. Secure in his thirty-four-year-old, five-foot-eleven-inch lithe frame, a light scrub of neatly trimmed beard and piercing blue eyes, he walked forward in anticipation, to think, to plan, to analyze—rowing.

"Evening, coach. How does the crew look?" a total stranger asked, recognizing him from his picture in the January 1904, *Annapolitan Chronicle* article that ran that morning. It was a question Glendon would hear a thousand times more in his seventeen years at Navy.

It was a question he would never tire of, one that would mingle with the cheers of 1920 Olympic crowds, letters of congratulations from Fleet Admirals, the voices of presidents, ambassadors, and movie stars in this, the cresting of his young adulthood. It was a question that would later echo with the cries of a grandson lost at sea, a son shot and killed in a hunting accident, memories—heroic, mythic, and tragic—that would mingle with the trophies in the rooms of his old age, where he sat legless in a wheelchair until his death in 1956.

How does the crew look?

It was the fundamental question.

"Not sure yet," was his response this night in a tenor voice. "Haven't even seen the boys yet," he quipped as the footsteps of the two men separated one from another in the darkness.

No, he *wasn't* sure of the crew yet, but on this night he was certain of himself and his abilities. He held a great passion for all things water. It had him. Little did he know that on it and through its currents, the adventure of a lifetime—the longest Olympic winning streak—had already begun. . . .

BORN 14 APRIL 1870, NEAR THE OCEAN ON CAPE Cod, in Harwich, Massachusetts, Richard "Dick" Glendon was the son of a fisherman. His family, the Richard Alfred Glendons, were from the west coast of Ireland. Leaving Ireland in the mid-1800s, the family settled in Nova Scotia. Richard A. Glendon, married to Alice McNulty, came to the United States from Nova Scotia in the 1860s. They had five children: Thomas, Mary, Richard, Alice, and John.[1] The middle child, Richard "Dick" Glendon, was destined to be an Olympic coach.

There is some family lore relating the Glendon ancestry to Scottish and English roots, which shows up in print in several newspaper clippings. But family genealogy records place the family in Ireland, emigrating over the North Atlantic to the United States at a time when Irish immigrants were considered lowlier than a good slave.[2] It is as if the family lore was altered in order to make a better life for the new American Glendons settling near Boston.

After attending Brook Academy in Harwich Center, young Dick went to sea at age thirteen, following in the footsteps of his father and family.[3] Working in the waters of the North Atlantic fishing grounds, he acquired hands-on watermanship skills that would shape the basis of his scientific oarsmanship in years to come. Here among a plethora of practical, commonsense, yet intricate things, he learned to gently rock compasses back and forth while filling them with oil to keep the air bubbles out, learned to adjust a boat's course to magnetic variance, learned how to hold a heading in the tide and wind, and how to feel the touch of the rudder in correction so as not to oversteer the wheel.

The decks of mackerel schooners, fishing piers stinking of herring and cod, harbor seals breaking surface with curious wet eyes, mooring balls steered up to with an effortless elegance by seasoned sailors, quahogs, and all types of ships, dories, and gigs—these were the images that filled his childhood days. On the Cape, where the family's white wooden homestead sat surrounded by sea grass and wind, the horizon of Dick's formative years was dotted with white sails, hulls, and seabirds. He learned the names of the types of ships by watching and counting masts and sail configurations further explained by his father.

His father was a man he honored for his courage and for the knowledge that the sea had given. The sea had taken him beyond Monomoy Point, beyond Great Point Light at Nantucket, to the deep and back. Dick's father introduced him to sea captains and fellow fishermen, and was proud of the young boy whose blue eyes watched intently and whose manner and innate sense of perception and depth led him to listen before replying to a question. This quality of reticence, perhaps learned from the hours at sea, perhaps learned from a father trying to teach him and give him both the knowledge and the joy of the sea, shaped the boy's character. His brow carried a line of tiny hair bleached white on the ruddy suntanned skin, and his flash of blue eyes twinkled as if part of and from the sea itself. So impressed would others be of the young Glendon, that a sea captain would one day give the boy a rough-cut pendant of green jade that he would keep as a watch fob forever. His father's world was mysterious, manly, ancient, and dangerous. Courage and character followed Glendon from the decks of the schooner, to the wharfs of Boston, to the boat sheds of his destiny.

HE TOOK PRIDE IN WHAT HE LEARNED FROM HIS father: A sloop had only one mast, one triangular mainsail, a jib, and perhaps a genoa. A boat with two masts, with the front mast higher than the one more sternward, and the position of the rear mast more aft than the helm, would differentiate it still as being a yawl. The aft mast being before the helm made it a ketch. Schooners had two masts also, but their graceful lines pleased the eye with the aft mast being taller than the bow-ward one. They were set with lines that held the entire ship's rigging aloft from stern to bow and starboard to port some 60 to 90 feet in the air; the skyward spiderweb of halyards, blocks and tackle, booms, masts, gollywoblers, spinnakers, and all manner of sail configurations were learned by young men on the Cape as easily as the rules of stickball were learned by young boys growing up on city streets. The sands and rolling grassy knolls of Nantucket, the Vineyard's cliffs, lightships, and lighthouses marking safe passage, the caws of terns and gulls, dirt roads, fog, sun, and weather of the windswept "elbow" of Cape Cod were his environs. They made the landscapes and seascapes of his soul.

From playing with small wooden homemade boats in puddles and tidal pools when he was a young child, to the first deck he walked upon, Richard "Dick" Glendon was learning the skills that would so deeply capture his imagination, his creativity, his musings, his dreams. Fish and boats and the men, the sounds, the sights of the fleets became so much a part of his nature that as he grew—there was no longer a beginning or an end to them. He no longer differentiated between what was the thrill of his first time in a boat pushing off the beach, rolling up over the waves, or being pushed back in by them in a following sea. The rocks, shoals, and ledges were slowly but surely etching their lines into the layers and fabric of his consciousness. Like Melville, his Harvard and his Yale were the decks of sailing ships—specifically the decks of a mackerel schooner—where following in the footsteps of his father and grandfather, and in the heritage of young boys who begged to go to sea, Dick Glendon sailed beyond the horizon line of sight in pursuit of elusive red schools of Atlantic mackerel.

He fished the Grand Banks and the Georges. He fished off of Grand Manan Island, New Brunswick, Canada, another country, another time zone—Atlantic Time. There is no other time there, no other name for the time there. There couldn't be—nor should there be. The place is of and one with the North Atlantic.

The North Atlantic. An entirely different ocean altogether from the southern latitude seas. As he left the Cape and his tiny Cape-side town of Harwich, heading north toward 44.7 degrees north latitude—nearly halfway to the North Pole—the moving tides, some reaching an extraordinary world-record 28 feet, would growl up the shingles, churning steadily toward the footpaths in front of cottage and cabin doors on the islands they'd pass. He'd watch securely from his midnight perch at the helm as a puffin flew by, or a whale breaking surface in the distance exhaled with a slight stench of fish that the discerning nose could recognize on a wafting breeze as they made an inside passage through Seal Cove to offload mackerel for salting and drying.

The black-green North Atlantic, whose slimy broad-leafed black kelp and temperatures of 55 degrees in summer do not invite even the bravest foot to frolic, he could distinguish easily from the diaphanous blue water of the beaches on southern Cape Cod. Glendon experienced seas of starry black liquid marble, calm enough to let moonlight skitter off it for a hundred miles—or at least as far as Nova Scotia, which could be seen in the rarified atmosphere. The breeze, a "Canadian high" ratified the air, making room in the sky for the moon and stars, pushing the weeklong fog bank away, back to sea, to the North Atlantic somewhere eastward, to the Georges Bank or perhaps farther still to the Grand Banks—those watery, infamous, fluidly defined regions of the planet reserved for currents, fishermen, whales, swordfish, cod, and folklore abundant.

Glendon sailed briefly on a whaling ship off Newfoundland where he studied nautical charts and learned the fathoms and meters of the bottom-world below. A young man who loved nature, he undoubtedly sat and stared into the moonlight at sea, for at Cape Cod, or 1,500 miles away on the Grand Banks, the moonlight would have been commensurately mesmerizing and dreamlike.

At the turn of the twentieth century, fishing reports on the North Atlantic fishing grounds were read by New Englanders the way other parts of America might follow batting averages. Its economy was based on barrels sold (sized by number one, two, three, four, with one being the biggest and four the smallest). A mackerel schooner that could bring back thousands of pounds of fish—sorted, barreled, and ready for the East Docks of Boston—was the preoccupation of the families, the crew, and the owners of the boats that risked their lives at sea in order for the well-to-do to dine in New York City, Philadelphia, and Washington, D.C. Where the fish schools were last seen by the masthead lookout, and which direction they were headed were daily set in newsprint. The price of the fish, which captains were sailing what ships, the weather "out there"—gales, squalls, seas, injuries, disasters, successes—flooded columns of the *Harwich Independent,* roiling or calming the shoreside anxieties of those who waited for the fishermen's return.

On land, some waited for money; some waited for loved ones. On board, some waited to reach the fishing grounds because it was only there among the walls and floorboards of air and water that they felt at home. Others waited only to hear the words, "Launch the boat!" so they could scramble into the seine boats, set their nets as generations had done for centuries before them, to set out, drop, pull in, and catch—fish.

Waiting was as integral to fishing as catching was. Dick Glendon spent hours, days, and weeks waiting. It was within those parameters of time spent, of watching and learning the skills of seamanship, that his greatest gift, his biggest prize of "fish," was being indelibly written in the sinews of his young body pulling on oars against tides, current, and net—filling the gray matter of his brain with possibilities, curiosities, and lessons hard learned of how to move a boat quickly through water. The schools of mackerel that shone red beneath the surface were his prey—for now.

Fast, sleek, elegant fish and the boats that sought them amalgamated to form a dynamic in Glendon's soul. As one of the eight boys rowing the dory—a 30-ish-foot-long wooden boat with a puller in the bow to retrieve the net, a helmsmen to steer, a setter to let the net out, and eight oarsmen seated two abreast on four seats— Glendon, with every set of the blade, every stroke and strain of his shoulders against saltwater, was gaining the empirical knowledge of how to maneuver a rowing boat.

Mackerel fishing involved dragging the top line of the seine laden with cork, its 400 feet of net coiled loosely yet precisely in the waist of the seine boat ready to drop into the sea, only to be pulled tight by weights on the bottom of the "purse" and by hands at the top. Only then did the diving mackerel get stilled, caught in the maelstrom of a school of living, breathing creatures thrown to the deck of a schooner to be butchered and sold. Glendon learned the inevitable—survival depended on the strength *and* the gentleness of his being. It depended on his ability to concentrate *yet* to not close his vision to the subtleties around him, and perhaps most important of all, to bury nothing in the depths of the sea to become like the carcasses and entrails thrown from the decks for chum and toll bait. His life, his world, would be the surface world. With an artist's soul, he loved the beauty of the seascape more than what was dragged from its bowels.

At age sixteen, Glendon, already a weathered seaman, left the decks of the schooner where he had gained an arsenal of practical nautical information and skill, and walked through Boston's East Docks to his uncle's boatworks on the Charles River, wanting to work near the wharfs and water he loved. Intrigued with the sport of rowing seen all around him and from his years of plying his oars in the dory, he took to a shell and discovered he was a natural sculler. Soon he was mingling with coaches, rowers, and boatmen at the nearby Boston Athletic Association's floating boathouse. Adept at anything to do with a rowing shell, he had found a niche. He knew this blend of water and boats was meant for him. Quick to acknowledge his practical roots, Glendon, when positioning himself for a coaching job, spoke of himself as "different from other rowing teachers in one thing: He came to his profession by way of deep water."[4]

He had indeed.

Starting at the bottom and working his way through various jobs, the tough young Irishman even took a few rounds as the sparring partner for John L. Sullivan, resulting in the blinding of Glendon's right eye, a condition he kept to himself and few others.[5] But being a natural at rowing and all things water, he found his niche in the rowing world and continued up the ropes of crew ranks rapidly, gaining success and respect in Boston's blizzard of rowing opportunities. He made a name for himself and his crews coaching a consortium of schools in the Boston Athletic Association schoolboy's program. The Boston Athletic Association was one of the oldest athletic clubs in the nation. Its objective was to "promote manly sports and encourage physical culture" among the finest prep schools, colleges, and well-heeled politicians and professionals of the area, and Glendon's being a part of it was no small miracle.[6] Well liked and with all the highly specific "hands-on" tools necessary, both figuratively and literally, to coach, row, and repair any boat or shell, Dick Glendon by age eighteen was considered one of the best and youngest professional rowing coaches in the nation.

The prestigious *Noble and Greenough Academy*'s bulletin stated their pride and confidence in the young Glendon, noting that he had "complete charge of the coaching, taking different crews at stated hours."[7] Between 1892 and 1893, as a coach and trainer of the highly competitive Boston Athletic Association, Glendon received much press coverage in the *Boston Daily Globe* and the *Boston Evening Record*. One article stated that he is "by long odds the youngest professional coach in the country." The same article renders him "quick to grasp an idea" with "just enough professionalism in his make-up which, together with his experience for the past three years with college oarsmen makes him almost indispensable. . . ." In another article, a glimpse into Glendon's genius is recognized; he is touted as "valuable to the club because he coaches differently."[8]

Boston sportswriter Bob Guild recounts when Glendon taught him how to row. He reminisced about the good old days when Glendon coached from a single scull—keeping up effortlessly with a four—or coaching from the coxswain's seat. Guild tells of Glendon overseeing and having his boats built in Cambridgeport.[9]

Other indications of Glendon's thinking in his formative days as a young coach appear in a comprehensive article about "Schoolboy Oarsmen" in Boston, which explained, "Coach Glendon was supreme in power in the direction of the work of the boys . . . in the first stages of the coaching, Glendon put the boys through a very careful drill, and devoted a good deal of time to the rowing machine in the clubhouse." And, "the candidates (chosen) were the largest and strongest boys of each school."[10]

He was credited with coaching Jim Shea, who won the National Junior Championship on the Charles in 1891.[11] His schoolboy fours and eights from Boston Latin, Noble, and Roxbury fed the crews of Harvard. And an article of that year outlines Glendon's initiative and progressive ideas in changing the old system:

> . . . having held several informal talks on rowing matters, and as a result there has been a complete change in the rowing system in vogue at the club for several years. Heretofore the crew candidates have been called to the gym and put to work on the rowing machines prior to the opening of the season on the water, but this spring they will be taken to the water and lumbering up in pairs, singles, and four-oared gigs. There appears to be excellent reason for this innovation. Heretofore the candidates on taking to the water felt reasonably sure of their seat in the eight, and if it were not forthcoming, they lost interest in their work. Under the present system a man will have to prove his right to a seat by showing form in pairs, and fours . . ."[12]

These early articles give hints of his initial training ideas that soon followed him to the apex of his rowing career at Navy. One such regimen was his decision as a trainer to "keep the men on body work" before they do any blade work whatsoever. This dovetails with the interview on his first day at work at Annapolis and his lifelong commitment to strong, well-built crews who knew their way around the inside of a weight room. He designed indoor rowing machines and indoor tanks for Navy that he felt was cutting-edge technology for building bodies as well as rowing technique.[13]

Rowing shells have no keel and therefore are particularly susceptible to drifting sideways in wind or choppy conditions. Glendon read the weather by smelling it, by feeling it on his cheeks, by sensing the direction of the wind across the surf, the time of the tide. His experience with water led him, and he had long ago learned to trust his intuition regarding it. He undoubtedly told his crews truisms he'd learned from fathers and uncles, particularly to his coxswains— for example, that anyone who wasn't afraid of water hadn't been out far enough or long enough. He was a man of few words but he spoke words his crew strained not to miss a syllable of.

Glendon was a formidable and beloved coach in Boston. In his eighteen years at the Boston Athletic Club he progressed rapidly and successfully in the stiff competition of the schoolboy ranks to the national limelight. It was during this time he met and married Mary Wynn and started a family. When Glendon gained an entry interview to take on the head coaching position at the U.S. Naval Academy, his decision to leave Boston hit the headlines.

Perhaps aiding his decision, the winter of 1904 had been a bad one. A late-season hurricane ripped up across the Atlantic Coast from the low country of the Carolinas to Cape Cod, leaving a vulnerable feeling in its wake. The record-breaking −46 degree cold in upper New York State settled across New England like a frozen blanket.[14] Out of this hard winter and the sweeping winds of the North Atlantic, Richard Glendon decided to leave the frozen bowels of the Charles River in Boston and turn his sights south—to the Chesapeake, to accept the invitation to be head coach at the U.S. Naval Academy. When Glendon boarded the train after spending

Christmas with his wife, Mary, and children, he was heading into history.

ON THIS THE VERY FIRST EVENING OF HIS FIRST day at Annapolis, like a sailing ship tacking back and forth across the prevailing wind of his life and night's thoughts, he was preoccupied with making headway. He wanted to meet "his boys." Arranging for a meeting of the crew the morning of the very next day, Glendon tried to visualize the crew out in the boats on the harbor, making their way steadily, solidly into the wind. He was already proud of them though he knew they would, at first, be unsure of him and of themselves. He would read the anticipation in some of their eyes and remember those boys in particular. He longed for the morning hours when he would see them and they him.

A master at reading potential, like a horse trainer summing up speed in the withers and the long smooth feel up a horse's legs and knees, Glendon knew what he wanted, knew what it took to make boats go fast while turning young boys into men. Oarsmen.

ACROSS THE UNITED STATES FROM PASADENA TO the Bronx another set of oarsmen were beginning their journey into Glendon's crucible of rowing. Names like Clark, Graves, Jacomini, Moore—names of strength and character that one day would be shouted from Olympic megaphones and broadcast across telegraph wires: Eddie, Johnny, Alden, and Vinny. These young boys, unbeknownst to them or their families, except in the quiet dreams and expectations of their proud fathers and doting mothers, were already on an intersecting course with destiny.

For the next few years as Glendon honed crews and hosted regattas on the Severn River in Annapolis, putting polish on a program considered outside the "real" rowing realm of the blue bloods of Harvard, Yale, Penn, and Cornell, the Navy "boys" were growing up, strengthening, learning life skills they didn't even know Glendon would tap into and pull out of them. America was in a state of flux. The country was bursting at its seams with expectations, fortunes being made, the future being sold as an endless horizon of opportunity—and everyone was buying it. It was a time of innocence.

The boys, the future crew of 1920, were "out there," waiting, with Glendon already waiting for them. Finally the waiting of his fishing years was paying off: He had grown wise in patience. He would wait. They were his elusive school of fish that he knew was out there and was confident he would capture on a "some day" that had not yet come. In the meanwhile, he would stitch his seams, as he had learned long ago at sail lofts and idle time made useful repairing threadbare jibs and genoas on a mackerel schooner that still swayed inside the balance of his being. He would sew one stroke at a time, one crew, one race, one season, one year until, in the trueness of well-tied knots and accurate skill, his well-made sails would begin to converge, from around the nation and the world, to take a bearing on Annapolis.

2. A CORPSE, AN OLYMPICS, AND A MIDSHIPMAN NAMED NIMITZ

Of all sports, I think rowing is the greatest. The big crowds and the joy of personal contact bring big thrills in football, but rowing is the greatest because it is a man's game in every sense of the word.

—Admiral Clyde Whitlock King, 1920 Navy stroke man

ANNAPOLIS WAS ABUZZ WITH RECONSTRUCTION. The Academy was in the midst of a makeover, 1904 was a time of flux and great changes were on the horizon. At long last, and after much deliberation, money from the nation's tax coffers had been allotted to erect a Naval Academy worthy of the U.S. Navy.

The Academy is built on a point between Spa Creek, College Creek, and the Severn River, a place which housed an Army fort in frontier days to monitor trade and travel on the southwestern shore of the Chesapeake. The fort was taken over by the Navy due to its magnificent, strategic waterfront location. At the outbreak of the Civil War, seeking to protect its fledgling Navy war school, the cadets and the school were moved to Newport, Rhode Island, and the base converted back into a Union Army fort. After the war ended, the base was in shambles, necessitating that the old fort and grounds be razed. A procession of building began, generating much interest over the next half a century. The new compound construction and architecture rivaled the granite edifices of nearby Washington, D.C., complete with the glamour and rigor of a modern military installation worthy of the heritage of Admiralty and the sea. The new addition of a domed chapel and dormitories like majestic Bancroft Hall—slated to bunk the entire brigade of one thousand midshipmen—with curved stairways clad in marble, slowly but steadily transformed the round and rustic area of Old Fort Severn right before Glendon's eyes.[1]

It was an exciting time and his new ideas and fresh face on rowing fit right in with all the other changes on campus. He wasn't so concerned about winning, not yet; what he wanted was excellence. He was in pursuit of the ancient, elusive *arêté*, the ancient Greek pinnacle of perfection, strength in grace of physical, mental, and spiritual balance. He would demand it of himself and his crew. At the first crew call-out eighty men reported and stood in front of the highly touted new coach. Among them was the makeshift crew of twenty-two first and second varsity rowers he inherited and was hired to whip into competitive shape. Glendon surmised and assessed the youth assembled before him—and God, how he loved each and every one of them. Notable among them was the young stroke man of the class of '05, Chester Nimitz.

Looking for sinewy types in the 170 to 180-pound range, tall, with a hint of athletic ability, Glendon saw arranged before him a young assortment of sizes and shapes that he would cull into a crew. Untanned faces, not yet stung with early spring practice rain on the Severn River, looked into his eyes and were sizing him up as was he them as crew and coach toed up man to man to see if the fit was right.

The 1904 crew he inherited consisted of two eights. The existent first varsity was made up of: Rodgers, Smyth, Todd, crew captain H. H. Michael, Farley, Goss, Laird, Court, Battle, Fitch, and coxswain Hart, with H. E. Kimmel as manager. The second varsity consisted of Nimitz, Marston, Coman, Jensen, Reichmuth, Taffinder, Root, Bartlett, and coxswain B. H. Green.[2] He called out each of the experienced rowers first, having them step forward, yet said nothing but gave an acknowledgement with the nod of his head and eyes as he continued to look them over.

He sent them out for a short warm-up run around him—like horses in a ring—and watched as they ran, asking himself who was taking the lead, who was dogging it? And after a time Glendon chose one on qualities of leadership as yet unproven, but that he intuited existed in this young man on the second varsity named Chester. Glendon put his hand on the hard shoulder of the fair-haired young man and said, "I don't know who you are but it seems you have the quality of a leader about you" and at that, Chester Nimitz became stroke oar in 1904, for Glendon's first Naval Academy eight.[3]

LITTLE DID ANY OF THESE ROWERS KNOW THAT stories of Glendon's impact on the Academy's crews—the strength of their mettle, the types of men crew turned out at Navy over the years—would shower the press for decades, particularly as the Navy middies grew to public stature as industrialists and World War II heroes.

"Fleet Admiral Chester W. Nimitz, who at the height of the Pacific war commanded over two million men and women, 5,000 ships, and 20,000 planes, was of humble and landlocked beginnings. Hoping for an appointment to West Point but offered a chance for an education at

Annapolis instead, young Chester studied early mornings and late evenings around his schoolwork and chores to prepare for the three-day Annapolis examination. His self-discipline paid off as he was accepted to Annapolis in 1901 at age 15 before completing high school. Because of the need for junior officers in Theodore Roosevelt's expanding Navy, the Admiral's class was graduated ahead of schedule on 30 January 1905, with Chester Nimitz seventh in the class of 114."[4] Through World War II, Glendon, and how the crew was doing in general, was of great interest to the larger Navy, more so than any other sport.[5]

On this day in 1904 little did they know that forty years later a World War II article would state:

> Navy's varsity crew has an unusual opportunity not only to sweep through to an undefeated season . . . but in doing so to bring more than a cheer to the lips of two old Navy Oarsmen who have proved in the few months since Pearl Harbor that they learned not only to be good crew men but good fighting men as well under the teaching of Old Dick Glendon. These two former pupils are Admiral Chester W. Nimitz and Rear Admiral Francis Rockwell, who was in Manila with Gen. MacArthur and journeyed from Bataan to Australia with him on their epic trip. Both Admirals Nimitz and Rockwell pulled in varsity boats under the elder Glendon during twenty years and more as head coach at the naval academy and both were outstanding oarsmen.
>
> Admiral Nimitz rowed in the days before Navy crews were permitted to leave the Academy and he was stroke oar of the 1905 varsity eight, one of the best crews the Navy ever had.
>
> Rockwell, known to his mates as Skinny, a nickname that

has stuck to him ever since, followed Nimitz to the academy. Rockwell was in the 1907 eight stroked by Ingram.

Glendon recalls Nimitz as a serious kid who would plot out for days ahead of time how he would stroke each race. Glendon says, "He was one of the best stroke oars I ever had. Had instincts for how hard to press and when to put the pressure on, a brainy stroke.

"Rockwell," Glendon says, "came back to the Academy on different times for numerous details, he was Director of Athletics, and crew representative—didn't surprise me that Rockwell made it to Australia with MacArthur. He visited me on the Cape before he left for the Philippines last fall, but had no idea what he was heading in to."[6]

And so it began. Nimitz was one. Around this stroke man Glendon now had to first build a crew, then a team, and finally, a program. Glendon picked his boys carefully, studied them, watched their reactions to downpours, rough water, near collisions, injury, and correction. Be it war with blades on the water or war with cannon shot above them, these young men were here to be trained as warriors. It wasn't just a matter of who among them was best. The individuals were less important than the whole—the brigade was the focus, not any one standout. No war was ever won with only one man. Though a brigade would follow a leader of one, that one needed a brigade to follow him. So, too, in rowing. The fundamental question was always "How did the *crew* look?" And the crew was not just each man in a seat; it was eight men rowing as one. The boat and the crew at large were a unit, the gestalt was the final equation, not the individual parts. In rowing truly the whole is greater than the sum of the parts.

A good man on a rowing machine, in training on land or in a

weight room, might not help a boat go fast. And that is the art of coaching, Glendon's artful ability to form a unit, a picture of grace and beauty, in strength. His boys and their boat were one with only one quest—to go fast in a straight line in pursuit of excellence. Let the medals fall where they may, pursuing elusive *arêté* would ensure a good day's row. When his boys put the boat on the boat-shed rack at night, they walked away knowing at least one thing if nothing else: The man who coached them knew them better than they knew themselves. He was the orderer of their chaos. His boys were beginning to reflect him as well as one another, and on this day in the waning days of 1905 with the pale, cold afternoon sun reflecting on the hull as it slid by, with the water glistening beneath them framing the Academy building and grounds, how proud he was of them, and how he loved them for it.

BY 1906, WHEN JOHN PAUL JONES'S BODY FINALLY came to rest at the Naval Academy, it was a bright clear April day. Dick Glendon strode with anticipation down the steps of his boarding house, the Annapolitan Club, around Church and State circles, to the main gate off King George Street amid a sea of dignitaries, midshipmen, and people. Having his first season under his belt and heading into the second, his confidence was growing—Glendon was in the right time at the right place. The New Chapel with its copper dome was to be eventually the final resting site of Jones's traveling corpse returned from an unmarked French grave with great fanfare; the central section of Bancroft Hall was a shimmering masterpiece, and would be the temporary crypt of the returned war hero until the final resting place was finished. New science and academic classrooms were being erected—it was the scientific era of more classrooms for weaponry, physics, mathematics, etc. Everything around Glendon was being beefed up, and the excitement, the rapture in the air was captivating and tangible. He smelled it, recognized it, wanted it. It was already infectious. Crowds like these with presidents' and diplomats' voices echoing over loudspeakers stirred something deep within the environs of his soul. He stopped and looked out across the length of the Yard to the water's edge. Not wanting the moment to pass, he took it all in, hoping to captivate it, internalize it, and gain in strength and stature from its presence. He took a deep breath, inhaled long and steady and held it there, closed his eyes, and during the funeral liturgy *he* said a prayer to the water gods. Spring racing was here. Georgetown came first and then Penn, Yale, and Columbia.

They did well. Winning came easily to Glendon, and the Academy approved. Taciturn by nature, being a New Englander, Glendon had a way with the boys. Unlike most other coaches, he carried his megaphone more or less for decorative purposes. He could be seen carrying it in the launch boat, leaning against it, keeping it handy, in case, but never picking it up for ten to twelve miles on the river. He was also known to look away from the crew for long stretches after studying them intently, but then never saying a word of correction to even the most egregious error like rushing the slide. But once back to the boathouse, he'd "take one man aside, and then another, and talk quietly to them. Then after the training table at dinner, he would talk with them individually again. He'd say, 'You were doing pretty well today but I wish you'd remember about that slide. Think about it tonight and tomorrow. If you can only get that smoothed out you'll be a good oarsman.'"[7] His gentlemanly fashion of concern and personal attention built confidence, and the midshipmen responded to it.

As the Academy grew and became more scientifically oriented, Glendon and his ever-present boatman, Chandler, took advantage of the scientists and laboratories to test Glendon's theories about water speed and hull design and resistance.[8] As the Academy changed its face to the world, so was the face of sports changing worldwide. . . .

IN THE SAME YEAR THAT GLENDON BEGAN COACH-ing at Navy, a gathering of sportsmen met in St. Louis to celebrate the World Exposition and Olympiad. This Third Olympiad was the brainchild of Baron de Coubertin, who revived Olympism with the Modern Olympic Games in Athens in 1896, followed in 1900 in Paris, now in St. Louis, and in four more years, 1908 in London, with the rowing events to be held at the legendary Henley Royal Regatta course, the British on their home waters.

Glendon felt he knew the British only too well. The most prestigious rowing club in the world was the Leander Rowing Club at Henley. Sportswriter Harry Cross revealed that Glendon had a secret ambition, from the early days, of beating Leander. Cross tells of a young Richard Glendon around the turn of the century, meeting the great Leander coach, Rudy Lehmann, who was in the United States, coaching the Harvard crews. Lehmann overheard Glendon saying that he felt Yale would beat the Harvard crew, and Lehmann summarily dismissed Glendon about offering the "the opinion of a novice."[9]

Glendon never forgot Lehmann's reproach, but his turn to race the best of the best was not at this time—not yet. Meanwhile, he honed his program year after year building rowing tanks, setting dietary concerns for the training table, studying speed and flotation, observing momentum, experimenting with blade and boat design. It is the collective combination of vision and manpower that elevate single bodies into the common greatness of a crew. How great this crew would be, and the effects of that greatness were only beginning. Glendon saw the possibilities coming together. Every nuance of rowing he considered and weighed. He analyzed the stroke, the boat, the men.

The racing world of rowing was in an exciting state of flux, too, developing and advancing as the newly revived modern Olympic Games butted heads with the long-established status quo of dual meets between Harvard and Yale, the Henley Royal Regatta, New England stuffiness, and the vast Victorian-era racing protocol that draped the sport in tradition not likely to change easily.

Baron de Coubertin, founder of the Modern Olympic Games, was himself a rower.[10] As he had done with most of the British sports, he included rowing in the first modern Olympic Games in 1896.[11] Ever the Anglophile, he saw rowing as "the most complete sport that one could imagine."[12] But the earliest Olympic races did not go smoothly. The inaugural Olympic boat race in 1896, an exhibition of eights only—no singles, doubles, pairs, or fours—was canceled because of bad weather.[13] In 1900 and in 1904, as exhibition sports linked to giant World Expositions of art and culture, the crew races encountered dubious timing practices and lacked a qualified international field. For example, Vesper Boat Club of Philadelphia won the 1900 Paris race but no multi-oared British boat was even present.[14] This would be like having a baseball play-off and the dominant New York Yankees of the 1920s not showing up. These problems alarmed

Baron de Coubertin because he wanted to see the Games thrive and not falter.[15] Similarly, the 1904 Games held in St. Louis were not attended by the British or the French and, therefore, the British hauteur in the sport continued to reign supreme.

The logistics of transporting eights (which are over sixty feet long) necessitated borrowing boats, a practice that deterred some countries from travel—as still happens today. But by 1908 and 1912, the Olympics were truly representative in both the categories of boats and the international character of the field. And, as expected, British crews dominated the racing.[16] Overall, as an Olympic event, the early years were a mixture of racing styles, boats, events, and venues. But one truth could be seen clearly by all: Rowing was without question a British sporting tradition, with British style considered the best in the world. Some claim that rowing was the premier sport of England, and prior to 1920 the global sporting world ranked the English style of rowing as far and away the world's best.[17]

To add to the stigma of the fledgling Olympic events being subpar, its rowing events were seen as inferior to England's Royal Henley Regatta, and the sacred rowing waters of the Thames beguiled and eluded foreign crews. How to solve this? Easy. Have London host the 1908 Olympics and use the rowing course at Henley-on-Thames, home of the prestigious Leander Boat Club. The International Olympic Committee (IOC) did just that. Favorably, the logistics of transporting eights were more easily overcome at Henley also. For crews in continental Europe, borrowing boats at Henley or shipping them by rail or boat set a new precedent for international racing. Inclusion and competing fairly began to overcome exclusion and not competing.

When the English launched the 1908 London Olympics on the

Henley Royal Regatta course, England's Leander Club was slated to win easily—and did. The international Olympic rowing field was undoubtedly amused and intimidated by the bastion of regalia, not the least of which being the Royal Swan Catchers clearing the Thames of the King's royal swans so that they would not be injured by rowing shells, while pink-and-white-striped caps adorned with their hippopotamus mascot logo were proudly donned by Leander crews poised to "Ready, shove!" And, "Row!"

Rowing and its hundreds of years of pomp and tradition were alive and well on the sacred waters of Henley. If the 1908 Olympics did any one great thing for rowing, it established a European rivalry and an American envy. Henley and the European waters were to rowers what Wimbledon was to tennis players—the shrine. And everyone wanted to pray there.

Additionally, "staged as a stand-alone event for sports—the first time since Athens 1896—the London Games of 1908, held at short notice, marked a new era for the Olympic movement. The World Expositions were spectacular, but lengthy, and seen to delude the emphasis on sport that de Coubertin envisioned. The IOC had planned to hold them in Rome but Mount Vesuvius, which had erupted in 1906, proved to be a force beyond the committee's control."[18]

The 1908 Games attracted a record 1,999 competitors, from twenty-two nations, in 109 events, including thirty-six women. The British, as host nation, had the majority of athletes and ended up with the majority of medals, which raised suspicion to partisan judging. This protest—which the IOC subsequently honored by ruling that in subsequent Olympics judges would be selected from various nations—joined the continuing controversy over competitions being held on Sunday. One American, Forrest Smithson, staged a private protest by running the hurdles while clutching a Bible in his hand.[19]

NOT SURPRISINGLY, THE SUCCESS AT HENLEY made rowing events for the 1912 Stockholm Games easier to stage. Boats borrowed at Henley could now be reciprocated in Sweden. Can't ship your oars? We probably have a set you can borrow. As problems arose and were solved, the next time the same problem was up for discussion the answers could begin with, "Well, last time we . . ." And the matters were more likely solved and the racing more likely to go on. The more Olympic Games that were held, the more likely that Olympic Games would be held, and succeed.

ONTO THIS EXPLODING BACKDROP OF ATHLETICISM and world involvement in sport with the modern Olympic Games, Glendon finally had a canvas worthy of his work. He would be the Renoir to his crew's individual hues of paint. The picture he yearned to pull out of them, they themselves pulled stroke by stroke under his masterful blend of color, application, position, and perspective. They were becoming art and they knew it; they could see it as their pale bodies were honed to Adonis-like suntanned gods.

Glendon, ever the catalyst, was skillfully refining the raw crystals of their "near glass," soon to be hardened into intricate clear vessels he'd seen hand forged in Sandwich, Massachusetts. By 1914, after ten years of trial by fire, his program was beginning to take shape. It was a winner attracting the attention of athletes who were interested in something more. Navy was involved already in the glorious yachting world of the America's Cup and took great pride in "assisting" America's involvement in beating *anything* British on the water. There was a contemporary perception of invincible British sea power that pervaded rowing and sailing in particular. Glendon could see it. This time, this opportunity, was the springboard he needed to thrust his crews out of the backwaters and into the headwaters of rowing.

3. NAVY'S LOVE AFFAIR WITH CREW

There is that point of nostalgia that we do so love—what Henry James called "the visitable past."

—Preface to *The Aspern Papers,* by Henry James

———————————⊃⊂———————————

NAVY'S LOVE AFFAIR WITH CREW INVITES ONE TO step onto a dock and emerge in Poughkeepsie, New York, at the turn of the century: The Rockefellers lean from their freshwater yacht floating among thousands of cheering fans who hang from the railings of anchored steamships in the Hudson River. They're watching the crews of the University of Pennsylvania, Cornell, Syracuse, and the Naval Academy streak by.[1] Through the mists of this bygone era, one also glimpses the world of American riverside leisure immortalized by painter Thomas Eakins, whose regatta scenes along the shores of Philadelphia's Schuylkill River invite one to pause, wonder, and enter in. In equal grandeur, strolling in England amidst queens and princesses, straw hats and suit jackets, spectators sip Pimms and lemonade in the Steward's enclosure at the coveted Henley Royal Regatta in Henley-on-Thames. On either side of "the pond," rowing—the oldest intercollegiate sport in America and the oldest international intercollegiate sport in the world—was a grand affair.

This was the world of the elite. This was the world Navy was poised to enter. To understand the mind-set of Glendon and his boys and rowing, one must grasp Navy's tradition with crew and their determination, first and foremost, to defeat the British and to lead the world in the time-honored military practice of oarsmanship.[2] Sitting in the classrooms of Academic Hall, the crew midshipmen listened to history professors tell of how the Academy's rowing tradition sprang from its roots in warfare and the needed protection of the United States' freedom on the seas for trade and travel.

American Naval historians discussed mastery of rowing as one of the keys to sea power. They argued that rowing began as a functional effort to propel Greek triremes and Roman galleys; elaborate naval-oared fleets are depicted in frescoes of the Battle of Lepanto and at Pompeii.[3] Oared ships had complex naval strategies, as did steam-powered ships, because they were easily aligned and not dependent on wind as with sail power.[4] Naval scholars concur that rowing was a central aspect of Greek, Roman, Viking, Italian, Spanish, French, English, and American navies, ensuring freedom for commerce across the oceans that was fundamental for national supremacy.[5]

The midshipmen were trained in sailing vessels and the art of rowing in gigs whether they joined the crew or not—the art of rowing and watermanship skills were part of their training. They rowed and raced gigs from the ships they were assigned to and the glory of past rivalries being common lore: One such rivalry exemplifying America's national identity being to succeed in military rowing comes from an 1872 race in Yokohama Harbor between an American Admiral's barge and a British Admiral's barge. The American barge, a fourteen-oared gig, defeated the British on open ocean and, upon doing so, hoisted a flag that read, "the boat that Uncle Sam built."[6]

Naval crews were still racing this type of lapstrait boat in 1921 at the American Henley Regatta in Philadelphia. These boats are commonly seen on beaches as lifesaving boats.

While sitting in their dorm rooms in Bancroft Hall or sitting at the Seniors or Juniors Gate and reading, in the handbook of each Naval cadet's training since 1902, they learned the fundamental idea that the United States "was born of the sea and the people who made this nation came over the sea."[7] The United States was heralded by American rowing enthusiasts as the most favored country in the world for crew due to its large freshwater lakes and rivers, boundaries washed on both sides by oceans.[8] This favorable geography coupled with climate and the zeal Americans had for British sports advanced rowing in this time. Therefore, rowing found practical uses for saving lives in the first volunteer coast guard associations and as the first lifeboats.[9]

British fleets at anchor launched flotillas of four-oared gigs and pair-oared shells in competitions to rank officers' qualifications. Both the American and British navies staged these rowing contests as essential training exercises and demonstrations of physical prowess.[10] The military gigs and barges, forerunners of the sleek rowing shells seen today, served the utilitarian aspect of rowing. And to be a student of U.S. military and naval traditions meant to be a student of the British military naval traditions also since our navy stems from the traditions of Britannia, as do other American sports stem from the English sporting traditions. In other words, rowing quickly crossed the Atlantic and invaded Britain's former colony.

The American Sportsman's Library of Rowing and Track Athletics reports that "in the period following the Revolution there were heavy boats rowed by the longshoremen in NY, Boston, Philly: A great rivalry between Long Island Sweeps and New York City. First race in

America that we have on record, four men of NY to row the best of Long Island from Harsimus, NJ to the Battery. Fall 1811—Knickerbocker Club and the Invincible Boat Club—built lighter than usual for the race though still heavy by our standards. Knickerbocker won. The rowing that was rapidly gaining in the latter part of the 1850s came to a sudden stop during the Civil War when there were five clubs in NY, Baltimore, Philadelphia, Milwaukee, and Detroit. After the war eight more clubs formed. Most, including the great Philly clubs like Malta and Pennsylvania Barge, are here today."[11]

On the college level, rivals Harvard and Yale began building the first college boat-clubs—first at Yale in 1843, followed by Harvard in 1844.[12] Intercollegiate rowing began in the United States with the first Harvard-Yale race in 1852, and the first international intercollegiate competition, with the Harvard-Oxford boat race in London in 1869.[13] American historian Joseph Mathews maintains that at the 1869 Harvard-Oxford race the examination of the respective merits of American and English character, culture, education, technology, and muscle, by their respective national press corps, had already begun.[14] Following suit, the U.S. Naval Academy's interest in crew resonated with the above in the triumph of an American-born strategy launched in 1890 when a Naval cadet, Winston Churchill (American novelist—not to be confused with the English prime minister Winston Spencer Churchill of the same era), after the boat houses and boats were destroyed by a hurricane, revived the Academy's oldest varsity sport—rowing—at the fledgling U.S. Naval Academy after a twenty-two-year hiatus from 1870 to 1892.[15]

Considered one of his greatest accomplishments as a midshipman—reestablishing crew through his first published literary work—Churchill made what he called "a glorious appeal to those interested in the Navy" in a letter to the editor on behalf of the crew.[16] Coaching and rowing as a member of the crew of 1893, Churchill challenged the United States to wrest international rowing supremacy—and by implication sea power—from the British.[17]

At this same time, Naval Captain Alfred Thayer Mahan's monumental text, *The Influence of Sea Power on History,* challenged and compared the American "national character" to the British, asking whether the United States was "fitted" to develop as a great sea power.[18] Mahan set a keynote of idealism and inspiration for the U.S. Navy to stand unequaled, second to none on the seas; to seize its own identity and supremacy.[19] Captain Churchill, rowing in an American institution founded to seek naval supremacy yet currently following second to Britannia and its traditions, accepted Mahan's challenge to set the United States above the British—and hence above the rest of the world—in "oaring." Failure to meet that challenge, Churchill fretted, would be a "disgrace, for there is every evidence that if the cadets continue to be enthusiastic in the sport, before many years have passed, the Naval Academy will be able to rightfully claim a place in the front rank of the rowing institutions of the world."[20]

The first Naval Academy crews existed sometime before 1870, but the exact records of those crews are lost. In 1893, Navy bought an eight for between 800 and 900 dollars, hired the former Columbia coach, Coach Lahens, and "turned out a varsity eight that won a race against the Neptunes of Baltimore."[21] In 1894, the aforementioned Capt. Churchill aspired to beat the British and urged the Academy crews to master the art of rowing on a world scale. In 1895, Penn defeated Navy. That same year Navy was also defeated by Potomac Boat Club, of Washington, D.C. In 1896, Navy rowed four races—winning two, losing two. A Yale oarsman was hired in 1897 to coach and Navy beat Penn but lost to Cornell. In 1898, Navy beat

Columbia but lost to Penn. The year 1899 shows no crew racing. In 1900, J. H. Ten Eyck was hired, and Navy beat Yale but lost to Penn. In 1901, crew Capt. Roger Williams hired J. Herbert Hall to coach Navy, beating Yale and Georgetown but losing to Penn. No races were recorded in 1902, and in 1903, Navy beat Penn but lost to Georgetown and Yale. Glendon was hired and began in 1904, ending the seesaw nature of Navy's success.[22]

The early cadets' enthusiasm reflected the popularity of the sport as a national pastime immortalized in art and writings, as a matter of nationalistic pride, and as a sporting tradition to emulate. Rowing prints, such as *The Champion Single Sculls* (1871), were so popular that Currier and Ives produced a professional print so people could hang them in their homes and not just see their heroes in magazines and newspapers.[23] Thomas Eakins chose rowing as his first major painting because he had studied the nude in Paris in the 1870s and in America, social attitudes discouraged nudes — but half-naked male rowers were acceptable! *The Champion Single Sculls,* which depicted Eakins's friend Max Schmitt, was his first major work. Eakins was a rower and from Philadelphia, his letters from Paris encouraged his sister to go down to "his beautiful Schuylkill where women were encouraged to row and to socialize amidst the most manly of all sports — rowing."[24] What burgeoning midshipman, soon-to-be naval officer, wouldn't want to impress his love interest with a restful row on the Severn, past the Annapolis Yacht Club as backdrop and up Spa Creek quoting Dickens and looking for all intents and purposes like they were inside a bucolic painting? Rowing, and its athletic as well as romantic indulgences, was a must.

Quixotic as it might seem, rowing was also central and uniquely important in British sport traditions in the United States, because unlike some other British pastimes that underwent rule changes and other adaptations from the original British to the American version (for example, the British bat-and-ball sport rounders to American baseball), rowing rules were not malleable per se. American rowers competed head to head with the British, highlighting rowing's link to England. Rowing remained fundamentally English. There was, therefore, a two-fold pressure on the U.S. Naval Academy. Navy had to win for their school *and* their nation, thus shattering the image of rowing as a distinctly British sport that Americans inherited and to whose development they contributed little.[25]

Cheered on by Captain Mahan's decree to win the "race of life" on the high seas, and with the United States admittedly running second to the British in naval might according to military historians at this time, the midshipmen were determined to "walk through" Britannia and grasp the lead, if fleetingly, on the medals stand. What greater ambassadors could the nation find than Olympic gold medalists who were dedicated to a "Sailor's Creed" of honor, commitment, and service? This nationalistic contest is crucial to the understanding of Naval cadet rowers. It is what makes them unique in American college rowing circles. Their concentration of effort to beat the British stemmed from a military heritage dedicated to achieving naval supremacy. Stoked by the fires of intercollegiate rivalry in the United States, Glendon's crews, who were Academy students as well, were sitting in classrooms learning their lessons well, being primed to lead the world in rowing.

On a more somber note, with World War I in Europe ringing in the ears of America, the need for the "common" American youth, the "doughboy," to excel physically led to exercises emulating the strenuous rowing stroke, and crew boat races were placed in physical education and military training manuals that are still used today. Mastery of rowing and its importance in war heightened the rhetoric in the "little red" boat shed of the Academy; Glendon and his men of the heavy-weight varsity eight were listening.

No U.S. crew was strictly an American creation in boat, oars, and style until Glendon's came onto the scene. In the shadow of Harvard and Yale, Navy developed slowly. Under Glendon, and through his innovations, the crew solidified and began to be a challenger for the medals in the great regattas of the American Henley Regatta in Philadelphia and the Intercollegiate Rowing Championships in Poughkeepsie, New York. Glendon, patiently putting together one boat, one season at a time, as he had learned to patiently stitch and mend fishing nets and sails, crafted his scientific oarsmanship from 1904 until on the eve of the Great War, when he, his boys, and America stood ready to challenge British hegemony.

4. THE WAR YEARS: 1914–1918

Though much is taken, much abides; and though
We are not now that strength which in old days
Moved earth and heaven; that which we are, we are;
One equal temper of heroic hearts,
Made weak by time and fate, but strong in will
To strive, to seek, to find, and not to yield.

—Lord Alfred Tennyson, "Ulysses"

———— ⊃⊂ ————

AMERICA FACED A QUANDARY WHEN WAR BROKE
out in Europe in 1914. Wishing to preserve its own isolationism, the
country was reluctant to interfere with what it saw as a European
dispute. The United States was experiencing its own growing pains:
The northern United States was undergoing a boom in manufactur-
ing with Henry Ford's assembly line. War politics and unions soaked
up pages of the newspaper, and radio and newsreels paid attention to
the money they could make by making the news.[1] Regions of the
South struggled to keep the secrecy of continued repression of
African Americans, which one historian has called a horrific American Congo.[2] Frederick Jackson Turner's thesis on the vanishing
Western frontier framed a new model for American history and en-
ticed thinking in psychological terms, embodied in Roderick Nash's
heroes of what would be deemed the American frontier spirit and

the implications of its demise.³ Not coincidentally, Zane Grey's *Man of the Forest* became a best seller.

The unconscious was discovered, and exploded into literature, medicine, and everyday dinner conversation from New York to San Francisco. Ernest Hemingway began writing short stories based on his experiences as a World War I ambulance driver in Italy.

The increased scientific curiosity and efficiency in the machine's promise to mechanize work and reduce the yoke of physical labor, promised a taste of the long-envied leisure-class life to the common man—who now rose on a pedestal close enough to the rich that the worker merited a symphonic composition titled "Fanfare of the Common Man." Aaron Copeland, its composer, would return from his music studies in France after the war to embed himself in America.

Woodrow Wilson was President, Prohibition was just around the corner, the stock market was good, and along the riverbanks of America and the world, rowing was still an equal to its upstart cousin, football, and ranked as one of the great American pastimes along with baseball and boxing. The European problem of war was a nuisance to Henry Ford's rendition of the American Dream's "a chicken in every pot and a car in every garage," soon to be carried on by his son Edsel.

It was an era when great nations were in races against one another to conquer the heights and vastness of the planet with Amundsen and Scott racing to the South Pole and Shackelton's *Endurance* entrancing the world in its epic struggle in the ice. Social reforms and consequences were brimming on the horizon as Gandhi initiated his peaceful, noncooperation movement toward British rule in India, while a physicist named Einstein was perfecting his Theory of Relativity, moving one step closer to the atomic bomb.

Most Americans just wanted to ignore the war and hoped it

would go away, but with pleas coming from England for money, food, and weaponry, the United States reluctantly entered in, on the battlefields "over there" and on the sporting fields over here. So in 1917, when the United States entered World War I, the military enlisted sports figures such as Walter Camp of Yale and Joseph Raycroft of Princeton to preside over Navy and Army athletic programs.[4] Formal intercollegiate athletic competition ceased; however, informal rowing contests persisted.[5] Glendon had been coaching a decade at Navy. The Naval Academy, savoring this fresh wave of patriotism and pride, set its sights on England. Indeed, rowing style may have represented one of the last great sporting umbilical cords between Mother England and the United States. Severing this tie, by excelling beyond the imaginable, became Navy's goal.

Harvard and Yale became veritable "armed camps" and "khaki campuses." Yale's Adee boathouse was taken over by the U.S. military for boat training.[6] War altered the running of American regattas, necessitating, for example, that the host crews share equipment because travel was difficult and expensive. The informal regattas being held were truncated and rowing ranks declined temporarily—but the top schools of Harvard, Yale, Navy, and Penn kept a semblance of crew alive. Navy competed through the war years, until a brief cessation of all athletics at the Academy midway through the spring of 1918.[7] Glendon continued to fine-tune his all-American system of seating arrangement of in-line seats, American blades, Belgium-style swivel oarlocks, and a new hull.[8] *The Literary Digest* ran an entire article on the Academy's new shell (broader and flatter bottomed than other designs so it could plane on the surface) that was designed by the ingenious Glendon and built by an American boat builder.[9]

During the war years, crew racing began including shorter,

straight-line courses in contrast to the traditional river racing as coaches recognized a need to promote greater fairness.[10] This was an advantage for the Naval Academy. Owing to the rigorous routine of their daily duties, Navy midshipmen could not take the time necessary to train for the long 5,000-meter distances typical of collegiate river rowing at the time.[11] Each college's home-river course yielded a substantial advantage to that school, which intimately knew its own home water's rocks and currents. New standardization practices, such as those being inaugurated in the fledgling Olympic Games for course length, timing, allowable wind speed, obstacles, current, and officiating, were employed. Collegiate crew racing was reduced from 5,000 meters to the international course length of 2,000 meters. Standardizing factors that might yield any one crew an unfair advantage eliminated many of the earlier problems rowing had experienced, particularly at the highly charged international and Olympic levels. Glendon and Navy now could train for distances that were their strength.

IN 1919, WITH THE WAR OVER, THE ALLIED nations with troops still stationed in war-ravaged Europe staged the Military Olympics as a sign of hope and transition. Nation-building and militarism were preeminent in the larger global picture emerging from the ashes—and sports, and particularly rowing, were part of it. The idea of the Military Olympics is a credit to the commanders of the Allied nations. These commanders, concerned about a demobilization process that left two million Allied troops waiting to go home, staged games to signal a new beginning, "a unique love feast of diverse races and nationalities, of a greater and hopeful peace than the world had yet known."[12]

Elwood S. Brown, Director of the Department of Athletics of the YMCA, described in 1918 to Col. Bruce Palmer his concerns regarding the demobilization. Brown, concerned about the moral temptations and dangerous physical displays that might erupt with two million idle men waiting, outlined the need to replace the physical aspects of active fighting with informal and competitive games.[13] Suggestions were made to host mass athletic contests in Paris for every serviceman in service during the Great War. Soldiers would participate in an elimination tournament running from regiments through divisions, with the finals culminating at Pershing Stadium.[14]

Brown's idea grew and was met with enthusiasm. The French indicated that they were "keenly interested in American sports and the fine spirit of play that permeates them" and hoped that the American sports would make a lasting impression on their society. The idea grew to encompass bands, choral singing, and artistic competitions paralleling the format of the Olympic Games held in tandem with the 1900 World Exposition (World's Fair) in Paris. From Brown's initial letter of suggestion and interest, the Allied nations eventually competed in twenty-six events. The expansive program favored no one country, and there was no single army named as overall winner. Events were intended to highlight the individual efforts of the servicemen.[15] Rowing was to be the culminating event of the "largest and most successful service regatta ever held."[16]

The Inter-Allied Games were held from 22 June to 6 July in 1919. Crew teams began taking quarters and practicing on the Seine in early July, waiting for the regatta competition—the last scheduled event of the Military Olympics—to commence. The prominence of rowing in this era was evidenced when the regatta date of 17–18 July was chosen to allow the international crews competing in the long-established Henley Royal Regatta in England to compete there first, and then join the festivities in Paris. The racing in the "Allies Eights" at Henley was for the King's Cup trophy.[17]

The Times reported the Henley Regatta of 1919 as a fairlike atmosphere with the American Army crew headquarters dubbed "Dreamland" conspicuously decked out in stars and stripes.[18] True to its heritage and popularity of the day, news of these rowing events hit the papers and healed the wounds of the vicissitudes of war. Rowing and all its accoutrements of regatta regalia, movie stars, sunshine, and muscular bodies being cheered by sweethearts and kings, queens, and presidents was center stage again. . . .

MEANWHILE, STATESIDE, INTERSECTING LINES were merging on the Severn River in Annapolis. Many American families, being first- and second-generation immigrants, had close ties or emotions with the European war. Posters at home and abroad had romanticized the war as an athletic contest.[19] The images of Navy recruitment posters showed men rowing as a way to "pull together" rather than shoot guns at the enemy or advance on a beachhead.[20]

Honor and country had sidled up with militarism and athletics and left its mark.

The war was over but the talk from older brothers and fathers and neighbors made younger boys dream. British youth had been invited to War "Games" in the trenches just a few years earlier and American youths were attracted to the military academies just as

European youths were attracted to the traditions of honor there.[21] And Glendon and Navy crew were reaping the influx of young rowing fodder that walked through the gates.

Enter, "his boys."

WHEN EDWARD PEERMAN MOORE, ONE OF THREE football terrors from the hills of Virginia, walked through Gate Three in 1919 to report to Annapolis, he carried the first and only pair of shoes he had over his shoulder, so as not to scuff them during his journey from Pittsylvania County to Anne Arundel Point. At the fortified brick gates a sardonic salutation of "Hey, Country" stuck, and he would be called that by governors, kings, presidents, and princes. Edward Peerman Moore grew up in Ringgold, a small dot of a rural crossroad so deep in the hollers of Virginia as to nearly make it part of North Carolina. Moore had literally just stepped off the farm and had no water experience at all, a tough row to hoe indeed.

He was born fifth in a line of two sisters and two brothers in a farmhouse so spare that, being last, he had no bureau drawer to sleep in. He was suspended from the ceiling in a makeshift hammock—thus becoming a would-be naval aviator before even entering Annapolis.

A quiet, good-natured young man with a stutter and a mop of red hair touting a silver blasé on the back of his head that distinguished him from birth, Country Moore was formed by the isolation of deep forests and rolling farmland. His was an upbringing of tradition, hard work in the fields, respect, and obedience to nature, seasons of corn, raising bulls, football, and a heritage of small-town sports and high-school sweethearts. The All-American boy.

Already tall in high school, he played football following the legacy of his two older brothers, Arthur and Lindsey, who earned their way up the gridiron to West Point. Walking to school barefoot across the state line to North Carolina and in the evenings to see his sweetheart, Daisy, shaped the hours of his days. Amid sweet Virginia tobacco farms, wooden front porches swathed in wisteria and quiet good manners, gas-station stores with screen doors that slapped shut behind you when you went in hoping to stick your hand in a chest of Coca-Cola brimming with ice and bottles, Country whee-dled away his formative years as the content son of a farmer. A Southern Baptist who loved to sing "Rock of Ages" and to stand by the side of the road on a grassy knob by the turn near the farm and shake the hand of the newfangled "machines" as they went by . . . any coach would want this big of a heart on his team.

Clyde Whitlock King, the stocky football hero stroked eight seat with Sherman "Cutie" Clark, in front of him as coxswain. King was from Grinnell, Iowa, weighed 178 pounds, was six feet tall, and was twenty-two years old. A varsity athlete in boxing, basketball, and crew, he factored heavily into the Navy defeat of Army that same year by kicking the two field goals that won the game.[22] Known as a gorgeous he-man with a silver tongue, was it any wonder he would become class president for two years?[23]

Sherman Clark grew up in Yonkers, New York, the son of a linen merchant. His mother came to the Annapolis area and was very much a part of the social circle, including bridge partner of author E. B. White. The Clark house became known as a place where the young midshipmen, bonding together as an Olympic eight as well as a naval unit, met their dates, their "drags," on Sunday afternoon to walk lovers lane. They read and were teased from popular texts from the days of Charles Dickens, who loved rowing and wrote whimsical quips sure to edge into the conversation of flirtatious young men and women. "'Are you fond of the water?' is a question very frequently asked in hot summer weather, by amphibious-looking young men, 'very,' is the general reply. 'Ain't you?'"[24]

Nicknamed "Cutie," Clark was twenty years old, weighed 113 pounds, and was five feet eight inches tall. This young man was as close to a hometown boy as the Academy might get. Needing to be lightweight to be the coxswain but heavy enough to pass the physical for entrance to the Academy, he ate bananas outside of the doctor's office to pass the entry test—not knowing at the onset of his career that being light for his physical actually benefited his chances for making the boat. His doctor told him, "Oh, go on then. If you want to be a middy so bad that you'll sit here day after day in front of my office and eat bananas—I'm not going to stop you."[25]

Clark, who loved golf and was in the drama club at Annapolis, had no idea of the path fate had called him to embark upon. A slight, trim man, he excelled in his classes, winning an academic star and the respect of the Academy as well as the newly amalgamating crew.

It is no wonder that football great Clyde King wielded his oar on the curious little man's orders. King, with his barrel chest and hardheaded courage, was a bull of a man not to be taken lightly in any arena: pigskin or rowlock. Known to his family and friends as "a puny kid who couldn't stand the guff of even the kids' games in the neighborhood," he was sent to his family's ranch in Saskatchewan when he was eight to toughen up and become a young man. "When he returned three years later he was a youngster with a man's physique. He played basketball and football in high school and entered Grinnell College. In keeping with a resolve to work his way through school, [without his parents' money] he bought a shoe shining parlor in the little college town from a Greek for $300. He decorated the place with college pennants and college trimmings and advertised it as a place of fair co-ed trade. His business grew until his staff of shoeshine boys working for him was swamped and he took a hand at the leathers himself. He made close to $1,500 a year for two years and then sold the business for $600, went to Marion Institute, where he prepared for Annapolis."[26]

His was a body and frame of mind ordained to lead, never to follow; to confidently claw a boat down a lane regardless of tide or wind or weather to front place—holding pace because he had the steely nerves to do so and the weighty mind-set to know that it was the right thing to do; it was best to draw a lead slowly with stealth—rather than give the opponent too early a glimmer of the speed he knew his boat possessed. Clark and King worked together, one viewing forward, the other viewing aft to sight the 64-foot craft through the needle's eye of victory.

Passing through the much-heralded gates and soon to be at seats seven and six, were two New Yorkers, one from the city, one from the capitol. Vincent J. Gallagher in seven seat was from Brooklyn, and Donald "Johnny" Johnston in six seat from Albany, New York. Johnston's movie star good looks were suitable for a Norman Rockwell illustration. A powerfully built six feet two inches and 190 pounds, this quietly intense man joined Alden Sanborn in the "engine room," the widest part of the boat. A romantic enigma to his male friends who often boasted about their female conquests, Don Johnston was a singularly driven man whose heart was captivated by one woman, an Annapolitan beauty from Duke of Gloucester Street named Margaret.

Gallagher in seven seat paced the starboard oars to King's portside. Gallagher, who did not row previous to college, started his college career at Rutgers but transferred to the Naval Academy when he received an appointment in 1919. He was a handsome, auburn-haired, gray-eyed man with a contagious fondness for slapping his knee in a big belly laugh and tilting his head back when humored. "Gal" went about as a young boy with his father, who was a horse-and-buggy-doctor in Brooklyn looking in on Swedish, Irish, and Italian neighborhoods, riding a white horse-drawn carriage to see his patients. His father's patients called him "Little Vincenzio." He would one day be buried at sea.

Seat five belonged to Alden "Zeke" R. Sanborn from Jefferson, Wisconsin. Sanborn started his career at Beloit College and received an appointment to the Naval Academy in 1918. He was handsome, with a gentle face and green-blue eyes that drew your gaze to his. He was so flat-footed, he took his Navy physical in the morning before his feet flattened out with the wear and tear of the day's gravity. On one hand he was a fierce competitor; on the other hand, he was a sentimental, shy man, known to be sweet around the ladies. He had suffered through the loss of his younger brother William to scarlet fever when William was just twelve. Zeke played football, basketball, and, making the varsity crew in his plebe year, he rowed all four years of twenty-four races in his Academy career—setting a school record.[27]

In three seat was William "Buck" Jordan from Cleveland, Ohio. His parents were first-generation immigrants from Prussia who gave their son a drive for success. A man who would later become the president of Hughes Aircraft and invite his fellow water-shoveler Sanborn to work with him there, stood as a midshipman in 1919 among the middies in the brigade as the image of authority and control. An athlete who wouldn't let himself succumb to ailments, he joked a lot and laughed heartily. His Presbyterian upbringing included churchgoing with his four brothers and a sister. The laughter and song in his parents' home echoed in Buck's bass voice that was quick to sing almost any song.

Filling out this true cross section of America were two men destined to be the bow pair of the eight, Edwin Darius "Eddie" Graves and Victor Jacomini. Graves, a monster at 182 pounds and six feet five inches who rowed two seat, was from Chesapeake City, Maryland. He attended the University of Pennsylvania before accepting the appointment to Annapolis, where he would star in basketball, football, and become captain of the crew team.

Victor "Jack" Jacomini was the fourth son of six brothers—Marius, Gus, Edward, Alfred, Victor, and Clem—in a first-generation Italian-American family, whose father was responsible for the lens and the care of the Mount Wilson Telescope by polishing it with diamond dust. A great high-school track star, Jacomini ran, high-jumped, and long-jumped for Pasadena High. After winning the state championships, his coach simply asked him, "Do you want to run track for Navy?" He said, "Yeah, I guess so," then spent a year preparing for the entrance exams to the Academy and was in. The tall, easygoing, good-natured, statuesque guy was stoically silent yet gracious about his accomplishments. Always impeccably groomed, he wore his dark hair combed up and back off his forehead, making him appear even taller. Always one with a steady gaze in his blue eyes, he looked people right in the eye with a no-nonsense demeanor and carried himself with budding confidence. He had captained his high-school track championship team, which included the Olympic great Charles Paddock, who would also be on the 1920 Olympic team in Antwerp and would later go on to be a sport journalist and write about Jacomini.

Jack was extraordinarily tight with his brother Clem. They were fishing buddies and loved camping; his brother was a World War I ace flying instructor whose dreams influenced the young. He had lost his third brother, Edward, to cancer and was determined to live life in a broad and big manner for him and for his proud family.

A farm boy from the hollers of Virginia, an Italian immigrant, a first-generation Pole who rode a buggy through the cramped and crowded streets of Brooklyn: a cross section of American male youth indeed had entered the gates at Annapolis to place themselves in the annals of history. Whatever came at them, their heritage and their training from these days forward would mold them and sustain them. Their awkward days of shoeless strolls from Virginia hollers and first-generation immigrant poverty were being given a spit shine and polish like no other. They were tough and drew their inner strength from a well within and each knew it was there and hoped they didn't have to visit and drink from its waters too often.

And as the United States could now take a sigh of relief that the war had not interfered too much with its sons and daughters, so, too, the British sons could return to their pursuits, not the least of which was the rejuvenation of rowing, the University Boat Race and the Henley Royal Regatta.

5. BRITISH ROWING ROOTS

So, if you cannot understand that there is something in man which responds to the challenge of this mountain and goes out to meet it, that the struggle is the struggle of life itself upward and forever upward, then you won't see why we go. . . .

—George Mallory, Mount Everest Expedition, 1922

GOING TO SEA, GOING TO CONQUER IS PART OF the British mind-set. As an island nation Britannia's navies ruled a world on which the sun never set. Brave hearts and strong backs left their shores for expeditions to the North and South Poles. The geo surveillance of the Himalayas, the conquering of Everest, and all such were taken in stride as if it was expected that an Englishman should be first to cross waves and snow and ice as surefootedly as if strolling through the combed grass of London's Princess Park. Rowing and rowing contests were to be no exception.

Essentially, the British rowing tradition stemmed from its military uses in war. The military gigs and barges, forerunners of the sleek rowing shells seen today, took the utilitarian aspect of rowing and made it sublime. "So important was the role of rowing in the tradition of the British military, that historian J. A. Mangan described British naval rowing races in Japan in 1883 as so popular they were attended by the Emperor. As in the United States, exposure to the sport through the military led to Japanese starting university crews."[1] Running historically parallel to these military practices and training exercises, came the waterman's means of rowing for hire, the recreational pastime of rowing, and the highly refined sport of crew.[2] The legendary Dogget's Badge was a boat race in London of watermen.

Those who plied their oars inadvertently developed an immensely popular pastime that surpassed practical need and encompassed professionalism, entertainment, private clubs, and a multitude of college rowing programs.[3] As early as 1800, rowing was a leisurely pursuit in England. Historian Richard Holt observes that these early modern contests drew enormous crowds and that rowing enjoyed a popularity that was "quite phenomenal."[4] By mid-1850, crew had become the premier sport at Oxford and Cambridge. According to English educator Archibald MacLaren, by 1870, rowing was considered the top form of exercise, competition, and rivalry, dwarfing "all our other national pastimes put together."[5]

The romance and beauty of being drawn to the banks of languid waters and whiling away idle hours with oneself or with a lover or friends, has been an alluring pastime, most likely since leisure time could be exploited. It was not uncommon for women and men to be seen rowing about recreating, picnicking, and just "messing about in boats."[6] Military, working-class, gentlemen amateurs all claimed rights to their particular bent on rowing—and each propagated a version unique to their own interests. Having said this, it should come as no surprise that the well-heeled interests of such famous rowing waters as those of Cambridge, Oxford, Henley, and Leander would eventually come to the forefront with flair and panache.

As American youth wandered outside Wrigley Field or Yankee Stadium hoping to catch a stray ball over the fence or get an autograph, on the Surrey Shore under Westminster Bridge in the heart of London, young British lads in the 1870s were watching rowing clubs called "Stars" and "Arrows" transform and meld themselves into what would become the most prestigious rowing club in the world—Leander. The original red and white stars and arrows of Leander's forerunners blended and became pink in the wash, or in the rain, or in the printing of programs for races—only history knows the mix for certain—but one thing is sure and leaves no doubt: The logo of the King of the River in England is a pink hippopotamus—and it is called Leander.

If the boys in America grew up reading and dreaming about playing for the Yankees in 1920, English lads were hoping to be Leander men. As young boys in the States collected baseball cards, in England there were Spy cartoons (hand-drawn portraits) of rowing greats from Cambridge and Oxford and Leander for youngsters to aspire to. As American boys would be reading Spalding's Sport series, the English lads were reading *The Boat Club* by Oliver Optic, the chapter on St. Ambrose Boat Club in *Tom Brown at Oxford*, *Grit the Young Boatman* by Horatio Alger, the *Bumper Book of School Stories*—"The Will to Win," or "Rowing by Straw Hat." In England, boat clubs like those at Eton fed college students to Cambridge and Oxford, which fed mature national heroes into the Leander ranks, much like American baseball and the farm teams that feed the Yankees. When Navy went to row against Leander, it would truly be David against Goliath.

C. M. "Cherry" Pitman, coach of the 1920 Leander Olympic eight, perceived the rowing at Oxford and Cambridge as, "in many respects carried on under more favorable conditions than are enjoyed elsewhere. Probably nowhere else it is a pastime that lasts the whole year round, winter and summer alike; and nowhere else have men, on the average, so much spare time to devote to it. The large number of different colleges [within the universities], and therefore of different boat clubs, makes the field of competition a very wide one, and the rivalry intensely keen. It is this spirit of keenness, and the *esprit de corps* which it evokes, that are perhaps the most marked characteristics of (English) University rowing. It would be difficult to find a scene of enthusiasm that would compare with the Oxford 'Eights' or the Cambridge 'Mays.' "[7]

Oxford University is a collection of colleges. Many of these colleges have boat clubs and one of the most famous boat clubs within Oxford is that of Magdalen College. Magdalen was founded in 1448 by Bishop William of Waynflete, who had also been Provost of prestigious Eton.[8]

As with Oxford, Cambridge University is a collection of colleges. "Trinity Hall, one of the most famous rowing colleges, was founded by Bishop Bateman of Norwich in 1350, making it the fifth oldest surviving college of the University of Cambridge. It was originally founded, in the words of William Bateman himself, 'for the promotion of divine worship and of canon and civil science and direction of the commonwealth and especially of our church and diocese of Norwich.' The rationale behind this stated purpose may well be attributed to the Black Death of 1349, a disaster which, among other things, had resulted in a shortage of clergymen and lawyers. To this day, the College maintains a very strong tradition in the study of Law."[9] And according to David Swann, the son of the 1920 British rower, Sidney, or "Cygnate" Swann, "at the Hall they produce two things—barristers and rowers."[10]

The schools, Oxford on the river Thames and Cambridge on the river Cam, were veritable rowing havens due, not in the least, to their proximity to water. Adding to the serenity and allure of water and oaring were the Water Walks of Oxford's Magdalen College, known for their peaceful reserve. The college has a majestic air of tradition laced with the beauty of formal gardens world renowned for hyacinths, daffodils, bluebells, snow drops, forested canopies contrasting with lush meadows.[11] And Cambridge, with its graceful arched footpaths crossing the parklike setting near the boathouses, beckons one to cast off booted feet, slip one's bottom on to a curved seat—and row.

It has been long understood that what most regard as play serves an underlying purpose—namely training for some future event. This event can be the skills of better citizenry by invoking local competition and camaraderie. Skills learned in one's youth are also frequently the skills needed for defense and military tactics . . . such as hunting, sailing, boat handling, ball throwing, archery, etc. All of these movements and muscle trainings can be exploited—if need be—at the right time for military or personal defense: They are valuable and necessary. They are also fun.

Given that the element of entertainment and relaxation go hand in hand with the human need to interact socially, friendly wagering, racing, and the eventuality of exclusiveness are natural progressions. For carefree spontaneous play to evolve with maturity to a more complex and ruled game—of say, bumping, or "tag you're it"—to eventually evolve on the water as straight course, highly structured racing, competition is natural. Moreover, like the ripples of water on the surface of ponds themselves, the initial input, the pebble, sends waves in all directions, catching the eye, passions and fancies of many and not a narrow, straight-line singular progression. Thus, rowing captured the mind and the imagination of every aspect of this Island Nation. From farmers needing to transport goods to sell, to royalty wishing to associate and mingle and enjoy, to familied Oxford or Cambridge boathouses steeped in generations of boat consecrations, to images of family crests mingled with boat club crests, all the way to admiralty, kings and emperors wishing to add their stamp of approval and be counted among the spectators *royal*—rowing flourished in England and on the continent, no less than cricket, polo, tennis, and horse racing.

Once two great universities were positioned on waterways and brought up in the tradition of excellence nothing less than a great rivalry could and did result. In a nutshell the history of the Oxford-Cambridge Boat Race comes down to a challenge issued to Oxford by Cambridge at the end of 1820. The first Boat Race so famous as to need no other appellation was rowed on the Thames at Henley. "Oxford wore dark blue jerseys, later to become the Oxford blue, whilst Cambridge donned pink sashes. Oxford were the first winners. The second race was staged in 1836 when Cambridge adopted their own light blue, and was rowed on a 5.75-mile stretch of the Thames between Westminster and Putney. The 4.5-mile race is held in March or early April, after the captain of the previous year's losing team issues a formal challenge."[12]

Certainly one can see the progression from the boarding schools of Eton and Rugby, for example, to colleges such as Oxford and Cambridge enticing others in Great Britain, the continent of Europe, and the world to come to these sacred waters and challenge these lofty schools, hoping to rub elbows with the sons of kings and diplomats while beating the royal pants off them in boats. What better venue to stage such rivalries than the pastoral river town of Henley-on-Thames and home of the most famous rowing club of all, Leander, and of the world-renowned Henley Royal Regatta?

In the midst of the university rowing clubs and the social rowing clubs, the University Boat Race and the Henley Royal Regatta, the British exalted their sport of rowing, perfected it, passed it from generation to generation for hundreds of years, and lastly, wanted to keep it largely for themselves. The necessity, the advancing, and the marching of the sport of rowing from the 1600s forward is as if the rhythmic pace of the catch and the finish within the rowing stroke itself ticked off the passage of time and became the very stone and building block of the next layer of tradition.

British oarsmen had long touted themselves as the greatest rowers in the world, with the richest and finest traditions of crew. Historian Eric Halladay, in his *Social History of Rowing in England,* states that the rowing clubs of London, such as the famous Stars and Arrows—forerunners to Leander—during the years before the Great War, were consumed with the task of having to defend English rowing against foreign invaders.[13] In 1896, an anonymous correspondent to the English sporting journal, *The Field,* predicted, "When the international element comes in, sport ceases to be sport and is turned into a branch of foreign policy."[14] To underscore the involvement of British national identity in crew in this era, Guy Nickalls, a British Olympic rower boasted that "he had never in his life been beaten by a colonial or a foreigner and that he had no intention of ever doing so."[15]

The onslaught of foreign crews impinging on England's famed Henley course previous to the Military Olympics provides a unique entrée into the British side of the pond's view of international rowing. Without going in depth concerning the amateur question and the gentleman rower/athlete debate, which has haunted all sports since the nineteenth century, it is relevant to look at the British growing pains that convulsed their inner sporting sanctums, and which Glendon and Navy were up against.

The British Empire, after spreading across the world, introduced sporting culture into their colonies and along the path of their military trails. While the British longed to spread their sports and culture, however, they didn't want to share them. This sounds like a contradiction in terms, but one need only look at the various examples of the British hosting of games to see that they tried to keep the winning and regulatory aspects of their games in their control. Flaunting this sporting hegemony in their colonies proved in particular to be a double-edged sword because the colonized nations imitated their imperialist leaders so well that later they invariably vanquished them on the athletic fields. Colonized people worked to overcome and surpass the imperialists. The colonial desire to beat the imperialist power was at the essence of the 1920 Naval Academy quest to beat Britannia. It is not unique; similar cultural tendencies throughout the British colonies have been traced by Allen Guttmann, who writes on the dynamics of these sporting scenarios, in *Games and Empires*.[16]

It is against this anti-colonial backdrop that the British defeats at Henley and the later defeat of the Leander crew in Europe must be understood. Rugby had already been taken from the pages of *Tom Brown's Schooldays* onto the American village commons; baseball had usurped British rounders, and cricket, a true British class sport, had already journeyed from the cliffs of Dover to Australia and the West Indies. Rowing was for the British one of their final sport sanctuaries. After all, the Henley course was in Henley-on-Thames. It could never be held anywhere but there, never pass beyond British shores. But what lurked beyond the British shores longed to pass inland to Oxfordshire and put Harvard and Yale shells on the sacred waters and test the nectar of the Olympic gods. International competition with Henley, with the national boat club of Leander in the 1908 Olympic Regatta at Henley, was just a matter of tides and time.

Just as crews putting in and taking out on the Thames in London had to deal with the tidal aspects of that ancient river, so, too, did the tides of persuasion, isolationism, and change obsequiously flow in and out of the awareness and dealings of the boat clubs and social gatherings of Britain. As rowing spread through the vast regions of the British military world from the United States to Canada, New Zealand, Japan, and Australia, so, too, did the very human aspect of hegemony. Beginning in the twentieth century, British rowing and stroke-style tradition were embedded in the rhetoric of British identity, and wresting that mantle away would be the stuff of epic lore.

6. HENLEY VS. THE OLYMPIC GAMES

There is a tide in the affairs of men,
Which, taken at the flood, leads on to fortune;
Omitted, all the voyages of their life
Is bound in shallows and in miseries.
On such a full sea are we now afloat;
And we must take the current when it serves,
Or lose our ventures.

—William Shakespeare, *Julius Caesar*, act 4, scene 3

TO APPRECIATE THE SIGNIFICANCE OF THE 1920 Olympic race, one has to understand the historical intersections of crew, naval power, and nationalism on both sides of the pond in the late nineteenth and early twentieth centuries. The 1920 Naval Academy crew, by developing a distinctly American rowing style that might lead to winning the Olympic gold, among other accolades, would force English rowing experts to concede that after the Olympic regatta, for the first time in history, they well might now have to adopt American ideas. Running perpendicular to the above, young British rowers were wanting to step outside of the traditions of their forefathers and *race,* head-to-head with all comers to see how fast they really were. It seems that the Great War brought the world closer together; and this time, this place, was a chance to really crow about being the best in the world. And there lies the rub: The Henley tradition and the Olympics, the past and the fervor of youth, had to go head-to-head to sort it out.

On the British side of the pond, the old guard and the new were divided over several issues pertaining to international participation at Henley, but essentially rowing and the Henley Royal Regatta were revered by the British as their own, with the Henley course considered as a more important race than Baron de Coubertin's revived Olympic Games.[1]

On the American side of the pond, Glendon's achievements had already distinguished him as the "venerable" Dick Glendon. The delicious synchronicity of these events, along with President Woodrow Wilson's plans for an American-led new world order in the wake of the Great War, set the stage for this important event in sport history—and the U.S. Navy's desire to surpass Britain provided the script. Furthermore, in their search for identity through science and technological advancement, and breaking out of their isolationism as a nation, a fervor rose across the United States, where fans found their heart's darlings in the "motley" 1920 Navy crew symbolically standing up against Mother Britain again.

HAVING FOREIGNERS ON THEIR ROWING WATERS appalled many British sportsmen. Ideologically, foreigners would bring new ideas challenging the status quo. Logistically, international competition, and the necessary money and preparation needed to compete, raised questions and were affronts to the standard British way of looking at sporting things.[2] Moreover, true athletes were not to work—as dictated in the British definition of amateur—for striving at sport and competition was considered work in British terms, thereby raising the athlete to the state of a professional. And if ever there was a Boston Tea Party in the making involving the infusion of British rowing hauteur into a caldron of bubbling, steaming, hot tempers, and words—the issue of amateurism versus professionalism in the gentleman's sporting realm was it.

The Olympic Games, therefore, in reference to more than one ideal, challenged what might be considered close-minded British views on rowing. Additionally, once you have rowed against everyone in the kingdom, there is a natural instinct for immortality, especially among the young, that requires one to know *just how fast are we anyway?* Such was the idea on the mind of young Gully Nickalls, member of the 1920 Leander Olympic eight, speaking against his father's era, his father being Guy Nickalls, Leander boat club Olympic gold medalist in 1908. Gully and his father held opposing views on the Olympic issue. His father was reported to have preferred to have nothing at all to do with the Olympic movement.[3] His son, an advocate of the younger generation's view, which sought international competition, "found himself frequently acting as deputy to Gold, the Chairman of the Amateur Rowing Association (ARA), who early on perceived, 'it did not take any particular foresight on my part to realize that the ambition of the majority of young men ... was to succeed internationally and to set their sights beyond the somewhat restricted competition to be found in this country.' "[4]

Therefore, the British debate over eligibility and governance heightened when the Amateur Rowing Association found "a breach in the amateur code" and took umbrage in 1912 with the British Olympic Association (BOA), issuing a statement "that in view of the efforts that are being made in other branches of athletics to raise funds by the public subscription for the expenses and training of competition at the next Olympiad, this committee deprecates such actions as tending to professionalism in sport, and calls the attention of the affiliated members to the fact that under ARA rules, oarsmen are no longer amateurs if their expenses are paid by funds raised outside their own rowing clubs."[5]

Following the conception of a recurring international sporting event such as the Olympics, countries formed new athletic organizations known as National Governing Bodies (NGBs), which reported to the Olympic Committee. This created a paradigm shift in the power structure within some countries that had enjoyed decades of high-level sport within their own borders. Many countries had elaborate committees and unions that set guidelines if not veritable rules for competition and practice within the individual sport.[6]

Suddenly, the inner workings of an old guard network dominated by an elite inner circle of families, politics, and lineage—which snubbed some and favored others—found their carefully constructed athletic bastions beleaguered with the superimposed Olympic organization casting an internationally wide net over many sports. This threatened the smaller social network of individual sporting associations that previously had found little need to communicate with other sports.[7]

A score of tongue-twisting new acronyms found their way into the minutes of amateur athletic unions, newsprint, and conversation. Britain found its ARA and its National Amateur Rowing Association (NARA) and the new BOA in conflict with *Federation International Societies d' Avignon* (FISA, the International Governing Body of Rowing) and the new International Olympic Committee (IOC).[8] The original association, the ARA, was considered old school in its adherence to the amateur code and touted as being backward-looking to the days of the Victorian era. The NARA had, previous to the forming of the BOA, joined ideas with FISA and dipped its toes tentatively into the pond of international rowing, by selecting a representative British boat for the upcoming 1920 Olympics and welcoming new blood into the Henley and continental college races.[9]

Thus, overseas rowing by international competition coming to Henley, such as the Allied Army crews of the Military Olympics had a significant impact on the amateur issue as well as the domestic affairs of the British. The sporting culture of Britain pervaded the British fabric of society in its schools and social clubs, in its betting patterns, and in its own national pride. The races held at Henley were considered "Little England" races for the select few—not for the colonies and certainly not for the uncivilized professional sporting world.[10] The Olympics of 1908, held in London, were initially not welcome to row the Olympic course on Henley water in what the Henley Stewards considered *their* section of the Thames.[11]

These matters of international competition, just stirring in the tidal pools of the Thames, would significantly come to bear on the 1920 Olympic contest with Navy and Leander. In a double-edged sword, England, by and large, didn't want international competitors *and,* previous to 1920, Navy had never been allowed to race in international competition. It was largely through first Athletic Officer Capt. Noble Erwin's "untiring effort and whole-souled interest in athletics at the Academy" that Navy (the Academy student crew) was allowed to leave U.S. borders to compete internationally.[12] So, fate would have to deal an *extraordinary* hand—moving the governances on two continents—for these two teams to race. And, there could be no suspicion of a professional internationally experienced crew coming to race the British. Navy was perceived as such an underdog by the British they were virtually unmentioned in the British Press.[13] The Leander Club was thought to surely triumph.[14]

THE LEANDER CLUB, BECAUSE OF THE MORE PRO-gressive attitude of the NARA and changing tides of thought throughout Britain, had benefited by the international exposure at Henley and elsewhere in FISA regattas. The 1920 Royal Henley, after a hiatus of five years due to the war, was revived to its full program of eight challenge cups. Nearly 400 crews were entered. Initial doubts regarding the quality of the crews, due to the diminished ranks from war, would soon be cast aside as *The Times* reported that "keenness and enthusiasm promise well for the future."[15]

Leander was housed near the Stewards' area at the finish of the Henley course. How they would fare in the upcoming Henley and Olympic Games would be sorted out in short order. Historically, for them, hundreds of lacquered plaques with their club members' names attesting to the winning the prestigious races at Henley lined the Leander clubhouse. The Olympic Games were newer but no less easily subdued. Leander won in the 1908 London Olympics on their home course at Henley. They set a world record in the 1912 Olympics at Stockholm of 6 minutes, 10 seconds.[16] There was no 1916 Berlin Olympics due to the war, and the undefeated 1920 Leander crew, Henley Grand Challenge Cup winners (consisting of E. D. Horsfall, G. O. Nickalls, R. S. Lucas, W. E. C. James, J. A. Campbell, S. Earl, R. S. Shove, S. E. Swann, and coxswain R. T. Johnstone) would have its chance at Olympic gold in Antwerp.[17] Sidney Swann and Ewart Horsfall were returning 1912 Olympic gold medalists.[18]

And the contention, long held in Britain and extolled in the press that "England has believed absolutely in the supremacy of its system in rowing over that of America," would soon be tried to the breaking point in Antwerp.[19]

7. AMERICAN SCIENTIFIC OARSMANSHIP AND THE CREW

Rowing is not a game, it is much more akin to riding, skating, or dancing, or any other form of locomotion developed into an art.

—Gilbert C. Bourne, *A Textbook on Oarsmanship*

WHILE THE BRITISH LANGUISHED IN DEBATES over professionalism, foreign crews on their sacred rowing waters, and modernity, British traditions in America were being challenged and scrutinized in ways never dreamed of. By 1919, Navy and Glendon had developed an identity separate from the British tradition. Seen being driven about, standing erect in his white shirt and dress pants in the center cockpit of the sleek wooden coaching launch *Dart*, ever present alongside the shells in what was to become known—out of earshot in the locker rooms as "the watchful *Dart*"— Glendon was forever studying, analyzing, and perfecting his own stroke: an American Orthodox stroke.[1]

Different from Harvard or Yale, which were patterned after the British style, Glendon was setting a course of changing the face of rowing forever. Since each American rowing club or collegiate crew cultivated its own traditions—generally derived from British models, which were often thought to be the secret, guarded ingredients to success—coaching protégés and fans were loyal to the mentor coach's program. Typically a rower thought that his school or club style and the coach who taught it were the best. A fierce allegiance to the traditions of a school or club characterized rowing. When a rower went on to coach, he typically coached the same style as his previous coach and ingrained the ingredients of that tradition of style in another generation of loyal rowers.

Walter Camp, who, in his role as athletic director at Yale was conversant of the various stroke styles of this era, understood the strength of this tie and the power of Great Britain in shaping the sport.[2] "To no branch of American athletics does this apply with greater force than to boating, because in that sport we still adhere in the principal points to almost the same general line as that prevailing in England for a long series of years," admitted Camp.[3]

From 1850 to 1920, heated tension over British orthodoxy of stroke raged across the Atlantic.[4] The search for an American orthodoxy to rival or surpass this British orthodoxy took place over this seventy-year period. Traditionalists Harvard and Yale rowed English orthodox style with English coaches and even English hulls when they could get them.[5] But most other American crews in this time period rowed a stroke that was either strictly English or a hybrid of English and American style. Most top American coaches were actually English trained, schooled, or born; they were either direct products of England who emigrated to the United States or were British-American hybrids.[6]

Britain took great pride in lithe rowers straining together, pulling graceful, stylized strokes. Concentrating on oar placement in the beginning of the stroke, they offset their rowers to the right and to the left from the centerline of the boat using a lightly structured vessel following the conventional wisdom that lighter was faster. On the other hand, Glendon set his boys in a straight line, in a heavier boat, and had them concentrate on powering their pull in the middle of the stroke. It wasn't pretty like the British stroke—it was called "homely and awkward" by the press—but it was fast.[7]

And Glendon's stroke was unique, for so proficient did American imitators become of the English style of rowing that on 4 July 1914, at the Henley Royal Regatta, Harvard beat England—on England's home waters. *The New York Times* crowed that "this is Independence Day, the anniversary of the date when America decided to be independent, and she has come forward today to show that the child has overcome her mother in oarsmanship."[8]

The British seemed to be flattered, and newspapers played up the imitation that in this great upset at Henley, Harvard rowed the English style. "Harvard's victory is popular in England," read the special cable to *The New York Times,* "as English oarsmen assert that it is a vindication of the English style, which they [Harvard] took from Eton to America."[9] Harvard's win was considered an amusing fluke that served to solidify British supremacy, unwittingly strengthening Glendon's Naval Academy All-American style soon to be unleashed on European and Olympic waters. Neither Harvard's win nor any other American rowing program brought a clear break from English orthodoxy until Glendon and the Navy crew.

Examples of early American rowing czars were Hiram Conibear and the Pocock brothers. Conibear, as portrayed by rowing writer Bob Harron, was an easterner, "who learned his rowing out of a book." Harron pointed out that Conibear trained baseball players before going to Washington before the Great War, where he taught a very eastern "leg and arm stroke" that was nothing new. Three other coaches, Leader, Callow, and Ulbrickson, all moderated the Eastern stroke learned from Conibear and added their own insights.[10] The Pococks, from Vancouver, though of England's Eton school lineage, produced a legacy of rowing at the University of Washington from 1907 to 1917 based on English style—yet were described by noted rowing historian Thomas Mendenhall as searching for an American orthodoxy.[11] Cornell, coached by the legendary Charley Courtney from 1883 to 1916, utilized the English style, with the sliding seat.[12] His style was said to be that of a natural sculler to which was "joined an import from England," which again was the prevailing tendency in America in the nineteenth century.[13] He was "openly courted" by Harvard in 1894 and served as Harvard's adviser and coach for a year.[14]

In describing American orthodoxy, not until 1920 did one style coalesce as "the best evidence of success" and this began with Glendon and Navy.[15] Up until then, no U.S. crew was strictly an American creation in boat, oars, men, and style until Glendon came onto the scene. In Glendon's own experiments with greasing up duck's bottoms to see if the added "water-proofing" would aid speed, he examined and tested principles of watermanship and physics that pertained to the rowing stroke. In his words, "Several tests with mallards, some of which were heavily oiled and others with natural oil removed from breast feathers, showed that those with oiled feathers swam several seconds faster than those without. In fact, the oiled birds seemed to float high on the water, while the others appeared to sink deeper than usual."[16] Looking at nature's solutions for speed and locomotion, Glendon also deferred to the oily substance exuded by fish and determined that oiling the bottom of a racing shell would reduce friction and increase speed. Whatever his methods, Glendon's success was concrete and recognized. Even the English Olympian Guy Nickalls, who came from England and coached briefly at Yale, subsequently warned the British of the Americans' speed before the Antwerp Olympics.[17]

By 1919, Glendon had directly challenged and altered the standard rowing rigging and designs through his innovations of hull shape for the shell, blade size, and design in the oars; seat configuration inside the rowing shell; the size of his rowers; and the point during the stroke in which they should apply power. In short, although the British and all the best crews in the world were using lightweight boats to support lithe rowers who focused on timing at the catch (the beginning of the stroke when the oar is in the water) and a highly stylized stroke, Glendon believed that bigger, stronger athletes, placed in a heavy, strong boat to support them, pulling hardest at the 90-degree point (the middle of the stroke when the oar is in the water) could generate more speed, a lot more speed. Glendon's Scientific Oarsmanship, or American Orthodox stroke, covered everything from training diet to hull hydrodynamics.

TO UNDERSTAND GLENDON'S INNOVATIONS IT IS necessary to understand the rowing stroke. The athlete sits inside the gunnels (sides) of a rowing shell (boat) with the feet facing the stern (rear) and the back of the athlete's head facing the bow (front). The boat, in most circumstances, is to be propelled by the athlete, forward, in the direction of the bow. The athlete cannot see in this direction and relies on a coxswain (a person who steers) who is seated facing forward. The rower sits on a seat that rolls over two tracks (the slide).

In sweep rowing, as opposed to sculling, the oars are longer and two hands rest on one oar; in sculling, an oar is pulled by each hand. The stroke in either sweep rowing or sculling is broken into distinct areas of transition: the catch, the drive, the finish, and the recovery. The catch is the point in the stroke cycle where the rower first places the oar in the water.

Fellow coach, Dr. Walter Peet, described the Glendon catch as long, but not as long as others of that era. To a modern rower, both catch and finish might look extreme, but Glendon did recognize the forces at play and began the shortening of the stroke—at least at the catch—toward the stroke used currently. Since Dr. Peet was a contemporary of Glendon and was a coach himself, he would have been capable of analyzing this.

The drive refers to when the oar is submerged after the catch and the rower is applying force through the legs, back, and arms to pry the boat past the oar plant. The finish is that point in the stroke when the legs have flattened, the back has opened, the arms have drawn in, the boat has been propelled forward across the water, and the oar is released from the water with a quick downward motion of the hands.

From the finish, the recovery begins again as the oar handle is pushed forward, away from the rower toward the stern of the boat. Sequentially the body of the rower is now sliding toward the feet, compressing the legs, readying to place the spoon (face) of the blade into the water at the next catch. The rower is now again ready for the next complete stroke cycle of catch, drive, finish, recovery, catch.

In terms of the effect of these transitions and positions in the stroke cycle, the catch is currently understood as the place where boat speed is the slowest. The drive, when the athlete is pulling on the oar handle and pushing against the footplate, is a place where boat speed is picking up and is greatest at the finish of the stroke. The finish is when the athlete releases the oar from the water at the end of the slide, and the recovery is when the athlete has the oar out of the water and is sliding back up toward the stern, getting prepared for another catch. One complete cycle from catch to finish to catch is called a stroke cycle and the rate is the number of stroke cycles per minute.[18]

The full experience of repetitive strokes to a rower would include periods of extreme exertion of the back and legs during the drive phase of the stroke cycle, when the blade is in the water and the boat is moving forward, coupled with a relaxed, slow return during the recovery phase, when the rower has the oar out of the water and is sliding back toward the catch and when the boat speed is slowing down. Like a car traveling at 60 miles an hour there are four points at a dead stop—these are the bottoms of the wheels in contact with the payment. So, too, when an eight-oared rowing shell is traveling forward, there are eight points at a dead stop—the wide spoons of the blades that are being anchored against the water at the catch.

The most critical features of the rowing stroke are the drive, when it is critical how the body applies the force, and the recovery, when the body weight is sliding back over the surface of the water, against the forward propulsion of the shell that the drive just created. The nuances of how to apply pressure and when, during the stroke cycle, is critical to boat speed and must be applied the same way by every rower in the boat, at the same time.

As stroke mechanics evolved through the centuries, rowers have gone from the British nineteenth-century stroke—what can best be described as a series of separate motions of legs, then back, then arms yanking—to Glendon's twentieth-century smoother, full-bodied stroke where the legs straighten as the back and arms open and draw. The motion that the athlete imparts to the oar handle translates through the oar, to the face of the blade into an action in the water. And how the oar works to deliver its force and power that cause the boat to move is determined largely by the placement of the oar in the water relative to the oarlock and the rower's center of mass. In terms of simple physics: The oar is a lever where the oarlock is one fulcrum, with the rower exerting pressure; the water is the weight that the rower pushes against, thereby driving the boat beyond the oar-plant. However, the physics of the rowing stroke are elaborate with the face of the blade in the water acting as a fulcrum, also. These intricacies were the world Glendon contemplated before sleeping at night.

The oar, through the stroke cycle, moves around the pin of the oarlock with the rower's hands on one end and the large spoon of the blade anchored in and against the water on the other. The speed and timing of the rower as they open through the stroke creates many turning forces—some act on the hull and some act on the water. These turning forces can make the hull undulate and veer from side to side as the sets of blades catch and release. Minimizing these forces—and indeed all forces except those that propel the hull straightforward with the greatest speed—is the goal of every crew and every coach.

Glendon recognized the importance and counterintuitive nature of applying more force in a smaller, yet more efficient area of the stroke than other coaches did who, in effect, wasted their crews' physical energy by having them apply power over a larger less efficient area, with the result of a slower boat speed. Intuitively, the unschooled rower thinks a big, long, powerful stroke, with a quick return for another stroke should move the boat swiftly—when in actuality, the controlled application of power in a specific, limited area, with careful, slow, balanced sliding in the recovery to the next stroke, actually makes for fewer strokes and greater boat speed. This balance of force and timing, and the counterintuitive nature of the stroke were inculcated in Glendon's crews in what became known as his creed.

Specifically, Glendon's creed is, "stick to the arc nearest the right angle," which ensures that the power applied to the oar by the rower is translated into forward movement of the rowing shell down the racecourse, rather than the power pushing water away from or toward the hull.[19]

Glendon's coaching notes and diagrams show a port oar that is at the catch, the point where the blade enters into the water, at 45 degrees, and at the finish, when the blade comes out of the water at 60 degrees. It is important to note that the boat moves past the oar-plant at the catch and through the stroke until released at the finish, rather than the oar simply pushing water past the boat.

It would be nearly half a century later that these types of indications could be readily determined with computer analysis as in modern rowing, but in 1919, it was only Glendon's careful eye and analytical mind that assessed these forces as described by Dr. Peet.[20] By applying the greatest pressure in the drive phase of the stroke just before the right angle (accomplished by traveling up the slide until the seat is through the pin in the oarlock) and grasping the effects of these hydrodynamics, Glendon adjusted the stroke technique to gain the advantage of rowing in the arc closest to the right angle. This minimized the turning forces that push water away from the hull (thereby doing nothing for making the boat go forward), and also minimized the turning forces that push water toward the hull at the finish (thereby causing turbulence and slowing the boat down as it exits the boat along the side of the hull, causing drag), and the boat goes faster. These forces are multimillion-dollar concerns on Americas Cup boats—particularly what is considered to be a more recent discovery of how water moves along and exits the hull.

The oar, from catch to finish, can travel a larger arc than what is most efficient to the forward movement of the hull. Glendon's creed of "row the arc closest to the right angle" was the most efficient arc to row in 1919 and is the most efficient arc to row nearly a century later. How did Glendon modify the stroke to achieve this efficiency and turn coaches' heads away from a style that had been rowed for hundreds of years toward a more advanced style? He had his rowers reach out less at the catch than other crews of the time (though his rowers still did have a moderate "Glendon layback" at the finish). This advancement of shortening the swing to the catch kept his crews sitting more upright at the catch and in the middle of the drive than other crews of the 1919–1920 period, which enabled them to apply more power.

This new application of power—perceived as a shorter, awkward stroke—required bigger, stronger athletes; for this, Glendon had another saying: "A good big man is better than a good small man."[21] Nothing would describe "his boys" better. One such giant was Vincent Gallagher, all grown up from his days as Little Vincenzio riding in his father's horse-drawn buggy, seeing the poor immigrant patients who lived in the tenement squalors and couldn't afford the Upper East Side doctors in New York. He would be the last man added to what would eventually be Glendon's Olympic eight. Gallagher was on the Hop (dance) Committee, and was not one to be shy around the "drags." At 190 pounds, six feet two inches, with huge deltoids forming a V on his physique, he stood arrow straight and let his muscular arms rest loosely at his sides. His hair turned prematurely iron gray while still at the Academy. He was a brainy kid with a propensity for science and math. A star man—he would graduate eleventh in his class. Gallagher was a perfect specimen for Glendon's new stroke mechanics, which required bigger, more powerfully built men to apply power in what was less a swinging motion (English orthodoxy) than a prying motion (American orthodoxy).

WHO WERE THESE OARSMEN AND WHY DID PEOPLE admire them? Exceptionally versatile Clyde King, who switched sides from starboard to port, to gain the premier stroke seat, no small feat in the pressure of an Olympic year, was the quintessential strokeman and of particular interest. In a dialogue in Vincent Treanor's "Looks Them Over," *New York Evening World* of 1929, he interviewed the famous athletic trainer Doc Barrett and Coach Dick Glendon, as they sized up the sport:

> Doc began, "I've been in all kinds of sports for thirty-five years and there's nothing that can compare with rowing. A boy has to be a he-man to get on those slides. I'd like to see some of those fighters get in there with an oar in their hands. They'd quit sure. And those husky football players don't fall over themselves trying to make the crew. It's too hard for them . . . now take those other sports," went on Doc Barrett. "Baseball first. They knock the ball out to the shortstop. He grabs it and tosses it over to first. Then he stands there up straight and relaxes. The football player gets into a scrimmage and then he enjoys a period of relaxation. And those fighters, what do they pull? Three minutes of slapping and then dance back to their corners for a minute's rest."
>
> Glendon cut in, saying, "Rowing is like thoroughbred horse racing. Like the racehorses, the crews start, and then they finish. There is NO in-between let up. They must give up all they have all the way. It's a real test of strength and courage."

Doc came back with, "They can't make any mistakes either. If one man goes bad, he spoils the entire boat."

"That," resumed Glendon, "is one of the chief worries of a coach. A sick stomach, or a touch of indigestion on the day of the race in any of the boys, and the best laid plans go wrong. . . ." What do the coaches look for? "A youngster who can get into the boat on the day of the race and just settle down as if he is rowing against one of his own crews, is the natural oarsman. But it's the same with crews as it is with good horses. You can tell a good oarsman sometimes just by the way he sits up straight in the shell."

". . . I [Glendon] once heard Clyde King . . . say that it takes more than nerve and courage to stroke a crew in a championship race than to do anything else in the sport line. There is a tenseness about the start of a rowing race that isn't associated with any other branch of competition. You can't move around like other athletes do. You must sit still, wait, and then get under way with the slightest possible loss of time."[22]

Glendon's ideas were radical, revolutionary—and considered a folly by some. The matchup between Navy and Leander, if fate could clear a path, would in essence be modern dance's Martha Graham meets Balanchine, or the finesse of football's Joe Montana against the hard-hitting Chicago Bears—style and grace against raw power and energy. In the eyes of the world this emerging saga truly was akin to the 1980 "Miracle on Ice," when the young American college students beat the nearly professional Russian hockey machine.

Glendon sought out certain elements in his men, particularly his stroke man, captain, and coxswain to fit his new theories of crew. Unlike rowers at Harvard, Yale, or Leander who had come up through the prestigious prep school rowing programs likes those of Kent, Exeter, and Eton, the would-be rowers at Navy had little or no rowing experience. From the stern of the shell forward, stroke to bow, Glendon's crews consisted of men from around the United States who were at the Academy first and foremost to be sailors, not rowers. Glendon had to mold them into the positions he wanted.

Glendon also had a set opinion about what was required to be a good stroke and good coxswain. He described his ideas about King and Clark:

> An ideal stroke oar should be able to set the pace according to the caliber of the crew he is up against, never forgetting for an instant the limits of his own crew. It is better to be beaten one-half or three-quarters of a boat length in rowing a heady race, than to row the crew off their seats trying some new stunt and probably get beaten by a dozen lengths.
>
> Clyde King, [stroke-oar of the 1920] Navy Crew, was an exceptional oarsman, inasmuch as he always seemed to know what his rivals were doing and the best move to counteract it. In his two-mile race against Harvard on the Severn he rowed the Harvard crew off their feet in the first mile of the race, forcing them to hold a stroke of 34 per minute, which was a little more than they were accustomed to. Although he was driving his own crew to the tune of 36, he was quick to notice the first break in the Harvard boat and immediately lowered the stroke, easing the strain on his crew without affecting the pace of the boat perceptibly, and drawing slowly away from Harvard. He eased his crew through the middle distance enough to leave them reserve strength to drive over the last quarter at 38 a minute, finishing with his crew in good shape five lengths in front.

A successful stroke-oar should have many qualities necessary in a captain, he should be a natural leader and must have the confidence of the whole crew in his ability to set the pace and hold it. A stroke oar should know the pace to set for his crew that will produce the best results; how to get off the starting line, and just when to lower the beat enough to hold his rivals through the middle distance, when to spurt if necessary and to always hold something in reserve for the final dash to the finish line. . . . [23]

A coxswain should be elected primarily for his weight. He should not weigh more than 110 pounds. . . . Outside of calling the beat of the stroke, and watching the watermanship of the crew, he should above everything else, steer the boat straight and keep a sharp watch ahead. Coxswains who are continually yelling at the crew, picking out faults in their oarsmanship, as a rule do more harm than good. Except to call attention to prominent faults, a coxswain should maintain a discrete silence in connection with this phase of his work.[24]

Stroke oar and cox were as one unit, as were stroke and Gallagher at seven. Stern pair, King and Gallagher, took their cues from Cutie Clark who steered their course with a quiet confidence in courage and inspiration. Clark's crew loved him for his decisive and direct manner that never criticized, never demeaned. Clark gave his crews a heady confidence and they gave him gold medals and the traditional toss off the dock that victorious coxswains were "entitled to"—and he loved every minute of it.

Another feature that Glendon perfected was using an American oar that was wider than an English oar, yielding the equivalent of a broader "sweet" spot (as in a Prince tennis racket), thereby extending the point of leverage to add more force. William "Buck" Jordan, one of the tallest members of the crew at six feet three-and-a-half inches, was a tree of a man with blue eyes and long arms to reach out and take advantage of the rigging and oar that Glendon perfected.

And then there was Victor "Jack" Jacomini, who at six feet five inches was the windbreak for the crew. His bow seat was the narrowest part of the boat and in the case of Glendon's designs, the part of the boat skimming over the surface of the water. Two of the most important seats in the boat are stroke and bow. Stroke sets the cadence but bow has the hardest seat to row and must have the cleanest exit from the finish to avoid a crab (a situation that can occur when the timing is off and one rower exits the water late and the forward run of the boat traps the oar under the hull and violently rips an oar from the rower's hand to smack him in the chest or chin or catapults him from the boat entirely); it's difficult to predict a crab, as the pulsing hull feels alive, light, and moving beneath him. Jack's seat was farthest from stroke man King and last in the line of rhythm. Even with wind or spray on his back, he had to enter and exit his blade perfectly clean.

Working with Jack in bow pair was Edwin Darius Graves in two. He was the captain of the crew and was twenty-three years old, weighing in at 176 pounds. Eddie, as he was affectionately called, "gave not only his good right, and his good left arms but his heart, his cheerful optimism, and his tireless energy to the crew."[25]

Since Glendon was experimenting and eventually choosing taller, heavier men than the English crews, the boat had to be able to float the increase in weight. So Glendon had a stiffer boat built. A stiff hull meant less flexion along the hull during the drive—less flexion meant the boat would track along in the water straighter and faster. Dr. Walter Peet described the boat as flat-bottomed and able to skim along in the bow; and due to its new hull shape, it also could withstand the heavier rowers. Heavier men needed a strong, well-built hull to structurally withstand the strain of their pulling and pushing. Glendon therefore considered hull shapes, hull material, and the slickness of the bottom of the shell to be important—results from oiling the bottoms of ducks to test their buoyancy determined the proper amount of oil to be rubbed over the hull.[26]

The boat, ah, the boat. So beautiful in craftsmanship, so elegant, strong, and sleek, crafted with all the shine, joinery, and smoothness of expensive furniture. The boats were up to 64 feet long, built upside down with smooth wooden bottoms steamed into a gentle "U" shape over the intricate latticed frame. The tiller was made of wood that tracked the boat by the coxswains' moving a line or wire stretched taut from the top of the tiller up the 8 or 10 feet sternward washbox to the coxswain's hands. A small keel, 10 inches long by 4 or 5 inches high and very thin, was attached near the tiller. The decks of the boats were canvas, fastened with hundreds of copper tacks along the upper edge of the shell and covered in varnish to waterproof them. These airtight compartments add buoyancy. The rowing "stations" were eight in number from stern to bow; each consisting of a seat raised up on a platform, that rolled on wheels up a two-foot-long slide. The rowers' feet rested on the bottom of the boat in clogs made of copper heal cups and "leathers," with ties like a shoe for the arch of the foot. Each station in an eight had an oarlock and a rigger bolted to its side, right or left, positioned midway between the feet and the knees. The oar protruded into the boat to the rowers' hands so that the main points of contact for exertion were the hands on the oar handle, the feet in the foot-stretcher, and the buttock on the seat.

The "engine room"—seats five, six, seven—was the power of the boat. It carried Sanborn, Johnston, and Gallagher. Alden "Zeke"

Sanborn in five was six feet three inches tall and weighed 183 pounds. His steady gaze and demeanor and strong nose caused him to acquire the nickname "Mr. Positive." Strong willed and someone who said what he felt, Zeke never looked back on a decision. Like Jacomini, he wore his hair straight up from the forehead, making him look even taller. Someone who tanned easily, he carried his heavily veined hands in an open, ready, confident gesture.

These men were the hardest pullers and were expected to haul on the oar. Power, pure and simple, was to be applied here. Forget finesse—pull the damn oar and make the boat go fast. This was the widest part of the rowing shell, making it the most forgiving. And in Glendon's design it was also the most fortified. He had strengthened the gunnels of the craft to withstand the pounds per square inch that these young Adonises were capable of generating. Horsepower pure and simple was the name of the game, as they were learning in their physics and maritime courses. Some unique features of Glendon's design were its broad, flatter bottom to get it up on plane faster, and its two-to-three-inch scalloped overhang built along the length of his eight that blocked rough water from coming in over the gunnels.[27]

Glendon was a student of physics and empirical knowledge. In short, his boats went fast because he built fast boats. This sounds redundant and overly simple but it is the essence of the art of coaching rowing: Consider every nuance of the whole—boats, oars, rowers—and then and only then do you have a fast crew. Experimentation all season long, year after year, built speed. There are no "lucky combinations" for a good coach. For a good coach, time-tested copious notes from which to build a methodology of performance is the winning combination—and Glendon knew it, followed it, lived by it.

The men are so much a part of the boat and vice versa that the seats are contoured to rest the buttocks solidly. The oar handle is scraped with a rasp to give the hand its grip, and foot-stretchers are angled to advance the forward lean necessary for reach and yet hold the athlete still in the finish. Unlike baseball bats that are thrown aside after a hit, or tennis rackets that can change sides or hands during volley, a rowing station once sat in, is it, for the duration of the race. From start to finish one can only catch, pull, drive, finish, recover, and start again: approximately two hundred strokes to a 2,000-meter course. The athlete is "pinned in" as it were, to a relentless station of wood, leather, and iron. The shell capable of accelerating to 18 knots generates the most horsepower of any human-powered watercraft.

The aforementioned stroke, oar, and boat refinements, and discoveries that Glendon had been tinkering with and perfecting for some fifteen years since his beginning at Navy, were about to finally be put into practice to complete the extraordinary picture. This is equivalent in motor racing to building the best race car, with the fastest engine, best tires, and best drivers. It was the combination of all the American Orthodox factors of Scientific Oarsmanship that Glendon was about to unleash.

8. THE AMERICAN SEASONS OF 1919–1920

I suppose it sounds archaic, but I cannot help thinking that the people with motor boats miss a great deal. If they would only use oars or paddle themselves, they would get infinitely more benefit than by having their work done for them. . . .

—Theodore Roosevelt

———

IN THE BITING HARSH WIND OF AN EARLY SPRING day in 1919, Glendon strode down the wooden steps of the Annapolitan Club, made a left at the sidewalk, and headed up Franklin Street toward the boathouse and tanks, much as he'd done for fifteen years since taking up residence at the club—his home away from home when not at Cape Cod. Coming from hours of speculating over rigging diagrams and lineups, talking late into the night on the leather overstuffed sofas in the parlor with crew backers and alums, Glendon brimmed with pride. Let the ice melt! Let the river flow! There was a readiness to his step as he walked the streets of Annapolis this spring morning, nodding with a wry smile to the onlookers' questions of, "How's the crew look this year, Dick?" "How are the boys?"

The war had left its mark on the Academy. If the war had

dragged on, it would have meant the end of the season at any moment; as it was, the brief entry into the war had left a heightened sense of purpose and dedication.

On his way to the first water practice of this new year, Glendon ruminated that 1919 would ultimately be an uphill battle. The war was over but its near brush of the campus had heightened the patriotic tenor and war mode around Annapolis. The Academy was, after all, a military school unaccustomed to relinquishing duty time for the year-round athletic training needed to stay competitive with the Ivy League (used as a popular designation for those schools) and private schools. Seasonal football practice in the autumn afternoon was one thing, but dedicating year-long practice time to the rigors of crew: water time, tank time, and weight training, for a mere three or four collegiate competitions that could be "blown out" by a strong wind and rough water was frowned upon by the Academy. Glendon had to make revisions in daily training table meals, arrange for critical, special transportation of boats, and for what? he wondered at times. Even if Navy were the greatest crew in the United States, Naval Academy athletes were forbidden from international competition and it would take an act from the Secretary of the Navy to unlock that door.

If problems within the Academy walls weren't enough, the occasional naysayers in the press were of no help. The Academy depended on public image for its recruits, so too, the crew relied on support of its alums to rally a cry of advancement. To succeed to the heights it envisioned, the crew needed to be top-notch to showcase in front of the alumni and athletic department administrators against the likes of Penn, Columbia, Harvard, and Yale, who boasted the sons of U.S. Presidents in their shells.

But Glendon was used to challenging conditions. Old New England salt that he was, he wasn't about to let a few bad storms or rough weather, literally or figuratively, deprive him of his goal. He felt that the tide was about to change. Indeed, something unique was happening at Navy—Glendon knew it and other coaches were starting to suspect it.

Due to the war and graduation, the crew of the 1919 boat needed to be filled mostly by inexperienced and untried underclassmen. Glendon's scientific oarsmanship continued to be honed, and glimpses of his strategy of bigger rowers can be seen in a *New York Times* article of 5 April 1919, that lists the physical statistics of all his crews.[1] Losing six of the varsity to graduation, Glendon looked to the ranks of the second varsity and the Plebe crew to build his dynasty.[2] His ideas were in place—and in crew the boat, the oars, the technique, coaching, and training were the real avenues of success. In rowing, a coach's vision is greater than the men in the seats. It is the collective combination of vision and manpower that elevates single bodies into the common greatness of a crew. Glendon saw the possibilities coming together. From bow to stern the 1919 eight was: Sanborn, Graves, Weidman, Skinner, Ballreich, Repplier, Harris, Ingram, and Crawford.[3] Glendon states in April 1919 that, "his material is the best he has ever had from a new class."[4] The article ends on the very optimistic note, "The Navy crews are progressing finely, and the finest rowing season in the history of the academy is anticipated."[5]

The 1919 season opener began with everyone from Penn and Navy on the banks of the Severn remembering this dual race in 1918 and one incident in particular which had been a turning point that began Navy crew's dignity and near mythical reputation. "The crew season of 1918 started but with only two returning varsity men . . . but 'Dick' took a hold with his usual snap and developed the raw material he saw at the first day of practice. His hopes hinged on a man named Ingram who needed to get under 185 pounds so Glendon could 'make a stroke out of him. Ingram did just that. When Pennsylvania came to race they were considered the smoothest and fastest team in the east and shown their rudder to every other crew that year.

"The weather was rainy and half a gale was blowing but Dick Glendon in a very generous and sportsmanlike manner gave the choice of course to the visitors, which is not much of an advantage on an ordinary day, but on a rough day gives an almost unbeatable one to the lucky man . . . the Pennsylvania crew had it all over Navy as they rowed down the lee side under the bluff, while the Navy crew, with more powerful men straining, tugged in the heavy waves midstream, gamely, but vainly, trying to catch her more polished rival. But an incident occurred which brought Navy more a greater distinction that even victory could have done.

"One minute and fifteen seconds after the start Pennsylvania's bowman snapped his oar putting the race on ice for Navy, had they desired to take it that way. But Navy stopped and after a new start were beaten, and although there were some who criticized the action of the crew—it is doubtful if there is one man in the Academy who does not feel that it was the sportsmanlike and gentlemanly thing to do and does not feel that any other action would have been unworthy of the spirit of the Naval Academy and of the Service."[6]

WHEN NAVY WON THIS DAY IN 1919, OVER THE University of Pennsylvania at home on the Severn River over a distance of two miles, *The New York Times* reported "Navy's Crack Crew Beats Penn Easily."[7] After much anticipation of a great season, the next race against Harvard and Princeton was crucial. Navy won again and never looked back. The press began to refer to the 1919 Academy crew as "the mighty Navy crew."[8] The Naval Academy won all of its seasonal regattas in 1919, which drew much attention to the national championship at the American Henley in Philadelphia.[9]

On 29 May 1919, *The New York Times* heightened the attention given the event by noting that, "The Navy crews that are to participate in the American Henley Regatta over the national course on the Schuylkill River on Saturday arrived in the city today. They came by train, but their shells and attendants were on four U-boat chasers, which anchored in the river."[10] The message was clear that Navy came to fight. One newspaper caption stated, "Navy Here with $65,000 to Bet on Crew; $13,000 Covered by Penn."[11] The article continues, "the Middies, always noted for their keen desire to bet, raised a pool of $65,000 but up until last night were only able to get $13,000 covered by [Penn's] red and blue followers. The other $52,000 may be swung over to the pool that has been raised to bet against the Army in the annual baseball game tomorrow."[12] (There was no Army/Navy football game to bet on since this annual event was halted in 1916 due to the war.)

Glendon, with crews arriving on the Baltimore and Ohio Railroad and shells arriving on the submarine chasers, knew and seemed to be practicing the art of intimidation as part of his scientific oarsmanship.[13] At 4:10 P.M. on Saturday, 31 May, they left no doubt of their superiority.[14] Navy crossed the line first to win the Stewards Challenge Cup, beating Syracuse and the University of Pennsylvania.[15] After winning the American Henley, so-named because the length of the course—a mile and five-sixteenths—is exactly the same as the prestigious Henley Royal Regatta in England, Navy had proved "beyond all cavil that it was the best eight in the East."[16]

Headlines on page 28 in *The New York Times* of 8 June 1919 crowed, the "Annapolis Crew Declared to be by Far the Best College Eight of the Season" even before the prestigious Harvard-Yale race.[17]

A revealing and stunningly important article by Dr. Walter Peet, past coach of Columbia, proceeded to dissect and analyze the empirical thinking of Glendon that in a nutshell is a synopsis of the Glendon stroke, which is the basis of the newly found and tried American Orthodoxy. Peet explained:

> Rowing enthusiasts are most curious to know why these middies are in a class by themselves, and what manner of stroke this *wonder crew* uses, especially as it has been 'pointed out' that their style is at variance with that of other rowing institutions, and not in accordance with the orthodox fundamental principles of the English stroke, which more or less closely, have been followed by our universities.
>
> The writer has been in touch with the Navy's rowing development for over twenty years and coached a Columbia crew that won at Annapolis. Dick Glendon has been the Navy mentor for seventeen seasons. This clever coach has worked along the ideas of the old professional sculler and has thrown all other theories to the wind. Also, he is a close student of the mechanics of rowing. Briefly, Glendon—teaching his men a homely, awkward stroke, according to all accepted theories— gets them to commence to put on their power while the blades are just a bit forward of the right angle to the side of the boat. Glendon's rowing creed is: "Stick to the arc nearest the right angle." According to the simplest mechanics this is where power properly propels. With an abnormally long reach the blades push water away from the sides of the boat and with a torso swing too far toward the bow they shove water inward— which is wasted energy and which does not count in putting the boat ahead. . . .

This is how Glendon does it: There is a fairly long torso swing toward the stern—much shorter however, than that of any of the others—and the slide goes a bit aft of the pin of the rowlock, which makes for a good beginning of the leg drive. The leg muscles are the most powerful in the human anatomy, and on the long sliding seats the middies get all there is to be gathered from them. At the beginning of the stroke the slides, (leg drive) body swing and arm work start together with the idea in each man's head that the eternal right angle is to be uppermost for the efficiency point.

Glendon has been a great student of rigging and shell construction. In rigging he places the stretchers (footrests) so that the kinetic kick comes precisely at the right angle.

The Navy coach's order for the shell that won from Pennsylvania in last year's final race and that won so consistently this Spring, covered a great many points. Al Ward of Englewood was the builder. Glendon had an exceptionally heavy boatload of men and his designs called for a shell with a flat bottom and wide floor. This craft, which was trimmed so that she rode up at the bow, floated the crew perfectly and "skimmed" over the water with consequent little resistance. Also the flat bottom and wide floor made for stability and an even keel, which always spell speed.

Glendon's theories certainly have made good. He has had no "lucky combinations," as so many coaches have had, but he has been a consistent teacher of winning crews for years. . . .

But it must be said that conditions and environment are all in favor of successful aquatics at Annapolis for these simple reasons: (1) Everybody has to pass a rigid physical examination on entrance, and he practically is in training throughout his four years; (2) the boat houses are right on the grounds. . . . And from the very nature of what is to be his life work, every prospective naval officer wants to "make the crew."[18]

In short, Peet described Glendon's empirical thinking as that of someone who deduced and intuited power and performance ratios and techniques that modern rowing coaches still use and have confirmed with computer analysis. Glendon's break from English orthodoxy led him to develop new stroke, boat, and rigging designs that are the harbingers of the modern era of rowing, as it exists today.

THE 1919 SEASON LED TO THE 1920 WINTER INdoor training in the tanks, with anticipation of the upcoming Olympic year, spring rowing, and scheduling. In early February, a special to *The New York Times* disclosed a change in the usual Navy home schedule. Princeton, Syracuse, Harvard, Yale, and Union Boat Club would be coming to the Severn River for a "brush with the midshipmen."[19]

The news "Navy Crews Quit Tank" was printed on 13 March 1920. The fact that a major newspaper would even publish the day the crew left the indoor tanks to practice on the water is indicative of the intense interest in Glendon's crew, from which he and the nation knew he might get the chance to eventually choose his Olympic eight.

In the dim yellow twilight after an early spring practice, reading *The New York Times* articles while taking his evening meal in the Annapolitan Club, Glendon had to have smiled. As he sat chewing on a cigar, in the overstuffed leather chair vaguely aware of other boarders whose steps creaked by on the hardwood floors as they passed through the entrance hall, or pulled up close to the manteled fireplace or climbed the white enameled staircase on the east side of the house, he watched as a new guest nodded and signed the guest book on the small wooden table to the right of the dining room archway, much as he himself had done sixteen years earlier.

His son Richard "Rich" had signed into that book, too, in recent years to help him—theirs was a coaching legacy. His other son Hubert coached at Columbia. America expected a great deal from the Glendons. Would they get it, he wondered, as he folded his paper and bade the small gathering of men good night and walked heavy-footed up the stairs and down the hallway to his modest room on the right. As he laid his thinning hair on the pillow, amidst a room of few personal mementos—family photos, letters, oiled-canvas coaching jacket, key fob, and pocket watch—he picked up a copy of Leander coach Rudy Lehmann's book off his nightstand and began his nightly ritual of reading about and analyzing his elusive opponent.

The rowers exhausted themselves on the water every day that spring, vying between first and second varsity for a seat in the coveted first eight. And the boatman, Chandler, ever present in his overalls and moustache, caring for the boys as much as the boats, himself a wry character and one of the keenest judges of oarsman, said, "It suttinly looks to me as though we're goin' to have a mighty fine crew this year."[20] He was right—1920 was replete with epoch-making occurrences.[21]

The first varsity, second varsity, lightweight, and freshmen (plebe) crews were all important to Glendon. Glendon would change rowers around throughout the season to get the ultimate combination. In March, the Navy crews of 1920 were set: First varsity: Bow, Jacomini; 2, Renard; 3, Jordan; 4, Graves (Captain); 5, Sanborn; 6, Johnston; 7, Weidman; stroke, King. Second varsity: Bow, Gallagher; 2, Reisenger; 3, Lee; 4, Moore; 5, Richardson; 6, Holland; 7, Litchfield; stroke,

Wanselow. Plebe crew: Bow, Schade; 2, Will; 3, Kirkpatrick; 4, White; 5, Jackson; 6, Bradley; 7, Browning; stroke, Huntington.[22] From these crews, after finding the right combination, Glendon would eventually choose his Olympic eight.

On 24 April, with Navy at home on the Severn River, Harvard came to row. It was the first race of the season at the Academy. After a long winter of training and "stirring the water in the tanks at the natatorium," and cold practices beginning on the water in late February, their home waters on the Severn River were still rough and choppy with small whitecaps. A heavy southwest wind made it impossible for the crews to row on Saturday. Navy and Harvard waited for the weather to cooperate. Sunday racing was "out of the official question." On Monday morning the weather cleared enough for the crews to go head-to-head. As was typical of the time, the competition ran from novices, to second varsity, to varsity.[23]

With few fans to cheer them, the Harvard freshmen and the Navy Plebes finally launched their shells and rowed "to the start of the two-mile race." The plebes got off the line first against the Harvard freshmen and never lost their lead. They finished four lengths ahead—Navy 12:24 and Harvard 12:40. The second varsity eight was about the same with Navy winning by six lengths—Navy 12:15 to Harvard's 12:38. The Harvard varsity, proudly touting what it considered its "Middy beating machine" in its varsity oarsmen, intended to save the day with a win. It wasn't to be. Harvard finished "about five lengths astern of Navy"; Navy with a time of 11:48 to Harvard's 12:28. Harvard, unaccustomed to losing, left the Severn with a resolve to wait and beat Navy later in the season.[24]

The news that Navy easily outrowed Harvard hit *The New York Times* on 27 April. The article praised the watermanship of the midshipmen as "easily superior to that of their rivals, and better prepared to meet the roughness of the water . . . in spite of this [the rough water] the midshipmen got a splendid drive to their shell, which was lacking in Harvard's boat." The article went on further to point out that Dick Glendon's son, an assistant on the plebe crew, scored a Navy win also.[25]

Columbia would arrive to race Navy next. According to a *New York Times* article, Columbia Coach Rice was optimistic to race but during a practice session on the rough water the afternoon before the race, "the superior physique of the Navy oarsmen was very plainly in evidence."[26] Two weeks after Harvard's defeat, Columbia fared no better. On the shortened Henley-style course of about a mile and five-sixteenths, the Navy plebes won by six lengths in 7:25 with Columbia's freshman at 7:36. The second varsity had Navy at 7:25 and Columbia 7:46. All eyes were on the varsity crews. Columbia jumped to a fast lead, only to be rowed down in the rough water by Navy, who won by five lengths. Times: Navy 7:19 and Columbia 7:36.[27] Not a Navy crew had seen defeat yet.

Heavy weather again stepped in to upstage scheduled events when Boston's Union Boat Club had to leave without racing its intermediate and senior eights. This was a grave concern to Navy, who had to face mighty Syracuse next. On the fifteenth of May the second varsity race was the closest Navy had seen all season. Navy just barely nosed out Syracuse 10:37 to 10:38. The varsity crews were next on the two-mile course. Syracuse took off to an early lead and was ahead by a length at a quarter mile from the start. Navy pulled even throughout the body of the race until nearing the finish when Syracuse handed Navy its sole defeat by 7 feet— Syracuse 10:20, Navy 10:21.[28]

Sources at the time hint that perhaps Navy lost due to overconfidence, and with its toughest races ahead, the loss to Syracuse instilled the "will to win" in Navy.[29] The college championships, American

Henley, and the Olympic trials would soon tell if Glendon could get the focus back into the crew.

At 5 P.M. on Memorial Day weekend Navy raced and won (7 minutes 3 2/8 seconds) in the heats for the Child's Cup (1—Navy, 2—Princeton, 3—U. of Penn, 4—Columbia) of the American Henley held in Philadelphia. This prestigious race has been annually rowed since it began in 1879 with a regatta between Columbia, Princeton, and University of Pennsylvania.[30] By special invitation the Navy crew was asked to row in 1920. The next day, Saturday, as part of the same prestigious regatta on the Schuylkill River, Navy was in the final. Racing against what were considered the best collegiate crews in the country, Navy won in 6 minutes 30 seconds (1—Navy, 2—Syracuse, 3—Princeton, 4—Union Boat Club).[31] Navy looked unbeatable, refusing to let the earlier loss to Syracuse deprive them of their goal—winning the Olympic Trials in July.

9. THE BRITISH SEASON OF 1920

You cannot stay on the summit forever; you have to come down again. So why bother in the first place? Just this: What is above knows what is below, but what is below does not know what is above. One climbs, one sees. One descends, one sees no longer, but one has seen. There is an art of conducting oneself in the lower regions by the memory of what one saw higher up. When one can no longer see, one can at least still know.

—Rene Daumal, Everest mountaineer

LOFTY, ETHEREAL THINKING INDEED.

The stage was set; a British routing was afoot. It was unthinkable. And as America went through its spring and early summer racing schedule to determine its National Champion, England's collegiate best, namely Cambridge and Oxford, were doing the same.

The Boat Race, a dual meet between Cambridge and Oxford held for the last seventy-two years, is *the* college race of the year in Britain. Like America's spring training for baseball camps, all eyes monitor the Cambridge and Oxford boats through their early-season ups and downs waiting for the March Boat Race, and a precursor to the British equivalent of the World Series in June—Henley Royal Regatta.

The British spring season of 1920 was no different. While American crews concentrated on races between Harvard, Yale, Navy, Penn, Union, and Syracuse, the top British crews, Cambridge and Oxford, concentrated only on Cambridge and Oxford. The Boat Race, early on in March 1920, was *the* premier race followed in the daily newspapers and *The Times* with all the flair and details of an Indianapolis 500. Daily wind direction, latest body weights of the rowers and coxes, whether they practiced on ebb or flow, which launches were up and running, how the Princes would be attended to, the Press launch, the Mile Post times, and the low water at Ibis's boathouse were all matters of national importance.

Omnibus tickets, car-paddock sites, and airspace above the racing was limited. Crowd control was published in the paper, as thousands of fans were expected to swarm the bridges and riverbanks of downtown London. The war was over. The country's spirit was light. The ebb and flow of the Thames tide ran again with peaceful currents without the knotted eddies of war. The gears of the British rowing world were churning along again at full throttle. Everything was in place.

The Brits once again could fill the columns of their newsprint with details of what really occupied their imagination: namely, everything to do with crew. And on 24 March, *The Times* rowing correspondent, for the first time since the war broke out five years previous, observed and reported on the progress of the Boat Race with a fine eye for every delicious detail; nothing can more vividly convey the English enthusiasm for rowing than the daily newspaper accounts of the practices and the race. Names of those lucky few boated, their latest weights, and style, were scrutinized on a daily basis. Cambridge was boasting H. Boret in bow, J. Simpson in two, A. Dixon in three seat, R. McLewen in four, H. Playford in five, J. Campbell in six, S. Swann at seven, with P. Hartley stroking and R. Johnstone as cox. As reported in *The Times*:

The crews had another glorious spring day for their practice at Putney. And with Cambridge due to row their first trial over the full course, it was no surprise to find a very large crowd along the towpath—one of the largest ever seen on a practice day.

Cambridge had much better luck with their trial than in their first attempt exactly a week earlier. On that occasion the conditions were about as bad as they could be, and, with the boat waterlogged, the trial was abandoned at Hammersmith. Yesterday the conditions were better than any crew has had for a practice row for some years past. The wind came from the NE, light, the best quarter for a row on the flood, the tide was a fast one, and there was a perfect sheet of water. Good judges were of the opinion that the trial should be rowed in 19 min., and Cambridge got within a second of this time.

The times with Oxford during their full course last Saturday, were under, although the comparison is not of great value, as the conditions were nothing like so favorable in the matter of wind and tide when Oxford went over: at the mile post Cambridge was 4'9" [4 minutes 9 seconds] to Oxford's 4'25", at the Hammersmith Bridge Cambridge 7'28" to Oxford 7'56", at Chiswick Steps Cambridge was 11'46" to Oxford's 12'23", Barnes Bridge had Cambridge at 16'4" with Oxford at 16' 55" and at the finish Cambridge 19'1" and Oxford 20'59".

The trial was undoubtedly satisfactory to the Cambridge supporters. The crew were well together, from the stretchers, and they kept their form right up to the finish. They were unable to shake off the Leander crew, which had come to pace them

from Chiswick to Barnes, but Leander had a very good crew rowing and they had the inside station at the start. The race promises
to be very open, but Cambridge will probably start favorites.

Prince Albert and Prince Harry propose to be present at
the race, which they will witness from the umpire's launch.

Oxford had S. Earl at bow, N. McNeil at two, A. Durard at
three, A. Bill four, D. Raskes at five, W. James six, H Cairns
seven and M. Ellis stroking with W. Porritt at cox. Oxford went
out at 11 o'clock. They paddled up to the football ground and
then tried three starts, the count showing 10 strokes in 15" on
each occasion. Turning below Harrods they dropped down to
try three starts from a stake-boat. The first two were tens
[strokes] and the crew then rowed a quarter, half, and a full
minute. The count showed 10-20 1/2-40 for the quarter, half,
and full minute. This was the fastest rate of stroke the crew had
attempted, and they got the boat moving very quickly. They
were out about half an hour.

Oxford were out again in the evening at 5:30 to row on the
ebb. They had with them London Rowing Club crew. . . . Some
good pieces of paddling and a few rowing bursts took the crew up
to Thornycroft's, London stopping at the Eyot. After turning,
Oxford paddled down to the Chiswick Steps to row to Hammersmith Bridge. They had a fairly good ebb under them. Ellis made
the rate 10-19 1/2-36 1/2 at the start and then dropped to 33. London took on the trained crew before reaching the lower end of
the Eyot, and then took nearly a length start. Oxford gained
steadily, and when they reached the Bridge, were nearly clear of
the scratch crew, stroked by J. Beresford. Along the boathouses
the crews tried a burst of rowing, in which Oxford took half a
length on Thames [the other crews were there to act as pacers

along the course] in half a minute. It was 6:30 when the crew came ashore. The crew will be out today at 10:45 and 3:15.

In the afternoon Cambridge went out just before 3 o'clock to row the full course under perfect conditions of wind and water. . . . The crews went to stakeboats [anchored starting stations], London taking three-quarters of a length start. Hartley made the rate 10-19-36 1/2 in the quarter, half and full minute, and 34 in the second minute. Cambridge rowed with fine dash, and drew clear of London in two minutes. Dropping the rate to 29 they reached the Mile Post in 4'9". At Harrods they were doing 28 and traveling smoothly and well. They reached Hammersmith Bridge in 7'26", still rowing 28. Along the Eyot, a strong Leander scratch [pace] crew awaited them, the order of rowing being: R. Barrett, bow, H. Peake, G. C. Brown, A. R. Wiggins, R. S. Shove, A. Garten, Honorable J. Fremantle at seven and E. D. Horsfall at stroke with Scott coxing. Leander led a trifle at Chiswick Steps, reached by Cambridge in 11'47". The crew had a headwind above the steps, and some disturbed water, but they kept going with a good length and swing. They spurted to 32, but failed to cut down Leander, and another spurt near the Bridge had the same result. Leander led by over half a length when Cambridge shot Barnes Bridge in 16'4", rowing 30. Leander then eased, as an Auriol Boat Club scratch boat was waiting just above the bridge, to pace the trained crew to the finish. . . . The latter took a lead of the best part of a length, but Cambridge gained steadily all the way in, and spurting up to 32 at the Brewery beat Auriol by a quarter of a length, and completed the full distance in 19'1". They finished very strongly, and were not rowed out. They took the boat in at the Ibis Rowing Club boathouse just above the finish, and returned by road.

A motor-omnibus service has been arranged to run on Saturday between 3 and 5 pm from Queen's Club to the Cambridge Rowing Club enclosure on the Duke's Meadows at Chiswick. Tickets, 3 shillings, will be on sale at the main entrance, Queen's Club, during the sports, or seats (prepaid) may be booked. . . . Tickets for the Cambridge University Boat Club enclosure are still on sale, and may be obtained by the public from . . . for 15 shillings, 7 shillings 6 pence including tea. The band of the Coldstream Guards will be in attendance, and a paddock for cars will be provided.[1]

AND SO WENT THE WEEK'S REPORTING ON A DAILY basis. Wind, ebb tide or flow, who was in and who was out of the boat, every maneuver right or wrong by a coxswain—everything was unsentimentally published in the paper. So keen was the public interest that the entire week's progress of the crews was carried in *The Times*. The significance of the status of workouts, which launch was in best working order, and whether or not the Princes were going to be in attendance the day of the race, were paramount. Even relatively quiet workouts were published for rumination:

"The crews had a quiet day's work at Putney yesterday. The period for long rows against the watch is over, and the coaches are now engaged in timing the crews up to get off the start quickly, and to row a high rate of stroke in the first minute or two. Yesterday the wind had veered right round from N.E. to S.W., and the sky was overcast, but the rain which threatened held off.

"Oxford showed great dash, and they are now able to row a much faster stroke than at one time appeared likely. They were rather ragged in the first minute, when bow caught a crab but made a good recovery. In the second minute they rowed uncommonly well, and went away from the Thames scratch crew very fast. It is evident that both crews are reasonably fast, and the result appears to be very open.

"The launch used by the Oxford coach has broken down, and yesterday Mr. Gold had the use of one of the Press launches for coaching. The Marltana was to have carried the umpire on Saturday with Prince Albert and Prince Henry, but as it will not be able to do so, an invitation has been sent to Mr. A. Hewitt to lend the Consuta, another fast boat, to carry the Princes."[2]

The Boat Race was scheduled for Saturday, 27 March. Final details of the last practices and crowd control were eagerly read by the waiting public. The rowing correspondent reported Friday that while Thursday's weather was favorable with a threat of rain, a good weather outlook for Saturday was not altogether promising. Bad weather with high wind and strong currents would make navigating a tactical nightmare—a coxswain's race.

Additionally, the following notice was in *The Times* and various postings around London, "The Air Ministry announces that the following Notice to Airmen (No.32) has been issued:

"The Secretary of State for Air has, in the interests of the public, issued an Order under the Air Navigation Acts, 1911–1919, prohibiting the navigation of aircraft of every class and description at a lower altitude than 6,000 feet, over the area within a radius of two statue miles of Hammersmith Bridge in the County of London, during the period from 12 o'clock midnight, March 26–27, to 12 o'clock midnight March 27–28, 1920.

"Owing to the abnormal crowds which, it is anticipated, will collect in the above area on the 27th inst. to witness the Inter-varsity Boat Race, the Inter-university Sports, and the F.A. Cup tie, this precaution has been taken to obviate the possibility of accidents to the public, such as might occur owing to the sudden movement of masses of people occasioned by the flight of aircraft overhead.

"Any infringement of the Order will be dealt with rigorously."[3]

On Saturday, the seventy-second race with Oxford the Challengers (since Cambridge won five years previous at the last race) was at last at hand. "The attendance probably was the largest in the history of the race. During the afternoon spectators swarmed the course and the brief rainstorm which swept along the river about 4 o'clock had not the slightest effect on the size or the spirit of the crowd. Every building which overlooks the course was crowded, and the launches, barges, tugs, and other boats along the banks appeared to be packed. The crowd was particularly dense at Hammersmith Bridge and at Barnes."[4]

One of the noblest moments of the race came before either boat was launched, when in a style of honor and sportsmanship representative of these caliber schools and rowers, the President of the Oxford Crew—Mr. E. A. Berrisford, who stroked at the 1919 Henley—"decided to stand down in favour of M. H. Ellis, the Shrewsbury Freshman, who stroked his school to victory in the Elsenham Cup at Henley last summer in a manner that suggested great possibilities in the future. It cost him his Blue [shirt], and he will go down to history as the only President without that coveted distinction."[5]

With the switch at stroke seat, the bow weight of the boat needed adjusting so the heavyweight R. Lucas from the 1919 Henley crew and a great rower from Eton, was replaced with A. C. Hill from Shrewsbury. Former Oxford President and Henley rower E. D. Horsfall, who had been coaching and advising the Oxford boat during this year's trial, also stood down for this year's Boat Race to make room for the shift in boat lineup due to the new stroke.[6]

The Oxford Crew was using a new center-seated boat from Rough boat builders, Oxford. Normally the English had their boats offset to the starboard and to the port sides but this new design—already in use by Glendon and the Americans—was just coming into favor in British schools. The Cambridge crew rowed a Simms of Putney boat. Both crews used Ayling's twelve-feet-three-inch-long oars, which were six inches wide in the spoon.[7]

Facing one another at long last, young, strong, handsome, and with a virtuous nature already tested, at just after five o'clock Mr. Berrisford of Oxford and Mr. Sidney Swann of Cambridge tossed the coin for stations. Cambridge won the toss and chose the Surrey station. As Swann walked away he thought to himself about the upcoming race. His counterpart—the Oxford President—because of a few practice pieces gone sour, relinquished his seat as stroke in this the greatest race of their careers, because he *chose* to. No one had forced the decision, he chose to step down and let what he considered a better oarsman step in, and thereby never to get his coveted Blue shirt—the symbol of greatness in the British college rowing ranks. Swann knew that all athletes strive for a toughness and strength of mind and body, but here on the bank he had met virtue; strength of character, of soul; and he knew it was going be a tough race to row indeed.

Swann wisely chose the advantage of selecting the starting position toward the Surrey Shore—the leeward station as it were, "with the wind varying between south and west blowing south-southwest when the crews went to the stake-boats . . . with a fair tide running."[8] With this, Cambridge had a good shot of winning. This would give a following wind (tailwind) from the start to Hammer-smith Bridge favoring the Surrey Shore, and at the finish a headwind at the curve in the course between Doves and Barnes. When Swann won the toss, his watermanship skills gave them the opportunity for victory—*if* they rowed and steered correctly. At the start Cambridge was away a trifle quicker than Oxford and led by a canvas at London Rowing Club. But the drama began at Hammersmith Bridge . . .

On this day, unknown to these rowers, the selection of the 1920 English Olympic eight began. Officials of the Leander Club, the British Olympic Committee, coaches, and the politically influential were all coming to the race and had been following the progress of the crews. From these two eights and from the best of Leander, one representative British crew would be boated for the Olympics. The best stroke, the best bow, the best cox. The selection of the coxswain's seat was the most precarious, for the two coxswains would be judged the harshest because in river racing, the coxswain's steering can win or lose a race. A bad stroke pulled by an oarsman can usually be over-come a few strokes later in the course of a long river race, but an error in judgment by the cox can cause the entire crew to fatigue, lose ground, and lose confidence. Great winning coxswains who "straighten out a course" by artful shaving of curves and hazards are thrown off docks in glee by the victorious crew, a losing cox with a flagrant error is usually scorned and cursed under one's breath as, "the little so-and-so who is just along for the ride; *damn,* you'd think he'd at least be able to keep us out of the current!"

At 5:40, straightaway, the race began with a flurry of blades and a lunge forward off the stake boats. Coxswains were shouting com-mands, and the Cambridge cox, Johnstone, "in making the shoot for the center arch swung a trifle wide and forced Oxford out. As a result

Cambridge added another half a length to their advantage by the time the boats straightened out at the Mall where Cambridge was stroking 29 to Oxford's 30. Above the Doves the boats ran into the full force of a wind, which rose a miniature sea, with white capped waves. The Cambridge coxswain promptly sought the shelter under Surrey bank and Oxford followed. At the lower end of Chiswick there was a length of daylight between the boats. Dropping the rate to 28, both crews struggled through the rough water and contrary to expectations, Cambridge showed superior watermanship under the trying conditions. Oxford lost some of their length and were becoming ragged, and two or three men showed signs of distress. By the time the crews reached Chiswick steps, with both crews rowing 26, Cambridge had increased their lengths (time 12'21") and it was evident that it would require an extraordinary effort on the part of Oxford to save the race.

"After passing Thornycroft's, the Cambridge coxswain wisely kept to the more sheltered water on the Surrey side, instead of making the usual crossing to the Meadows. Ellis spurted again at this point, but he could make no impression upon the leaders, and Oxford lost more ground when their coxswain by an error in judgment crossed over rough water to the Middlesex bank, opposite the Cambridge University Boat Club (C.U.B.C.) enclosure. As a result, he had to come out again to make for the center of Barnes Bridge where Cambridge led by 3 1/2 lengths in 17'34", both strokes rowing 30. The water was much better from the bridge to the finish, and Cambridge raised the rate to 32 before reaching Mortlak Brewery. Ellis made another effort to reduce the gap, but he had a tired crew behind him and there was not much life about the effort. Cambridge, on the other hand, rowed with fine length and dash, and, working the rate up to 34 in the final burst rowed in easy winners in 21'11". Mr. Adcock, who acted as distance judge, gave the verdict of four lengths over Oxford reaching the post 13" after their rivals."[9]

On this day the better boat won. Praise and print went toward Cambridge's stern three—Hartley, Swann, and Campbell—with Campbell seen as the best oar of either college. Oxford's James was singled out as the best Blue in their boat. Earl in the Oxford bow section was seen as "too strong for No. 2," causing the cox to have to steer with a strong rudder to compensate in this race—but in an Olympic boat of *all* strong men, Earl would be seen as a magnificent addition. Clearly Johnstone was the superior coxswain who made the right choices against wind and tide and in so doing guided the Cambridge boat to the calmer waters of length, steadiness, and victory. While steering wide at the first bridge in order to line up for the center arch might be seen as a foul in river racing—a slight, sly, intentional line taken to advantage yet looking as if done by current or wind will be excused by the judges and umpires—though never forgotten by the opposing cox and crew.[10]

THE GUTS OF THE 1920 LEANDER CREW BEING made from Cambridge's Swann, Johnstone, Campbell, Oxford's Earl and James, and existent Leander rowers Horsfall (an ex-Oxford rower of only one year absence), Gully Nickalls, and Shove (an ex-Cambridge star oar) started to materialize in the imaginations of those looking toward the Olympic Games.

And while Leander men and Cambridge and Oxford Blues dueled, something unique was happening at Navy: Glendon's crew was heralded and described as not only being an exceptional combination of speed and power, but collectively rated as one of the best crews of all time.[11] Would Navy be the best eight in the world in the 1920 Olympic year, capable of beating the British? It was unthinkable, yet if it were so, what could it mean for America? The answer, a forty-year winning streak—the longest Olympic streak—would stun the world.

10. THE U.S. OLYMPIC TRIALS

The oarsman is not a man alone. If his crew is to succeed he must become perfectly synchronized with the other men in the boat. Sometimes, for thirty or forty strokes—more if the crew is really good and well matched—all men in the boat will move together. Every move the stroke makes will be mirrored by the men behind him, all the catches will hit hard and clean, like a trout going after a fly . . . when that happens the boat begins to lift up off the water, air bubbles running under the bow, and there is an exhilaration like nothing else I have ever experienced . . . literally like flying.

—Brad Brinegar, *Dartmouth Alumni Magazine,* 1977

THE NAVY ADMIRALS' ACCOMPLISHMENT OF winning the American Henley was nothing short of miraculous. From that event, every aspect of the crew's journey to destiny made the papers. The Olympic trials of 1920 were scheduled for 23–24 July on Lake Quinsigamond in Worcester, Massachusetts. Glendon took 20 oarsmen, 2 full eights, 18 men total—8 rowers in each shell, 2 coxswains and 4 substitutes. This is a typical method of training used even today. Two boats of equal numbers allow the coach to switch rowers from boat to boat to find the fastest combination. Glendon made a critical seat change from the American Henley lineup in May: Weidman at seven seat would be out and Gallagher—the youngster—in. The selected men were given a short leave from school and were exempt from their summer naval cruise required at the Academy, to begin training on 14 June.[1]

In the interim, while the crew was away visiting home on leave, Chandler had the luxury of a few weeks to work on the equipment. The oars needed to be gone over and inspected to check for splits in the spoon on the water end of the oar and handle issues on the rower's end. The handles needed to be kept clean and scrubbed with lye and bleach to sanitize them at the end of every season. Oarsmen's hands would go through stages of "toughening up" through the season. The hands rested on the oar handles near the butt end of the oar. The hand closest to the butt end was called the "outside" hand because it was the farthest position to the rigger arm. The other hand was called the "inside" hand because it was closer to the rigger arm. The two hands during the drive pull equally, but at the catch and finish they do very different tasks. The inside hand feathers and squares the blade by turning the handle, while the outside hand sets the height of the oar handle through the stroke. When the oar gets wet due to splashes or rain, coupled with the constant movement of the oar handle, blisters usually form, and these eventually turn into calluses. This toughing-up process and the wear and tear of the hands on the handles through hours of practice and racing leaves blood, sweat, dirt, and loads of bacteria on the wood, which needs to be tended to several times a season.

The long shafts, the loom of the oar, need to be sanded and varnished. Oar handles once cleaned were sanded rough with a rasp to give the rower a good grip. Lastly, each oar was looked over and eyed for pitch and/or warpage.

The shell tended to get beat up over the course of a season. Normal wear-and-tear issues such as chips, scrapes, and breakage had to be repaired before the all-important trip to Worcester. Boats were usually crated and shipped by rail and the Academy had the additional challenge, should they win, of having a ready means of attaching the relatively fragile shells to the steel plate of a destroyer deck to cross six thousand miles of North Atlantic. A challenge not for the faint of heart.

Chandler worked methodically over the hull with the ever-present Glendon overseeing and rolling up shirtsleeves to sand and varnish, to eye the oarlock pitch, and to check the spread and work-through on all sixteen seats. Taking two boats meant twice the work but ensured double the safety—just in case.

When the boys showed up for practice, they were well rested and eager to get in the boats. The campus was largely empty and they enjoyed the privileges of relaxing amid the beauty of flowering magnolias, tulips, daffodils, and green lush grounds. The weather was warm now and the Severn flat, without the ever-present chop of spring thaw. They relished the sun and beauty of the steamy green-blue Chesapeake that stretched before them: land and sea and sun melding into one world—their world. They owned Annapolis that summer. They were the talk of the town and everyone in the shops and fish houses up and down the cobblestone streets knew what Glendon and his boys were about.

The fundamental question was always being asked and answered from the Annapolis Yacht Club sail loft to the Maryland hotel. "How did the crew look?" They were looking great.

When Navy boarded the train for Worcester, they knew they faced fierce competition for the right to represent the United States in the Olympic Games, including rival Syracuse who had beaten them in the college season. Many members of that crew formed a club team named Duluth Rowing Club under the coaching of James

Ten Eyck, but rumor had it that that the stroke man, Rammi, of the Syracuse boat, would not be with their club boat. Rammi was indeed replaced by the six seat of the Syracuse boat that won the Intercollegiate Championship earlier that spring, a man named Loakamp, who did a good job stroking, but not good enough to beat the unstoppable midshipmen.[2]

The regatta in Worcester proved to be one of the finest-run regattas in the history of U.S. Nationals. There was little wind, a bright New England day on the lake nestled into the hills of central Massachusetts. It was the debut of Glendon's winning combination—the names of Jacomini, Graves, Jordan, Moore, Sanborn, Johnston, Gallagher, King, and Clark at cox were printed in the program for the first time. Every event was started on time and at intervals along the 2,000-meter course colored smoke bombs were sent up to let the crowd that was waiting at the finish know who was in the lead.

A CREW RACE IS UNIQUE IN SPORTS COMPETITION because, once the start is given, there are no time-outs, no injury delays, no substitutions—just a mad dash down a corridor of lanes to the finish. If someone gets hurt or an oar breaks, the coxswain has the responsibility to tell that seat to jump out of the boat if necessary—to lighten the craft if that rower is no longer contributing to the power and speed. This is where the term "dead weight" comes into play. If an oar breaks, better to cross the finish line with only seven rowers than to cross with eight, with one man just sitting taking up space, adding dead weight, and slowing down the boat. The rowing stations are very close together and when the seats are sliding, any interruption or stoppage of the movement can cause chaos in the boat. Things happen very, *very* quickly in an eight-oared shell thrusting at full power to the finish. Everyone must be alert and be ready to obey without hesitation to a coxswain's commands—even if that call is, "SEVEN, you're out of the boat in two! One, TWO! On THIS one!" And with that the rower is expected to pitch himself over the side of the hull, and stay underwater to the count of ten to let the length of the boat and thrashing oars go by overhead. Once he's surfaced, the safety of the umpire's launch awaits to haul the soaked rower in.

On this day in 1920, the 2,000-meter race was all Navy's. The eights raced in such harmony that they looked as if they were gliding over the water, perfectly synchronized. When rowing is done well, it is a beautiful thing to watch; when it is done poorly, it is ugly and labored. But on this day, Clark and King gave one another a bright knowing exchange with their eyes as they held the lead down the course. The catches felt solid. The boat wasn't rocking, it was perfectly set in balance—it was easy, beautiful—and they knew it. Water whispered as it ran smoothly down the hull. The bow cut into the cool water and a straight track of slight turbulence exited the stern of the boat. Clark held the tiller lines tight, King and Jacomini kept the boat running straight—the bow of the shell needing to be perfectly aligned so that all the heads in front of him, Gallagher, Graves, Johnston looked like one mat of brown hair, not seven separate heads bobbing. Shoulders were square; chins level. Any extraneous movement unessential to the stroke had been drilled out of them months earlier by Glendon. The boat was running "hot, straight, and normal" as Navy men say.

King watched the eight puddles left by the strokes. He wanted to have enough power per stroke to stretch out the puddles so that his stroke puddle did not fall into Jacomini's as they drifted past the boat. He wanted the boat to run between the oar-plants, glide in its speed as they powered through the stroke's release before catching again. The puddles stayed spread, the key to fast rowing. The oars, finishing precisely at the same moment, made one kaa-thunk at the finish of each stroke; the wheels rolled on their seats in unison. Clark saw only one body in front of him—King's. He saw no one else's chest or knees leaning too far to one side or the other; ports, the even numbered seats split to his left, and starboards, the odd numbered to his right. He only saw their arms reach out at the catches, their disciplined bodies keeping their center of mass over the keel. God, it was a thrill to *execute*! And they all knew it! *Finally,* as eight individuals they had congealed into one body and the boat ran light and true beneath them.

Surging over the finish line first, smiles beamed in the Navy shell as all eight let their oar handles rest lightly between their knees and chests, oar blades flattened on the water's surface 90 degrees to the boat, as it glided effortlessly to a stop. Jordan scooped up water and splashed it over his head in glee, Clark and King were embracing; other crews drifted past them, disappointment and exhaustion racking their faces.

It was all Navy that day. They rowed the mile and a quarter course in 6 minutes 20 seconds, for a course record.[3] They were in—they were going to the Olympics Games. They had won with Syracuse second, the Navy intermediate crew third, and Duluth Boat Club forth.[4]

EXCITEMENT OVER THE NAVAL ACADEMY'S CHANCE to beat the British grew as the 1920 Olympics approached. In the growing excitement of the fervor toward the Olympics, American Olympic Committee (AOC) President Kirby was certain that this 1920 team would be the best ever and certain they were headed for victory due in no small measure to the fact that this was "the first time that the government has given official recognition to the participation of American athletes in the Olympics."[5] Up until this time athletes participating in the Olympics went on their own nickel or by club or private funding. President Woodrow Wilson signed the Senate Amendment Joint Resolution 179 on 2 June 1920, to give money and essential sponsorship for the first time to this or any Olympic team.[6] This was consecrated in order to, "Hold up the name of America in these Olympic Games this year."[7]

In July 1920, the Anglo-American rowing controversies over orthodoxy of stroke, equipment, and tradition were poised for the transatlantic showdown, to be decided on a canal outside Antwerp, Belgium. The thrill that this possibility provided to the Academy, to Annapolis, to the Navy, and to the nation at large is reflected in several newspaper articles. *The New York Times* of 15 August discusses not only this current Olympic crew but also the prospects for the next several years of rowing at Navy, claiming that "the whole standard of rowing at the Naval Academy will be elevated by the trip to Antwerp" and "Rowing, already highly regarded by every Navy man, will be given additional and lasting impetus whether the Academy crew wins or loses in the International event."[8]

The people of the United States were embracing these young men as their team, representatives of themselves and of a cross-section of America. In an article of unknown origin, found in the July 1920 Olympic Trials program, Navy's crew is labeled as "Lads from 7 states" who were "truly a representative American crew—it's the best eight in the country, college or club and it's the big favorite to prove itself the best in the world after the competition with the European and English crews."[9]

As Navy began provisioning to proudly transport its crew to Belgium on the armored cruiser USS *Frederick*, many of the other

Olympic athletes were slated to suffer through the crossing on Army transports. W. Pitt Scott, the Captain of the USS *Frederick*, reporting on the transport mission, gleaned the prestige and importance of the trip by summing up his armed escort as "indicating to what extent the Government was back of them."[10]

American fans rallied behind the Navy boat as more than just men and wood. The boat and its crew became a symbol of the United States, something to be protected, the underdog up against ghosts of the Boston Tea Party, British General Thomas Gage, and the like. Department of the Navy records indicate numerous transmissions and special arrangements made for the USS *Frederick*, including a special docking permit and live-aboard arrangements for the duration of the stay in Antwerp harbor arranged by the United States with the Belgian ambassador.[11] In contrast, the other Olympic athletes sailing on Army transports were to be housed in a schoolhouse in Belgium, living under what would be substandard conditions. Track and field, swimmers and boxers, runners including Jacomini's track squad classmate, the famed Charley Paddock, were on the Army transport ship *Princess Matoika*, which had been used to bring back 1,800 bodies from the war and was stinking of formaldehyde and rats, and crowded with less than adequate food and sanitary conditions. Athletes would find it reprehensible.[12]

As it turns out, the accommodations and transport would raise umbrage, prompting the athletes to compile an indignant letter of protest. *The New York Herald Tribune* on 7 August 1920, highlighting the differences in the treatments of the Olympic team athletes, carried both stories ("U.S. Olympic Athletes Threaten to Go on Strike: Dissatisfied with Accommodations . . ." and "Navy Olympic Team Arrives in Antwerp in Good Condition") juxtaposed in adjacent columns.[13] But despite the inequities, a potential Navy win over

England in the Olympics was indeed generating attention and excitement. With the U.S. Navy athletes readying to steam to European shores, the rivalry heightened.

NAYSAYERS NO LONGER, EDWARD R. BUSHNELL OF *The Pittsburgh Press*, in a preview shortly before the crew was to set sail to Europe, wrote that "experts who have seen the middies [midshipmen] row are confident that they can beat anything Europe has to offer."[14] The nationalistic attitude of the day—that not only the "middies," but also all the athletes in this Olympiad embodied the ideals of America—surfaced again in early August as the Olympic fever heightened at the onset of the Games. Ralph Davis of *The Pittsburgh Press* summed it up: "Uncle Sam is confident that his boys will come through with another victory." Davis spelled out exactly what victory would mean. "The example of a super-type of athlete we would hold up to the world—strong of heart, clear of eye, clean of heart, lovers of honor—all." Davis concluded with a rhetorical flourish: "Is it any wonder if they are proud, or that we are proud of them?"[15]

11. THE CROSSING

In years to come when the younger generation ask to hear a story of the Great War, the oft-told submarine sinking yarn can be passed up in favor of the story of the Olympic Cruise to Belgium, a land devastated and destroyed but not dry . . . to its members, this sea going voyage will ever remain a midsummer night's dream. . . .

—Foreword of the chapbook *USS* Frederick *Olympic Cruise: August–September 1920*

ON THURSDAY, 15 JULY, THE CRUISER USS *Frederick,* with Captain W. Pitt Scott at the helm, took on fresh stores and boots (personnel) at the Philadelphia Navy Yard. Three days later it went in search of "black diamonds" (coal) to Hampton Roads Virginia, and on the nineteenth discovered 600 tons of the stuff alongside on barges ready to be put on board at what was sardonically termed the "Coalpassers Ball." On the twenty-first it had arrived in Newport, Rhode Island, awaiting the Navy crew athletes, who had just won the Olympic Trials, to join the other Navy Olympic swimmers and athletes already aboard.[1] Entering into the venue of Newport and the American aristocracy of the Vanderbilts, the Breakers, and Marble House—especially that of yachtsman Harold S. Vanderbilt—Glendon and his crew stowed their rowing togs and travel clothes in preparation to dine and mingle with the upper crust.

Newport, the northern jewel of the New York Yacht Club and sailing's world-famous America's Cup, was pulsing with the 1920 resurgence of the America's Cup race after World War I had delayed the contest. The Navy, having a base inside the harbor, was no stranger to the maritime pride taken in America's Cup racing. When America's *Resolute* declared it was running into rigging problems, its aging designer, Herreshoff, was carried overnight on a U.S. Naval destroyer to the races offshore of New York City to save the day and adjust the *Resolute*'s rigging that would beat Britain's *Shamrock IV*.[2]

The young rowers, brainy, suntanned—Olympians all—destined to be Admirals, captains of industry, and dashing pilots, donned tuxedos for a reception that evening. Striking in their formal attire, they mingled and conversed easily in the crowd, particularly with Miss Muriel Vanderbilt, known to frequent Army-Navy football games, and others of the Newport yachting and equestrian scene.[3] They were in the limelight. Thanks to Glendon, these young men, from the farmlands of Iowa and the hollers of Virginia, were among the socialites of the nation and *they* were the main attraction.[4]

AT LAST, THE DAY OF DEPARTURE: 24 JULY. EVERY-thing was set; everything was in place. The Navy crew's departure was not only the focus of Newport, but of the nation. Moving-picture men came on board to photograph them and the all-reservist crew.[5] Standing proud in their navy blue sweaters with the gold varsity Navy "N" center front, the crew posed, arms crossed, with rowing togs revealing chiseled quads and soft leather lace-up ankle-high boots. As the day warmed and the ocean breezes tossed their sun-bleached hair, the crew was filmed working out on the makeshift rowing machine on the starboard foredeck in their white Olympic shirts with American Olympic Committee shield. Glendon, ever present in his rolled-down white Navy cap, was explaining the rowing stroke to the reporters. Clark, the only one wearing long pants and a blue blazer, knelt along-side the crew on one knee offering slight suggestions to pace and stroke. Mr. J. Jenkins, a press representative of the Navy Department, hovered about. He would be making the crossing to drum up publicity and in the hope of promoting the voyage as a sort of "cruise with the stars" to stir up athleticism and the thrill of life on the high seas as something wonderful and coveted, intriguing enough to lure re-servists and recruits into the regular Navy.[6]

THAT AFTERNOON, AS THE LINES WERE CAST OFF from the pier in Newport amid a rash of waves, the men felt the ship's movement come alive to the sea. They left in the midst of well-wishes, and many missed family and friends who couldn't make the long journeys to see them off but who were nonetheless in their hearts and on their minds.

Glendon, in his old fishing waters, spotted the Vineyard Sound Lightship at 2:14 P.M. just south of the thrift and dunes of No Man's Land and at 9:12 P.M. Nantucket Shoal Lightship was a mere three miles away.[7] Little did he know that these light vessels, which com-forted him now, would serve as objects of pain and terror years later when his grandson Tommy would be lost at sea, unable to row against an outgoing tide and an offshore breeze that would bring him and his friend within sight and earshot of the Stonehorse Shoal Lightship—the last human contact they would have—before being swept into the vastness of the water and the night.[8]

On board, the last glimpses of land would soon be lost in the westward sky, and to the east, only sea, darkness, and the largeness of the ship acting as exclamation point to the event. Each member of the crew was torn between private thoughts, adventure, and what the future might hold. Darkness cloaked the ship's sides and deck as small vee'd-waves, generated by the steam-driven propellers, ran the length of the hull. A constant hum of horsepower vibrated underfoot.

On deck, in the dim light of a round globe, Country Moore held a letter from his sweetheart Daisy in his hand, and smelled the air of the sea mixed with his memories of the deep-scented woods of Virginia and North Carolina—and of her.[9] In the distance an inbound Boston or New York ship's lights dotted the horizon, a sentry to the ever-widening distance speeding them apart.

A few of his crewmates, standing one-legged, leaning on the rails, and laughing, were confidently poised for the days ahead. It was their time, their destiny. So many thoughts, so many prayers surrounded them. How could they fail? Moore felt certain they simply could not.

A deckhand appeared from a passageway, and Country turned his thoughts momentarily to the sailor who was like him, but not. Moore was aware that the sailor was in awe of him. Though both were Navy men, each knew they would never be equals. In this rare circumstance, the Navy Department declared the Olympians onboard as passengers, not crew. As such, the Olympians were placed on a pedestal, set apart, unique.[10]

The Academy and the Olympic crest sewn on his Navy sweater he wore to keep off the evening damp chill separated them.[11] He was already, as was the entire eight, part of the elite. In this transatlantic crossing his metamorphosis began. At the Academy he was different, a country boy with a good-natured laugh, known among his friends as being a country bumpkin. But here and now, just this moment, as the reality of the passing of waves and time and distance, real distance, an ocean of distance complete with an ocean of realization, he knew in an instant that he, they, would never be who they'd been before. Self-realization hit him as hard as the steel riveted boilerplates of the hull. His future world was in the darkness somewhere there, ahead, off the bow, while in the churning wake of the *Frederick,* his past was being stripped from him, shed, reptilian in nature. His new skin at this moment was emerging brighter and shinier—he would never sit in a rowing shell the same again. Confidence was the man he'd become.

The sailor, finishing his deck task, moved on. And with that Country reached the bulkhead door; and tucking the letter from Pittsylvania County into his pants pocket, he slipped through, his eyes and gait pausing momentarily—but only a moment—to adjust to the new light from the passageway within. There he saw his crewmates, ship's officers, the ever-present reporters and movie-men, and those engaged in animated conversations about having acquired a Vanderbilt's invitation for this party or that event, especially Jacomini, who seemed to have struck up a personal chord with Muriel Vanderbilt.[12] He entered into the gaiety, music, card playing, and revelry of Admirals, railroad magnates, and Olympians. . . . [13]

AND SO NOW THE GREAT BURDEN BEGAN; IT WAS all up to them. It was time. Sea watches began. Steering 82 degrees true, standard speed 13 knots, all quiet about decks. To taunt the homesick first-timers, mail buoy watch was posted for those wanting to leave letters in the middle of the North Atlantic for a fictitious mail-boat to pick up, and fantastic reasons for the paravane-rig, to stop sharks, were discussed at length.[14] A lightness of step and a playfulness was awash on deck. It was their ship, their captain, their crew. On the sea they were in charge, masters of their own destiny. How they fared now was largely up to them.

Glendon and Chandler, as coach and boatman have done for ages, privately monitored and observed their rowers. They had done so these four seasons from the plebe squad to senior year, and they would do so even more on the long hours of this journey. They worried about them as individuals, not just as numbers and names in seats. Sustaining a comfort level to keep them focused on future events was critical, and every detail of a rower's needs was attended to. Glendon discussed with the ship's personnel just what would be needed to keep the boys in condition. "Give them good food, plenty of it, and good quality, from the first day to the last, and we will win medals," Glendon said confidently. "Athletes do best in routine. Get the routine started, stick with it, eliminate surprises. Then, and only then, will they be able to execute their training and discipline."[15]

Glendon also insisted on trainers, doctors, and masseurs so his boys would have the same treatment as some of their European competitors who had the opportunity, while still at home, to indulge in the same.[16] The trip would be part of the physiological taper. The wait to board the ship, the crossing from Newport to Southampton and then on to Antwerp, required careful occupation of their minds and bodies, which the coach had completely in hand.

But, more important in Glendon's mind was the condition of their spirits. Those they were leaving behind, coupled with the "rising star" impact of the last year, still played havoc on their concentration at times. And there were the personal interior shackles that held some bound. There was the tragedy of Zeke Sanborn's closest younger brother William, who'd died of scarlet fever at twelve and whose death still haunted him. Zeke was seen frequently alone at the rail, his green-blue eyes staring at the waves. When engaged in conversation, Zeke was quick to add a "For the love of mud" or "What the deuce" to a sailor's conversation strewn with curse words, and Glendon loved him for it.[17] Jacomini's brother and idol, Clem, the World War I flying ace, had just recently crashed and died on a routine instructor's mission at the flight school.[18] Jack was devastated and, in his grief, at times still lacked concentration. Glendon monitored him and always had a positive word for him.

Then there were Country Moore's and Johnson's sweethearts.[19] Love is a powerful motivator and Glendon was certain that these two men would be like oaks—solid—as are all those who have found the key to happiness in giving, letting go, and getting beyond themselves and their own imperfections by being seen, touched, and healed through the love of another. He knew this, as mature men do, for he himself was leaving his wife, Mary, and their seven children, yet he carried them with him. He was proud of her and their brood. He loved her and that love was part of his strength and hers—a strength and a bond great enough that allowed him to leave them these summer months to fend for themselves on the Cape, a place he loved. She dreaded the long nights of loneliness over the years he was away at Annapolis. She was not a woman who fit into the yacht clubs and society of the Baltimore, Washington, and Navy wives' crowd. Mary loved Boston, was a mother of seven, a New Englander whose home and comfort was there.[20]

No doubt Glendon took a long glance as they passed the Cape. Last looks at Nantucket's Great Neck light and the faint yellow house lights barely perceivable on land tore at his heart as it did the others'. They were passionate, selfless men who would die for a cause and, therefore, live in pursuit of one, too. That is why the

Academy sought them. That is why Glendon chose them for his eights and that is why they were the ones on this ship this night.

THE SHIP WOULD FOLLOW THE NORTHERN CIRCLE route close to the coast of Cape Cod, then toward Nova Scotia, the home of his ancestors.

All had a checklist. The athletes, the coaches, the crew.

The deck of the *Frederick* had been fitted with rowing machines bolted to the deck and the shells strapped to a scaffolding on the starboard foredeck. Besides the crew squad, there were Navy track men, fencers, wrestlers, boxers, and swimmers on board the *Frederick*. They all took daily exercise of some kind, and any morning about ten o'clock the quarter-deck of the ship resembled a floating gymnasium, complete with trainers and four tons of ice—at the ready for sore muscles.[21] Moving pictures were shown every evening on the quarter-deck and the ship's specially commissioned 23-piece band furnished music.[22]

Glendon was ever vigilant. The equipment he entrusted largely to his boatman Chandler, with his ever-present pot of grease and quid of tobacco. But Glendon was constantly monitoring the condition of the crew, the preparation and maintenance of the physical stature of his boys, as well as their need for laughter, camaraderie, and relaxation to distract them from broken hearts, missing home, family and friends, and the ever-looming intersection with destiny: the VII Olympiad.

Captain Scott was responsible for the safety of the crossing, muster stations, navigation, ship's stores, comfort, and monitoring the weather. Converting a U.S. naval warship into a modified passenger ship was both a challenge and a pleasure. More than just a listing of the ship's officers and hands, the USS *Frederick*'s manifest read like a who's who of the Golden Age of Sport. *Vanity Fair* in the United States and *Punch* on the British "side of the pond" were taking advantage of names like Kelly, Vanderbilt, and Rudy Lehman, the British coach and rowing authority, who was himself a contributor to *Punch*.

The utter calmness of the sea pleased them. They needn't arrive for their Olympic debut green from vomiting; yes, even Navy men get seasick on occasion. But not on this trip. Clyde King, from Grinnell, Iowa, boasted he was too tough to let it bother him even if it had. Being a Central Plains landlubber and midwesterner more accustomed to wheat fields and rolling prairie, he relished the absolute flat-as-a-pancake seascape as far as the eye could see.[23]

THEIR WORLD WAS AT PEACE. THIS WAS AN OPTI-mum moment in time and space, indeed. Glendon had the crew working eight-in-a-line, stroke to bow, in the modified rowing machines that he had designed himself. Their coxswain, Clark, nearly always wearing a neatly tailored suit jacket over his sweats, drilled them on what commands would be used during the race by 500-meter intervals, the 2,000-meter course being broken up into four sections of 500 meters apiece. The first 500 included the intricacies of the high-powered start; the second got them into their settle and race pace; the third 500 was a no-man's-land, an area of anaerobic deficit and fatigue that begged the rower to stop and rest; and then the final 500, with the sprint to the finish, told all. Cutie Clark had them all etched indelibly into his brain and imparted his enthusiasm and confidence to his crew, not through yelling and barking orders, but by a sort of calm assurance. His was the only voice they would hear on the race course. Even Glendon at this point in their training imparted corrections and suggestions to Cutie to execute, lest there be too much reliance on crew to coach rather than crew to coxswain.

Glendon knew it was time to let Cutie be the coach in the boat. Time to let the calm, confident coxswain shine and stand as a giant among these trees of men. His crew was large, with Jordan and Jacomini towering between six feet three inches and six feet four. Clark needed to tower in respect and confidence among the crew for them to win. The crew was aware of the withdrawal of Glendon day by day. He distanced himself more and more to let his crew solidify.

Glendon knew he had done his best with them. And in a telegram sent from the ship he assured his wife that "the boys were looking absolutely fit and able." She had no doubt as she looked eastward through her Cape Cod window near Harwichport overlooking Monomoy Point that he was right.

King and Clark exchanged musings with certainty. "Coach is turning it over to us. Have you noticed? He thinks we're ready. So then we must be, right? British be damned!"

And they spread their quiet confidence fore and aft in a tangible new wave of "victory might really be ours" murmur.[24]

Maturity leaves an indelible mark and perhaps none was so astounded by its arrival than Vincent Gallagher. The baby of the crew, he could feel respect deepening. He had made the boat at the last minute, ousting Weidman, who had rowed all year for Glendon. But Gallagher's strength and command of an oar, his sheer physical stature, and his affable nature won him nearly instant shell-mate trust. He wanted to be great, greater than himself, and he knew that he would be now in the communion of the eight-become-one. He had felt it in the pulling of the oars in practice on the Severn. There was a self-seeking obsession in all of them, which ultimately and inadvertently led to unexpected collective freedom as they finally shed their singleness and "star" quality to become one boat. He knew, as did everyone in the boat, that any of them at any time would give all they had now and in the future for the others. It was a great feeling.[25]

Near 41 degrees north latitude and 53 degrees west, they passed within miles of the *Titanic,* the 1912 tragedy still fresh on their minds. They knew from newspapers and stories of friends and from their classes that the *Titanic* had rowing machines of shortened wooden oars connected to a heavy metal oarlock and bolted to the floor with a sliding set of seats and footrests—such was the popularity of the sport with the British and Americans of the day. Words and images about the ill-fated ship—like the band playing "Nearer My God to Thee," 15 April 1912, the White Star Line, survivors being rescued by Cunard's *Carpathia,* a death toll of nearly 1,500, Captain White's last words to his crew, "Be British"—gave them pause to wonder just what was the fettle of these Leander men they would face?

The crew, ever aware of the military and political situation in the world, reverenced their position of safety and Naval superiority. With the Great War over, the North Atlantic was slowly returning to its reign as a veritable railway of shipping. Ships obeyed and followed long-established commercial shipping lanes not unlike ocean high-ways passing port to port if possible. Westward, London–New York traffic generally took a more northern track, and eastbound traffic took the southerly track. Any sight of sail or plume of steam-powered vessels caught their minds and imaginations, for these young rowers were Navy men and this aqueous world was theirs to dream in and traverse. They were taking it all in.

They knew that no mariner worth his salt would be caught dead not knowing they were on Georges or Grand Bank by the look and smell of the sea, or just by the clouds and seaweed floating by. Sargasso weed drifted by off Georges Bank and here, the second day, just beneath the Tail of the Bank, the southern end of the Grand Banks, the shallow water was slightly greener in the plankton-rich water. Porpoises surfaced off the port side—an ancient sign of good luck—and this murmur spread through the crew. All of them looked for a whale to sound as Glendon was overheard talking to the officers about his days fishing these very grounds in his youth.

Here in the deep sea there was no more need for soundings as the depth in this, the second largest ocean in the world, was two miles beneath them; and the Tail of the Bank rose up from the depths to a mere 120 feet. On this very still day the mingling currents, warm and coaxed even faster from the depths of the Atlantic basin to those cascading off the Grand Banks shelf, smoothed the water's visible surface to large poolings of satin green-blue mirrors where the wind's cat's-paw area of patchwork was trying desperately to take hold and raise even the tiniest wave—with no luck. One could *see* the waters mingling in their eternal thermal columns that took ships and passengers to the deep or carried plankton and warm biospheres followed by game fish and light to the surface world. Such was the seascape readily changing before them as they slipped across it—one with it—at 13 knots.

These water and poolings were some of the richest fishing grounds in the world. Swordfish, mako, and blue shark thrived in the columns of warm and cold water silently rising and sinking in the depths. Once past Newfoundland, the Labrador Current mixed with the Gulf Stream, or the North Atlantic Drift, and soupy weather closed in on the ship as they headed toward the middle of the North Atlantic. The feeling of a real sea voyage was setting in. Only a few small birds were following the ship. They flew very close to the surface and Glendon mused that they resembled Chimney Swifts in flight. They were Storm-Petrels, also known as Mother Carey's

Chickens, and their appearance was the indication of a storm. They followed the ship day and night across the Atlantic (approximately 3,000 miles), yet never once were seen on the surface of the water, or on anything floating on the water, demonstrating what a remarkable power of flight these small birds have.

Three or four days out the ship gladdened in the Gulf Stream. Glendon remembered his fishing as a boy and the journeys on mackerel schooners and took solace and saw good fortune in the color of the water in "the stream," a deeper blue than the surrounding body of water, approaching ultramarine. One day he noticed tropical vegetation in the form of kelp and seaweed floating on the surface and also transparent jellylike formations and a large sea turtle apparently sunning himself on the surface of the water. It was about two feet long and probably weighed about 200 pounds. Glendon remarked to no one in particular along the rail that it was a small specimen though. He had seen them on the New England coast weighing 600 pounds, and they were known to attain a weight of 800 pounds.[26]

During the rest of the trip they saw porpoises, dolphins, flying fish, and one day a whale. The boys of his crew, and anyone else within earshot to listen, were astounded at the breadth of marine knowledge Glendon possessed and, ever the teacher, passed on in monologues like, "Porpoises belong to the whale genus. They come to the surface to breathe, are four or five feet long, and weigh four or five hundred pounds. They are gregarious, and some of the old-timers call them 'puffin pigs,' on account of the puffing sound when they come to the surface to breathe. They much resemble revolving wheels in the water while swimming.

"Dolphins also belong to the whale family. [They ran into a school one day and they gave an exhibition of speed swimming that made the swimmers on board the ship hang their heads in shame.]

They can gather such speed in the water that they are able to make a broad jump of fifteen or twenty feet through the air, which is a remarkable feat, considering the size of the fish. They are gregarious and are found in every sea from the equator to the poles. It is said that they have a very acute sense of hearing and are attracted by regular or musical sounds."[27]

Some of the landlubbers aboard never really believed the stories they had heard of flying fish until actually seeing them. Glendon explained, "They are small fish about five to twelve inches long and much resemble 'whiting.' They have extended fins which resemble wings, and I have seen them leave the water and travel a distance of seventy or a hundred feet. They do not move the fins but seem to glide through the air, resembling a small monoplane in flight."[28]

MIDWAY ACROSS, LATITUDE 45 DEGREES 41 north, 40 degrees 28 west, 1,500 nautical miles away and 1,600 to go, they were halfway to Europe to the east and equidistant to the North Pole as from the equator. The North Atlantic was still behaving itself with only the slightest whitecaps, unperceivable swells, and a following wind of 15 knots, which, when coupled with the forward speed of the ship of 13 knots, made for a negligible breeze on deck. All of these factors lent themselves to the training of the athletes on board.

The clear purple-blue waters of the 3,500-meter-deep Atlantic swirled and churned away from the hull, mesmerizing the thoughts of those rail-gazers where dreams were rapidly closing upon them. The question on every crew member's mind was, "What are the Leander men doing today?" The other teams they would be competing against were considered, but the possibility of triumphing over Leander was the cornerstone of all their hopes.

Flicking some salt off the rail into the passing sea, Johnston and Graves made small talk about the newspaper reports of the Henley Royal Regatta. Leander had won handily. Johnston's long stares off the starboard side, noticed by Graves, were met by the captain of the crew with compassion and a gentlemanly understanding not to pry. Sea crossings being what they are, the long hours led each man to his own thoughts. Johnston's letter writing and his sauntering away to quiet parts of the ship to read letters and to write them told any who noticed that he was in love with Margaret Hill back in Annapolis.[29]

With the ship's gaiety and noise behind bulkhead doors, on deck small groups clustered for a smoke, drinks, concerns about the equipment, the shells riding piggyback up on the starboard fore deck, and, of course, the ever-present heightened consciousness of the upcoming race.

Friendships, in the long hours of the crossing and with the near hypnotic lulling motion of the sea and ship, eased tensions and beckoned for men to speak up and talk of the things in their soul. Along the rail, Glendon and Chandler talked about their counterparts Rudy Lehmann and Cherry Pitman of Leander. Glendon joked that he had read Lehmann's book, *The Complete Oarsman,* in the Chatham Library. Feeling like he knew the man, Glendon looked over the rail and gestured toward Belgium whispering, "Lehmann, you have your science and I have mine."[30] Glendon felt confident he knew Leander's strategies and also intuited that Navy's relative anonymity and enigma status would work to their benefit. He was sure of it.

Leander's confidence might work against them, as well as their having to peak twice, as it were, with Henley—their showpiece regatta—the third week of June and again in the Olympic Games in a matter of a mere two months' time. It is hard to get one's body to peak once in a season, let alone twice. Glendon felt his boys were going to benefit from this long rest during the crossing, whereas the British would be training still, perhaps to their disadvantage. There are some Olympians who swear they really only peaked once in an entire lifetime—not to speak of twice in a summer season.

Jordan in three seat and Jacomini in bow wondered about their British counterparts, Earl and Swann. What were they like? Who were these men and what were they likely to be doing and thinking? For Jacomini and Jordan, whose parents had just immigrated from Europe, these waters and the people on both sides of it were the stuff of their grandparents' dinner conversations.

Jacomini wrote home often, telling his mother and father that he had gained his sea legs and was bunking with eleven other athletes in the captain's quarters. Glendon, realizing he had a young crew, and having encouraged all the boys to write home to keep homesickness at bay and to keep them focused on the upcoming events and their shipboard training, saw Jack writing and prompted a discussion of the movie-men on board. "Did you tell your parents about the Associated Press and the International Press snapping your picture all day long?" Jack responded that his face felt like it was going to crack from smiling so much. "Well, if they have this much interest in you now, think how they will be after we win!" Jack jotted that line down, knowing his coach "surely knew what he was talking about since he has been in the game for 32 years."[31] Finishing the letter in time to give to the pilot boat as they entered the English Channel Jack wrote enthusiastically that Coach Glendon told them "all contestants would be given bronze statues of 'Marathon' and the winners would receive diplomas and medals." He reassured his parents that many of the officers and crew were going to come to the Games to see them row, and "the First Lieutenant wants to buy us champagne as they surely think we will win."[32]

MEANWHILE, BACK IN HENLEY-ON-THAMES, AT AN-gel's Tavern, conversations were likely to revolve around rowing and the upcoming prospects at the Olympic Games. Horsfall and John-stone might have sat comfortably sipping an evening's Pimms and lemonade after just putting up their shell. They would have had an unremarkable row, perfunctory, as theirs had been this whole year—they were that good.[33]

To any questions sizing up the competition, Horsfall undoubt-edly quipped, "Most crews are known to us except the Japanese and the Australians. Norwegians and Swedes we can get by and the Americans are reportedly awkward—and two weeks at sea can't help them. I shouldn't think we have much to worry about there."[34]

"Cable reports say the Yanks are halfway here, mates. Should have taken a toll on them, I think," the barkeep probably agreed without solicitation.

And the Leander men would have tipped glasses to him with a smile and drank their last bits of fruit and dregs before shoving away from the bar rail, picking up their knapsacks of row togs and John-stone his rudder, and exiting the pub into the quiet streets of Henley.

They were the elite. The best that England had ever boated. They were young and strong, confident, with a European home-court advantage. The odds favored them.

ON THE *FREDERICK* THEY WERE NOT EVEN AWARE that their progress was being monitored—a sporting invasion, as it were, crossing the same North Atlantic waters for de Coubertin's "higher, faster, stronger" Olympic mottos of peace that only two years previously were notorious hunting grounds for sinkings by German U-boats.

On the last leg of the journey they encountered a storm, which drove them from their course. The gun-metal gray hull of the ship joined the gray overcast skies seamlessly. Every three minutes the *Frederick*'s foghorn blew as they entered the comparatively shallow waters of the Celtic Sea. Winds freshened. Crew and passengers braced for a storm. Chandler and Glendon checked and rechecked the boat straps and scaffolding holding the eights on the foredeck, which was now awash with the boarding seas. The vessel rolled and gave way to breaking green-black seas with streaked white faces that drew the ship off course nearly a hundred miles. A damp hush shrouded the ship amid the roar of the wind taking the tops of the fetching waves off their crest and slapping them onto the super-structure of the ship, nudging it hour by hour to destiny. The waves running before them in the following sea were like so many sentinels in advance of troops. Dew so heavy that it rolled off the armored plates and hand-railings dripped from gangways and bulkhead doors, watch lights and ring buoys, the unrelenting sea submersing the entire ship in a watery skin shroud. The silvery white air was soaking, not thin.

Rain pelted from time to time, sounding a hush drone beat on the decks, air rushing by opened doors with its unseen hands reaching through fog into the passageways, howling eerily of the ages it spent in the watery world of the North Atlantic. The fog bell rang as lookouts peered into the mist, their minds sorting out water from sky, cloud from water, gray ship from gray ocean.

The insular mood was taken advantage of by Capt. Scott, who

The 1869 Naval Academy Boat Club, the oldest sport at the academy.

Oldest Photographic Record of Naval Academy Athletics
BOAT CLUB—CLASS OF 1869
Back Row (left to right): S. C. Paine, J. C. Wilson (cox), J. Garvin, G. F. Wright, T. D. Bolles.
Front Row: A. P. Osborn, D. D. V. Stuart.

Richard A. "Pop" Glendon.

The three Glendon coaches in 1929: Hubert, Richard A., and Richard John.

Coach Glendon with son Richard at the dock.

The childhood environs of Richard Glendon, Chatham, Massachusetts.

William "Buck" Jordan and Edward "Country" Moore.

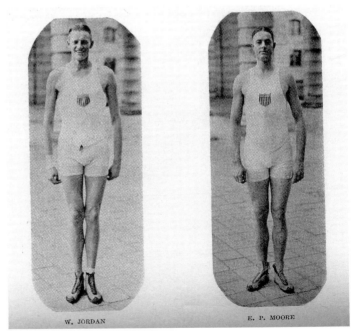

W. JORDAN

E. P. MOORE

V. J. GALLAGHER

Vincent "Gal" Gallagher.
DUNCAN GLENDON, THE GLENDON COLLECTION.
USED WITH PERMISSION.

Bowman Victor "Jack"
Jacomini.
DUNCAN GLENDON,
THE GLENDON COLLECTION.
USED WITH PERMISSION.

V. V. JACOMINI

E. D. GRAVES, CAPTAIN

U.S. crew captain Edwin Darius "Eddie" Graves.
DUNCAN GLENDON, THE GLENDON COLLECTION.
USED WITH PERMISSION.

CLYDE KING

S. R. CLARK

Navy strokeman Clyde King and coxswain Sherman Rockwell "Cutie" Clark.

A. R. Sanborn and D. S. Johnston.

A. R. SANBORN

D. S. JOHNSTON

Chandler, the 1920 U.S. boatman.

Leander's Sidney "Cygnate" Swan and Al Swan.

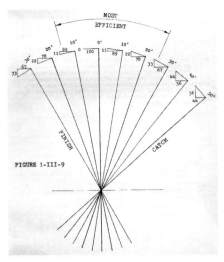

FIGURE 1-III-9

Glendon's creed: "Row the Arc Closest to 90 Degrees."

Michael Purcer. Used with permission.

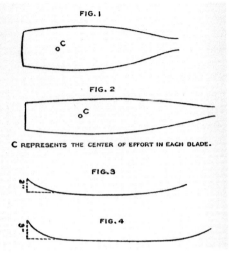

FIG. 1

FIG. 2

C REPRESENTS THE CENTER OF EFFORT IN EACH BLADE.

FIG. 3

FIG. 4

Glendon's American orthodoxy: the American blade (Fig. 1) is wider than the British blade (Fig. 2).

Duncan Glendon, the Glendon Collection. Used with permission.

S. EARL (MAGDALEN).

Sport and General.

WINNER OF THE OXFORD UNIVERSITY SCULLS IN RECORD TIME.

Sebastian Earl of Magdalen College (Oxford University) and the Leander Boat Club.

The Rowing and River Museum, Henley, England. Used with permission.

Indoor rowing machines at the Naval Academy.

The 1920 Naval Academy crews, with the Olympic eight on the left.

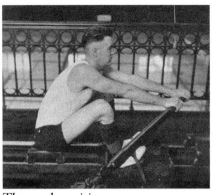

The catch position.

DUNCAN GLENDON, THE GLENDON
COLLECTION. USED WITH PERMISSION.

The finish position.

DUNCAN GLENDON, THE GLENDON COLLECTION.
USED WITH PERMISSION.

The USS *Frederick*.

DUNCAN GLENDON, THE GLENDON
COLLECTION. USED WITH PERMISSION.

Captain Pitt of the USS *Frederick*.

U.S. NAVAL ACADEMY ARCHIVES. USED WITH PERMISSION.

The 1920 Navy
eight on board the
USS *Frederick*,
Sherman Clarke
and Richard
Glendon kneeling.

BARBARA GALLAGHER,
THE GALLAGHER
COLLECTION. USED
WITH PERMISSION.

The Navy eight exercising on rowing machines onboard the USS *Frederick,*
with rowing shells tied on the racks and King at the stroke.

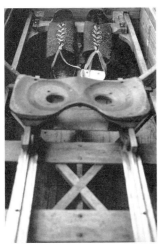

A 1920-era foot-stretcher, seat, and slide.

The challenges of transporting
eight-oared shells in 1920.

The canal boat *Sophia* transporting the Olympic shells from the USS *Frederick* to Vilvoorde.

Antwerp's Olympic Stadium, 1920.

The tavern converted by the U.S. rowing team into quarters; notice the American flag hanging from the second story.

Camaraderie between some of the European crews and America in the boat tent.

The 1920 Leander crew launching, heading toward the start for the Olympic finals.

The 1920 Olympic finish: Navy wins by half a length.
Duncan Glendon, the Glendon Collection. Used with permission.

Joy in the streets as Moore and Graves celebrate after the race.
Duncan Glendon, the Glendon Collection. Used with permission.

Glendon standing on platform "one" receiving the Olympic gold medals.
Duncan Glendon, the Glendon Collection. Used with permission.

The 1920 World Champions.
DUNCAN GLENDON, THE GLENDON COLLECTION. USED WITH PERMISSION.

The official program of the
VII Olympiad, Antwerp, 1920.
OZ SANBORN, THE SANBORN
COLLECTION. USED WITH PERMISSION.

A Norman Rockwell illustration of a 1920 crew member.

The Richard A. Glendon Trophy.
DUNCAN GLENDON, THE GLENDON COLLECTION.
USED WITH PERMISSION.

A photo of Adm. Chester W. Nimitz signing the Japanese surrender papers, with a personal notation to Richard Glendon beneath.
DUNCAN GLENDON, THE GLENDON COLLECTION. USED WITH PERMISSION.

The Leander Boat Club, Henley-on-Thames, England.
SUSAN SAINT SING.
USED WITH PERMISSION.

The 1920 crew in dress whites, with Richard Glendon in the center front row and his son Richard J. Glendon in the center back row.

The U.S. Naval Academy 1920 Olympic gold medalists' crew reunion, 1958. Left to right: Clyde King, Vincent Gallagher, Donald Johnston, Alden Sanborn, Edward Moore, William Jordan, Edwin Graves, and Victor Jacomini, with Sherman Clark in front.

used its imagery in the Sunday worship service to urge the crew to go deep inside on this day and settle in with themselves and ask, "Who is it I will be in three weeks' time? Olympic champion or a name fallen off the rosters, unheralded, forgotten like all the souls we are quietly slipping past, lost in the deep? Go deep inside yourselves, not in your mind, not in your young heart, but deeper still—into your soul—and fashion your destiny. Greatness lies within, not without. Champions are personages, not a mere medal for one race. Pursue excellence in all things, and the winning and losing will take care of themselves. For on any given day on a field of play someone wins and someone loses. It is only a 50/50 proposition. But what I ask of you and what you need to ask of yourselves is 100 percent excellence—in character, in honor. Easy to win with honor, difficult to lose and retain it. But should you lose a race, you still have won yourselves if you pursue personal excellence. You will not be unsportsmanlike, angry, or petty, nor stubborn and mean-spirited toward anyone. Yours is a slice of time and opportunity given to many yet sought by few to advance and achieve civility and virtue through competition.

"At the Games we use sport, tomorrow we may use business or education or science or technology but whatever the vehicle we must compel the hours and actions of our daily lives toward honor—toward others. Use every grain of your intellect and will to do so, for then and only then will you be champions—Olympic medal around your neck, or not.

"Pursue excellence in dealing with one another, your teammates, judges, fans, family, friends—seek to live above reproach in all things and you have won the race of life. Take counsel not in yourself—for one's mind is deceptive and self-seeking—no, take counsel as do the waves, joining in and falling upon one another, not just those that please you—in an endless succession of effort, exhaustion, trying to rise again, moving forward, pushing the mark and the bar ahead, then giving out and settling only to rise again and again in the glorious effort of trying mind, body, soul to exhaust oneself in virtue. Seize it. Relish it. Capture it as if taking a bulkhead for your country, for today in your health and agility of mind and spirit and body, you have opportunity. Write your names in the ledgers of Olympic glory and celebrate your seeking as equal to the heights of its gods."[35]

OUTSIDE, FATE RAGED IN A NORTH ATLANTIC storm attempting to rip the shells off the foredeck and steer the ship off course. Aboard the *Frederick,* radio compass messages were received from England and France. The directions from which the messages came were indicated on the chart by two straight lines. The point of the intersection of the two lines showed their position and at the end of the storm they found that they were 100 miles north of their proper course, and continuing in that direction would have landed them in the Irish Sea. After a course correction at 8 A.M., they passed Ireland and by the next day the storm had abated and the *Frederick* and its passengers got their first sight of nimble fishing boats seesawing in the swells, dotting the coastal waters of England. Steaming south they rounded the Isles of Scilly and the Bishop Rock Light with its two white flashes every fifteen seconds atop the 167-foot pillar of granite.[36] The lighthouse reared up isolated offshore on a reef and was a morose sentinel of the western boundaries of the Isles of Scilly and Land's End. The crew marveled when they heard that giant waves in the 1800s hit topmost sections of the light.

Coming from the north back down toward the English Channel, Glendon was comforted by the lightship *Seven Stones,* anchored in

1879 with three white flashes every thirty seconds. Their passage through the Strait of Dover stirred their primordial souls. As the white, chalk cliffs stood out sharply in the pink and purple hush of ambient twilight, the echoing cliffs of France were equally smothered in sea haze and history as they steamed past Cape Gris Nez Light dimly visible in the distance—the channel at this point being only twenty miles wide.[37] Off the coast of Dover at the southernmost tip of Kent, Dungenness Light with its black and white bands stood proudly flashing five white every thirty seconds. Its circular brick bade them farewell as it stood as a testament to British tenacity.[38] At 9:32 P.M. they passed Calais Light abeam and headed for the ancient port of Antwerp and West Hinder Light.[39]

At last, nearing the coast of Holland, the *Frederick* procured a pilot and proceeded up the river twenty miles to the ancient city of Antwerp, Belgium. The crew awoke to find the ship lying off the dikes in the Scheldt River, waiting on the tide. At 6 P.M. on 7 August, they tied up to Quai 8, Antwerp, anchored in the river Scheldt, two or three hundred yards from the big dikes of Holland, after twelve days at sea.[40]

Leaning over the rails of the ship and marveling at the environs, the crew saw Holland as a very picturesque country with its big dikes, canals, windmills, and quaint little homes. Some of the big dikes, sloping 300 feet toward the sea, were forty feet above highwater mark and forty wide on top; and they accommodated roadways and service railways on the same dike. Some of the homes in Holland seemed to be situated twenty feet below the level of the sea and the dikes were patrolled every half mile. The united length of the canals of Holland stretched on out of sight and the tall poplar trees that lined the canals on both sides gave a very scenic effect to that part of the continent.[41]

The long siege of coaching, training, discipline, and anxiety under which the coaches and crew labored was soon to be tested in the elimination heats, which would only too soon be past history, leaving the two greatest eights to battle for the supremacy of the world.

12. 1920 HENLEY AND LEANDER

"What, after all is a sportsman?" he asked. "As I understand the breed he is one who has not merely braced his muscles and developed his endurance by the exercise of some great sport, but has, in the pursuit of that exercise learnt to control his anger, to be considerate to his fellowmen, to take no mean advantage, to resent as a dishonor the very suspicion of trickery, to bear aloft a cheerful countenance under disappointment, and never to own himself defeated until the last breath is out of his body."

—R. C. Lehmann,
coach and honorary secretary of Leander[1]

———— ✦ ————

IN ENGLAND, INTEREST WAS KEEN. ENGLISH NAVAL and Military Intelligence posted the following regarding the movements of the U.S. crew in *The Times*: "For the conveyance of the American naval representatives who will take part in the Olympic Games at Antwerp, the Navy Department has ordered the cruiser *Frederick* to be commissioned for a trip to European waters."[2]

To the person on the street the upcoming Olympics were a time for glory again. For thousands it was a time to heal battle-torn wounds and to mend the soul of humankind that had been rent in the trenches and hedgerows of Flanders Fields. Belgium had been a staunch ally, and rallying support for the Olympic Games became a stake in the national honor of Belgium, England, and all the Allied powers, as well as the cloak of goodness to be draped over the land that had successfully driven back the aggressive arsenal of military destruction. For Europe, World War I was a giant, hateful brawl among families and friends with the direst outcome of decimated allegiances and social interweavings that had solidified over centuries. The war was fresh on their souls and in their consciousness; indeed, the eyes of the living could see in the walking memorials to the black testaments of war that survived among them—armless, legless, sightless some—that the oozing wound of viciousness ached to be healed with lightness of spirit. Fresh was Lt. Col. McCrae's poem "Flanders Fields," published in England's famous magazine *Punch* in 1915.

In Flanders fields the poppies blow
between the crosses row on row,
they mark our place; and in the sky
the larks still singing fly,
scarce heard amid the guns below.
We are the dead. Short days ago
we lived, felt dawn, saw sunset glow,
loved and were loved
and now we lie in Flanders fields.
Take up our quarrel with the foe,
to you from failing hands we throw
the torch; be yours to hold it high.
If ye break faith with us who die

we shall not sleep in Flanders fields,
though poppies grow in Flanders fields.[3]

Fresh was the memory of the dead, of the money spent, of the soldiers gone from home, of the suffering to those who felt that it was a time for healing at home. In the summer of 1920, a brief flurry of "should we, shouldn't we" engage in the upcoming Olympic Games was exchanged in newspapers' Letters to the Editor, and in conversation in the local pubs, but in the end the chance to hold the torch of virtue high through sport and goodwill won.[4]

Secretary of War and Air (and soon to be Prime Minister) Winston Churchill, in a moving speech to rally support for the team at a luncheon given by the British Olympic Council at the Criterion Restaurant, reflected the optimism of the day. "It is important for the public to know how matters stand so that there is no risk of England being unrepresented at the Olympics."[5] Furthering the cause, at the same luncheon a message was read from the Princes also: "The Prince of Wales, the Duke of York, and Prince Henry wish every success to the British Olympic teams and hope they will receive every support from the public."[6]

Amid the shuffle of waiters attending the crowd and food being served, Churchill proposed a toast to "success to the teams of the Olympic Games," a rallying call to meet that day to make a real effort in securing a fair chance for British teams at Antwerp. . . . "There is a great wish on the part of the Belgian people, which was suitably expressed by the heroic Belgian King, that the next celebration of the Olympic Games should be held in Belgium to signalize her vigorous effort at recovery and her full assertion of revived, renewed, liberated national life after the long suffering and oppression of the German invasion. . . . However if we look at it only from the point of view of British sport and of our record in international sport, we might feel more inclined to advise the postponement of the competition until another year had elapsed after the close of the Great War. . . . [But still] the character and quality of many of the British competitors afford very high hopes for a reasonable share in the honors."

Cheers rose in the room as Rev. de Courcey Laffan continued with Churchill's charge as a matter of national honor. "It is sometimes said that we were making too much of sports," but he believed there was no time when they needed to make more of sport than today. "If we are to have a democracy with the right qualities, every man must learn to live, in the first place, for his country, and in the second place for himself. The man who has learned to play his side and not for himself has learned the first lesson of citizenship and will carry it through his whole citizen life."[7]

And what greater symbol of peace and goodness to the world than to send the "Flowers of England" to what was one of the worst battlefields in the Great War? Let the might of the very names that would be called out and echoed on the loudspeakers jar memories to the attention of goodness and righteousness and chase the darkness of petty war cries of greed and invasion to the sidelines and outside the boundaries of dignity. Let the might of a tradition of gentility overcome.

The British had spent centuries spreading civility throughout the world. And they believed that in this war and future wars the lessons of sport—courage, honor, fairness, a will to win, and a will to be fair and honorable in victory—was engrained in the very soles of the runners' feet at Rugby School. As the future Prime Minister Churchill said, the Battle of Britain *was* won on the playing fields of Eton. The value of virtue bore no small price tag in British consciousness, and the urge to come to the aid of the Belgian king and his people tore at the heart and soul of English pride and sentiment.

The Great War had partially been started through belief in Alfred Thayer Mahan's ideology that command of the sea was vital for a great nation. Let the navies of the world carry swimmers, fencers, divers, and rowers to Belgium now instead of troops. Let the Japanese and Australians cross thousands of miles of ocean without fear of mines or torpedoes. Let them come, let them all come—and they did—by the tens of thousands.

Indeed, Pierre de Coubertin himself had commented twenty years earlier that British school lads *needed* to spend more time in sports to toughen them since the French were trained in militaristic fencing and the Germans in tumbling and Turnerbrand. Why not prepare youth for sport in case of war? And if war never came, at least the lessons of conditioning and fairness abounded. But with the assassination of Archduke Ferdinand of Austria by an errant Serb in Sarajevo, the wheels of war *were* set turning and grinding through the lives of those who would become some five million dead and four million missing. Belgium had declared neutrality in Austria's quarrel with the Serbs. It was sympathetic to the European houses of past glory who needed to expand their empires toward better ports and freer trade, much as the British had, but King Albert of Belgium wanted no part of a war, even though his country was the first casualty as Germany vaulted its attack toward France though Belgium. Could a cry for peace and resurrection from the throes and scars of war from the gentle and heroic Belgian king with his brave young family now be forgotten?

Never. For just as the Great War had dredged up romantic notions of fighting for family honor (most of the royal families of Europe are intermarried and indeed the English throne has Germanic bloodlines in it) and past heritages—so, too, did a quick and certain momentum and romanticism play a part in the 1920 Olympic cry for brotherhood and peace, and a show of strength in virtue, honor, and civility throughout Europe.

And who better to bring home the glory again than the British crew Leander? Immortalized in the Greek epic of Hero and Leander, Leander was a great and determined lover of Hero, a priestess of the Goddess of Love, Aphrodite. Hero would light a lamp in her tower on the edge of the water near the Hellespont for Leander to see as he bravely and steadfastly swam, nightly, to secretly lie with her. One night a storm came up and Hero's lamp blew out and Leander, losing his way, drowned in his quest while swimming the waves. Leander men always likened their legacy to that of the gods. So esteemed is the Leander tradition of rowing in the annals of English valor that no fewer than five ships had carried the name *Leander* in the Royal Navy since 1780.[8] Leander was the all-star, highly coveted goal for those rowers good enough to represent their schools at what was essentially the national rowing club of Britain.

TO UNDERSTAND LEANDER ONE MUST THINK OF IT as a national honorary rowing club. If you are the best of the best in your college you are invited to be a member of Leander. And because it is nearly impossible for one college boat to have all eight of the greatest rowers at any one time in the kingdom, Leander crews, which had their own club rowers of past Olympians and varsity rowers, frequently were made up of the freshest, brightest, young college fodder that could be found. So it was possible for the best of the college eights to row for Leander in an "all-star" venue for the Henley Royal Regatta, the great postseason race, while other boats might be confident enough to win with their season-long boatmates or with past alumni greats jumping in to join them, as would be allowed in the summer, when collegiate rowing rules and stipulations are suspended, allowing for many combinations of winning crews for club races.

As the Boat Race was to the universities of Cambridge and Oxford, the Henley Royal Regatta was to Leander and the rest of the rowing clubs of Britain and the world. Leander stemmed from the humble roots of the Stars and the Arrows Rowing Clubs in London's highly trafficked wharf district near St. Johns Hospital in the 1700s, when river watermen were followed by betting barges that placed bets during the racing. Needing to grow with the city and to remove itself from the filth and stench of inner-city Victorian London's riverbanks, the racing was moved to a more pastoral and socially acceptable club setting on the Thames at nearby Henley, where the grand Leander Club now boasts its sumptuous boathouse and the fastest racing in Britain.

The Henley Stewards of the 1920 Leander Club offered invitations to Cambridge's great Swann and Campbell, and Johnstone at cox, to row with their own Leander Club's Horsfall and Shove. After Henley in June, another set of invitations went out to add Lucas, James, Earl, and Nickalls for Leander's representative Olympic eight, cementing together what were some of the greatest and fastest rowers England would ever see.

Coupled with Cherry Pitman as coach, and undoubtedly the wisdom of the ages in the flock of Olympians manning Leander's hallowed halls, terraces, boat bays, and foyers, were decades of rowing, racing, and coaching strategists who carried themselves equally in Parliament, banking, the clergy, and royalty. For all of England, the upcoming Olympic Games was the time to put on the dress again and go and do what the British do best—be British.

13. CUTTING DOWN

In eight-oared racing "cutting down" tactics are almost invariably adopted. "Try to beat them in the first minute; if you are unable to, then beat them in the second; if that is impossible beat them in the third, and so on."

—Gully Nickalls, British 1920 Olympic crew

GREAT BRITAIN'S LEANDER CLUB BEGAN PRACTIC-ing for the Olympic Regatta at Henley-on-Thames after the Henley Royal Regatta. *The Times* coverage of their practicing for the Olympic Regatta was summarily upbeat: "The crew rowed in the new Sims boat which appeared to carry them admirably."[1] In the same article, they'd reportedly tried a new set of oars on 16 July and sent their Sims boat ahead to Antwerp, finishing their practices at Henley in a Magdalen boat.

Accolades by *The Times'* rowing correspondent included, "The rowing was a long way in advance of anything seen at Henley during the last two regattas."[2] The confidence of success for the Leander crew was evident: "The crew promises well and with another fort-night's practice should make a really first-class eight likely to retain the trophy which Leander won at the Olympic regatta of 1908 (Henley) and 1912 (Stockholm)."[3] England's best—Horsfall, Nickalls, Lucas, James, Campbell, Earl, Shove, Swann, and cox Johnstone—feared not;

there was no debate in their minds. They were the best that ever was, plain and simple.

On a warm summer's night in August, after five weeks of concentrated rowing together, the nine men of the British Olympic team gathered with friends and family. Sitting in the beautifully terraced and manicured wrought-iron and brick, palatial Leander Club at Henley-on-Thames—the most prestigious rowing club in the world and looking across the ancient and graceful Isis and Tamesis Bridge—how could they not feel superior? After all, England had never been beaten in any Olympic rowing they'd attended, and many of their fathers—legacies in their own right from Cambridge Blues and Oxford's Magdalen, and Henley racing—had won before them and had come this night to see them off.

Strolling across the bridge they sauntered to the elegant Red Lion Inn and dined beneath the steeple of the squat, square church tower.

With proper tablecloths and neatly folded linens abounding, a good dinner of beef or lamb and potatoes, with beer or hearty red wine blazoned with polished silver goblets, the British crew solidified their hopes and confidence through conversation, stories, and laughter. All of their breeding, all of their schooling, had prepared them for this very moment in time to be Olympians. To represent Britain and Leander, to be Olympic champions, was their due.

Other diners and fans, nodding hellos and reestablishing old acquaintances, if only in their memories of seeing these legends stroke by at Henley or the University Boat Race, reassured them even further that they were the best that England ever boated. Confidence became them.

Their Henley Olympic Regatta of 1908 was the stuff of bedtime tales, a Camelot of blades and boats spoken about with pride and longing by their fathers, uncles, and schoolmates. Stockholm in 1912 had been a victory, so there was no reason to believe that Antwerp would be any different, nothing more than another feather in the rowing cap of England. Like the swan feather proudly protruding from coxswain's hat worn in the Royal Swan Upping days, pomp and circumstance, tradition and pageantry, was theirs to relish and preserve, not feign. They were unlike the young Americans from Iowa and the Bronx, whose families boasted no rowing lines or heritage, but only boasted of being of the American working-class blood that presumed to counter England's privilege with spunk and grit.

And after dinner, they stopped at the boat livery beneath the tavern where gray swan goslings drifted past with their elegant white swan parents flanking them for protection, much as their own parents and siblings were doing now.

From the depths of Henley's winning waters, Moor hens, coots, and mallards drifted beneath them in the calm placid water through the elegant granite arches of the bridge. Royal Mute Swans floated gracefully by. These were swept up and protected every year by the Royal Swan Catcher. With his red coat and swan-feathered cap, on Swan Upping Day, he would count, ring, and, among other duties, transport them to safety during regattas in order to protect them, the guarded property of the Royals.[4] These men shared a kinship with the feathered things that drifted beneath the bridge in elegance and buoyancy, leaving vee-ed chevrons behind them on the water's surface that dissipated into the depths again. Water passing under the bridge from the foothills toward London and to the open North Sea and to Antwerp beyond, beckoned them as sure as the figureheads on the bridge lured them onward. Mute gray goslings, yearning to grow into exquisite mature white swans, strained at the young men's sense of comparativeness, as the goslings drifted on the currents and winds of the ancient Thames. Oh how these young Leander men wanted to linger and mingle in the ancient waters of the anthropomorphous and feel the cool hands of the goddesses Isis and Tamesis empower them to the stuff of glory and legend in and on the river as their fathers had done before them. Would they not have paused on the apex of the gently sloped bridge and have wished for glory for themselves? For family? For God? For country?

Swann, Nickalls, and Horsfall all came from great rowing families and many a tactic and encouraging word would surely have been uttered in toasts and glasses raised to "Triumph!" and to Leander Club's traditional toast, "Corpus Leandri Spes Mea!" (Body of Leander My Hope!)[5]

Many of these men and sons had never known defeat on the water, why should it begin now? Ewart "Dink" Horsfall was considered one of the greatest strokes in the history of English rowing. After Eton he went to Oxford and in 1912, won the gold at the Stockholm Olympics. In 1913, at stroke, he and Oxford defeated Cambridge. In 1913, he became the first stroke to win the Boat Race after being behind at Barnes Bridge. He won the Grand at Henley four times—three times as stroke—and he stroked the winning crew in the Stewards' Challenge Cup on the only two occasions he competed. He joined the RAF and won the Distinguished Flying Cross and had the rare distinction of being awarded a double Military Cross. After the war he returned to Oxford to reestablish rowing there, which kept him in training and brought him to this, the eve of his second Olympic appearance.[6]

Nor was Gully Nickalls a stranger to these Henley waters. He was the son of one of the most revered Oxford Magdalen oarsmen who won the Stewards' Cup seven times, the Goblets six times, the

Diamond Sculls five times, and the Grand four times. At age forty-one, his father was one of the oldest Olympic rowing champions who then closed his illustrious rowing career by winning gold in the 1908 Olympics at Henley-on-Thames.[7]

Gully was first taken to Henley when he was six years old where he rode in the umpire's launch—"to watch daddy row."[8] "I remember it so well. I was sitting in the bow of the launch and as my father was backing down his pair-oar to get the stern of the boat on to the starting point, he glanced up and winked at me. My heart was very full and a thrill of pride surged through me. That god-like creature had seen me and, oh joy, he winked at me. What more had life to offer? I was hooked."[9]

Sidney Swann, nicknamed Cygnate ("Cyg"), was from a great rowing family whose father was a Cambridge Blue and a great runner. Cyg was a Cambridge friend of Olympic runner and barrister Harold Abrahams of *Chariots of Fire* fame and a 1924 Olympic gold medalist from Great Britain. Abrahams and Swann were both members of the elite Trinity Hall of Cambridge—where all they make are "lawyers and rowers." When Cyg Swann first entered there, knowing that it was dear in money for his clergyman father to send him to one of the finest schools in England, he asked his father what he should do, and his father sent him a telegram with the mere phrase, "AT THE HALL, THEY ROW." In a letter home to his parents Cyg thanked them for the two shillings for food and the three shillings for paper and then signed off with, "Well, I'll 'easy off' now," using a rowing coxswain's phrase for ending a rowing outing and letting the boat drift to a stop—and then added, "As you can see, I'm quite rowing mad now."

In Henry Bond's *A History of the Trinity Hall Boat Club,* Cyg Swann is considered one of the greatest rowers and in fact perhaps one of the greatest athletes in Cambridge's history.[10] Educated at Rugby and Trinity Hall, his father rowed in the Boat Race three times, won the 25-mile bicycle race against Oxford in 1884, and rowed the English Channel single-handed at age forty-nine. From a family of sweet, earnest men with "blue eyes and thinly hair," Cyg was quick to laugh and always had to do anything that needed to be done straightaway.[11]

In 1910, on his first appearance at Henley, Sidney Swann stroked Trinity Hall to victory in both the Visitor's and the Wyfold. He was in the Cambridge "blue" boat in 1911, 1912, and 1913. In 1913, Swann was invited into the winning Leander eight in the Grand and won the Goblets that same year, partnered with his brother Arthur. The Swann brothers repeated this feat in 1914, winning the Goblets again at Henley. He won gold in the 1912 Leander boat at the Olympics in Stockholm, and following a family tradition, entered the Church after the war.[12]

Was he waiting now this night, perhaps saying a prayer in the twelfth-century medieval St. Mary the Virgin Church at Henley-on-Thames? Was he standing in St. Leonard's Chapel or St. Mary the Virgin Chapel with its sixteenth-century steeple a backdrop to Henley and the Regatta? Did he kneel beneath the Perpendicular-style vaulted wooden ceiling and pray for what, Excellence? Safety? Gold? Did the entire team walk past the flint-knapped flushwork (flint chipped and split in half with stone set in mortar) into the silent world of filtered stained glass light in hopeful reverence, just as the U.S. team was doing in Brussel's Cathedral?[13]

Steve Shove in two seat was the captain of the Leander Club. In the heart of the Leander shell were the formidable Sebastian Earl of Oxford's Magdalen College fame who had just defeated Cambridge in the Boat Race and won the right to sit in three seat in the Leander eight with I. A. Campbell, stroking the bow four, and "Jimmy" Walter James at five, and with R. S. Lucas, "Luke," at six in the engine room. Nickalls and Horsfall were the stern pair. Coxswain R. T. "Bush" Johnstone—son of Banner Johnstone, who captained the 1908 Henley Olympic boat—had just steered Cambridge to their magnificent and unexpected win over Oxford in the Boat Race a few months earlier that year.[14] Henley's streets were quiet tonight, but in the shadows and crags of stone walkways and ancient moss he and his father both could hear the echoes of 1908 when flag-draped Henley streets swelled with fans and rowers from around the world. Enthralled and fully immersed in the Olympism regalia, fanfare, and spirit the crowds burst into cheers when England trounced the Belgians by two lengths. Surely they would do the same in August.

LEANDER HAD IN CHERRY PITMAN AND R. C. Lehmann the best coaches, and they had the newest equipment—they were ready. The crew walked back against a cool breeze, over the bridge from town, and entered the redbrick entrance of Leander, sheltered beneath the chestnut trees. As their senses filled with the scents of the Thames' still, black water, the walking paths and fields beneath the rolling hills of Oxfordshire, they surely felt the strength and virtue of youth. They were the pride of England. And in the night air, where none but water birds and water gods could hear, their strategy was born.

Nickalls, one of the elders of the crew spoke in hushed certainty, "Spurting, of course, should be initiated by Horsfall, or at any rate, by Horsfall and me, though as we have suggested, it is up to every member of the crew intelligently to anticipate the possibility of such a move. It is usual for the cox to call on the crew for these special efforts.

In some cases the cox" and he looked at Johnstone straightaway, "calls for a spurt by banging the bungs of his rudder lines on the saxboard of the boat, in others he is furnished with a press-button bell which rings in the bows of the boat and is audible to the whole crew. [We shall have to be on our toes with eyes and ears open.]

"The only sure means of surprising our rivals is by passing the information up the boat from the stern by word of mouth or by watching and following so closely that no sound or verbal exhortation is needed. This latter method requires we have a perfect understanding of our stroke."[15]

With all the lads enthralled, he continued, "Expend all your effort and maintain your form throughout—that is the way to win races.

"This holds good always except in the last minute of a very close race; then it is best to go 'mad dog' getting in as many strokes in the minute with all the power you have left to you. Many desperate finishes have been won by these methods and it is the only time when an oarsman may be excused for neglecting a little of the niceties of style and form."[16]

Further along the road he says, "When our opponents spurt, unless it is in the last minute and a half of the race, we do not immediately reply. Thus you avoid becoming hotheaded and hasty. It is best to make sure of keeping your length and your cohesion and to make the suitable reply just as soon as the other crew's effort begins to die away. Landmarks are very useful for knowing how far you still have to travel. Johnstone, you will have to reconnoiter the course with Horsfall well ahead of the game, but the race itself is a surer and more reliable guide on which to base your tactics."[17]

"This is our time, 'every oarsman here, will be treated as a thinking intelligent unit,'" Pitman added. It was a consummation devoutly to be wished.[18]

"Look," Nickalls continued, "I had gone up to Oxford in the Summer Term of 1920. Henley was to provide me with my first experience of that regatta as a participant. With incredible good fortune, I, we all, found ourselves rowing, I in seven in the powerful Magdalen eight, which won the Grand Challenge Cup with the greatest of ease."

That this crew showed exceptional pace is generally admitted. Just how much it was capable of was never proved. And they were captained and stroked with superb aplomb by none other than E. D. Horsfall, who had rowed in the Oxford crews of 1912, '13, and '14.

Gliding on enthusiasm Lucas spoke for the first time to Shove, "Sure, some of us have seen war service. Our age therefore for undergraduates is above average, though that could scarcely be claimed for our experiences of first-class rowing. We are older and therefore stronger and more skilled, all the better."

Shove, Honorary Secretary of Leander, couldn't agree more. "As soon as Henley was over, our rowing representation at the Olympics came up for discussion. The Committee has all the faith in the world in us."

As a crew at large, with the exception of Shove, they did not know of the labyrinth of compromises and positioning undertaken by the Henley Stewards and Leander Club officers in consideration for their Olympic eventuality. The Olympic Summer Games were to take place in Antwerp that year, and it was decided for economic reasons to send only an eight and a single sculler.[19] In regards to this composite Leander eight, four of the Magdalen crew won places with the inclusion of Cambridge oarsmen at bow, four, and cox, with Leander's Shove and Horsfall at two and stroke. (There are those who aver that had the Magdalen eight been left as it was, it should have won the Olympics. They argue that the new material, though in some respects an improvement as regards individuals, robbed the crew of that wonderful morale, which had put such zest and dash into their racing and wining at Henley in 1920, and that as a result the new combination of Cambridge, Leander, and Magdalen was slower than the old. Others retained an open mind on this question and felt that this year's selection of seats against any competitors would prove superior.)

The truth is that almost no one had the faintest conception of the extent to which American rowing had developed in the previous eight years, so no one seemed worried. But Swann, up to this point quiet as they strolled along, and who had been to the American scene as a coach, interjected, "Don't underrate the Americans. They will be much faster than you think."[20]

Nobody paid the slightest bit of attention to him and he delved back into his private thoughts on English rowing style. "A crew composed of the following has usually been found most effective: Bow should be neat and easy with his movements, above all a good waterman. Two is ditto, but slightly heavier and stronger. Three, four, and five the most powerful oarsmen available. They constitute essentially the driving machinery and need not be considered from the point of view of watermanship or neatness. They must be powerful men, and provided they are intelligent, they can be taught to row well for their strength to be made effective. Six seat should be a clever oarsman as well as being powerful, and of course, a most reliable racer. Seven should be the most finished oar in the boat. Stroke (eight) is the most difficult man to find, as he must combine so many qualities, but first and foremost he must be a man of the right personality, a real leader who will not be discouraged by adversity. His weight is immaterial."[21]

Swann assured himself, after going through the above rhetoric, that they needn't worry about the Americans because American shortness of swing made the American style more suitable for bad watermen and large clumsy men. The English long swing means more freedom of movement and enables the human spring to be fully utilized by "opening up" from the stretcher, yet, he remained uneasy about the reports of the "large" Americans.[22] He kept his opinion to himself among their group and walked on.

Earl, an absolute rock of dignity and propriety—handsome to a fault with a chiseled chin that spoke of his strength of character and will—spoke for the first time. "When we come up to the start, we should have but one idea in our mind, and that is *to drive from the heels our hardest every stroke.* Our training has been with a view to getting the body and the hands into such a position and can happen as frequently as possible. If our training has been sound all will go well."[23] They all nodded and agreed with quiet murmurings and a sure light in their eyes as if ignited from the light of determination in his. Certainly Leander's training had been sound. They were comfortable in assuming all would go well. It was becoming in their minds a simple matter of execution as outlined in their evening of elocution. Their heritage, their lineage, their honor for family, club, and country buoyed their self-assertion for success.

Leaving on Wednesday, having gotten the last possible training in at Henley before leaving for Brussels—the rest of the British team athletes had already gone ahead and been to the Opening Ceremony—they were reading of the other chaps already participating for God and country and, by God, they wanted to throw their lots in with them.

"To Leander!" Earl cheered as they rounded the alley toward the club just off the bridge. "To Leander!" they all cheered amid back slaps and hugs, handshakes and goodbye kisses to mothers, fathers, sisters, and family all.

The fathers' hands lingered in some handshakes. Cyg Swann's brother, Arthur, also a rower but not chosen for the team, looked him in the eye saying, "Row for us both, will you?" "Done," was Cyg's reply. And with that, the evening was over as cars and footsteps, doors and well-wishing quieted and died away. The muffled sounds, cares, and dreams of eventide became one and were carried by the water gods of Tamesis and Isis beneath the waters of the bridge, downstream through the locks and past the Parliament of London, across the Channel's dark waters, north to the waiting shores of Flanders, Antwerp, Vilvoorde, and the floats of the VII Olympiad.

14. VILVOORDE

Blue of the seven seas, Gold of God's great sun.
Let these our colors be til all of time be done.
By Severn shore we learn Navy's stern call.
Faith, courage, service true with honor over, honor over all.

—"Anchor's Aweigh," third verse

WHEN THE USS *FREDERICK* ARRIVED ON FOREIGN shores, Glendon reported in a letter to his wife:

We procured a pilot at this point and proceeded up the river Schneldt 20 miles to the ancient city of Antwerp arriving at the dock at 6 P.M. on 6 August after twelve days at sea.

At this point the officials in charge (these being the Olympic committee officials) seemed to take the line of least resistance. There was no receiving committee for the athletes, and no arrangements had been made for housing the racing shells; in fact, no one seemed to know even where the races were going to be held! The result was that the crew squad was [stranded] on the *Frederick* for five [more] days while the other athletes were in training. I decided to keep the squad in condition by taking long hikes about the city and viewing points of interest.[1]

One day we visited the "Steen" or ancient castle of Antwerp, which dates back to the tenth century. It was very interesting as the castle contained many relics of the middle ages. The dungeon was the most interesting part. On payment of a few centimes to the guide we were furnished with candles and allowed to explore the dungeon, which was famous as a torture chamber during the Spanish Inquisition. We saw a chamber with smoke still visible on the walls in which victims were smoked to death. In some places dark blood stains had soaked into the stone floors and were still visible. Rusty chains and hooks hung from the walls and ceilings. The ancient water-torture machine was in one compartment and consisted of a stone seat over which an arrangement was hung which allowed a drop of water to fall a drop at a time on the victim's head, which finally drove him crazy. In another part a deep well led to the river underneath into which the victims were thrown alive.

One day we visited the Antwerp Cathedral, which was started in the fourteenth century and finished in the sixteenth; a period of 200 years to complete. The cathedral contained many beautiful Flemish oak carvings, and paintings by the old masters. Peter Paul Ruben's masterpiece, *The Descent from the Cross* is there. It was taken down and hidden during the war and twenty minutes afterwards a German shell crashed through the window and exploded a few feet from where the picture had hung. The Belgians attach some spiritual significance to this incident. A gold line ran diagonally across one part of the floor, and a hole as large as a quarter was cut in the glass skylight above through which the sun's rays came. This arrangement was an ancient time-piece and the Belgians could tell the time of day by the position of the sun's rays on the gold line.

We finally procured the canal barge *Sophia* and transported the racing shells twenty miles through a series of canals and locks up to the Royal Nautique boathouse (the King's own) at Three Fountains. This was another interesting trip. Ruins of churches and homes could be seen in the distance on either side. We stopped at one of the locks and bought some wooden shoes from the little Belgian children for a few centimes. Before leaving America there was much talk here about the starving children of Belgium, but they appeared to be very well fed to me, and looked as healthy, if not healthier, than any group one would see in [our] country.

The Belgian shells housed here during the war were in disrepair. The Germans had occupied the boathouse for a year and put the wooden shells outside exposed to the weather.[2]

We put up at the Steamboat Tavern a short distance from the boathouse. The windows had been shot out during the war and had not been replaced and living there was much like camping out. There were many small children in the vicinity whom natives claimed were born during the war of German fathers. We visited a beautiful Chateau nearby the grounds which were nicely laid out and well stocked with game. One morning about sun-rise I was passing through the grounds and saw as many as twenty Belgian Hares in one small field.

During the two weeks of training the crew rowed an average of fifteen to twenty miles a day, and most of the coaching was done on a bicycle or in a broken down army truck, driven

by one of the most reckless daredevils it has ever been my pleasure to meet. I could tell some stories about this driver and his
truck but will not have time.[3]

Mary read the letter over and over, sharing it with neighbors on the
Cape and her children who were so proud of their father's fame.

NEWSPAPERS COVERED LEANDER'S PROGRESS TOWARD
what was seen as a perfunctory necessity to go to Antwerp in order
to bring home the gold, whereas when the Americans first arrived, it
was to relative anonymity due to the confusion among the local
Olympic organizing committee. Undaunted, Navy set up camp and
got down to the business of rowing.

When the press photographers arrived, wagering on the rowing
events began. European spectators, abandoning ancient rivalries,
bonded together as one community of Europeans rooting for the
British rowers against the Americans.[4] Brand Whitlock, the American Ambassador, came to watch and have his picture taken with the
crew.[5] Feelings ran so high that the amount of riverbank betting
against the United States by the largely European crowd was considered extraordinary by the press.[6]

In contrast to the granite columns of Annapolis and the pastoral
setting of Henley-on-Thames in England, the racing for the VII
Olympiad was to be held in an industrialized section of the Wille-
broeck Canal between Trois Fontaines and Marly, just a kilometer or
so from Vilvoorde and more toward the outskirts of Brussels than
Antwerp. It was described in the *Field* as having, "On the right bank
looking from start to finish was a rough paved road, bounded on the

right by a dreary, dusty wall and odoriferous ditch. On the left bank of the course was an almost continuous line of factories, some of which discharge streams of hot water from their condensers into the murky waters of the canal. The average depth of the water was from 15 ft. to 20 ft., and compared to the Thames was a little heavy to row on. From an artistic or picnic point of view [it] was unprepossessing. From the purely business point of view of boat racing, it was as good and as fair a test of the merits of competition as it is possible to imagine. There was never for one single instant the slightest advantage in either station."[7] So wretched was the site that Pierre de Coubertin labeled it sardonically as, "a place so hideous that no attempts have been made to try and disguise its ugliness."[8]

No matter: scenic beauty aside—what of the water? That was the real question. Beautiful scenery along the bank does nothing for a rower's soul compared to good water. Water without current, without tide. And the water in Vilvoorde was still and flat as a tiddly-wink; it was a thing of beauty to any rower.

Still water under the boat has a tone unlike any other when rowing. Still water sucks in the catches uniformly—as should be—like toast dropping into the slots of a toaster. The sounds of the slides rolling, the breaths of each rower, the grunt and slight wheeze as they execute the drive and the telltale kaa-thunk, kaa-thunk as the oars drop to their flat face at the release to finish the stroke, eight-as-one, in hushed elegance readying for the next. Still water soothes the side of the shell, accepts the forward run as it slips along. "Stroke her like a gentleman and she will be a lady, stroke her rough and hard and she will be a bitch," runs through the minds of the crews. And in this water they have a lady beneath them. Something classy and beautiful, working with them, reaching the harmony of the elusive heightened speed called "swing." And on this water—still water—the men, the "woman," the boat, the oars, the effort are poised to explode into ecstasy as these, the fastest human-powered watercraft, reach 18 knots seemingly effortlessly in a dance of effort, strain, relaxation, push, and shove till "easy off" is heard and the water's surface heals from the frenzy and the boat and the rowers retire from it as in a dream . . . until tomorrow's "hands on" is heard again.

WHILE THE TRAVEL-WORN AMERICANS WORKED out the kinks and staleness of nearly a month's travel to Belgium, the Leander crew was still in England where fans discussed details laid out in the daily news briefs: "The Leander eight for the Olympic Regatta completed their training at Henley on Wed. morning, and by the time this note appears should have reached their quarters at Brussels. The weather for the last week of training on the Thames was very pleasant, with brilliant sunshine and light winds. Mr. C. M. Pitman took over the coaching duties from Mr. H. W. M. Willis, and will be with the crew until the racing is over. The new center-seated boat built by Sims was used until Saturday last when it was put on the road for the docks for transshipment to Belgium. The new craft carried the crew admirably, and appeared to run very smoothly between the strokes. The Magdalen boat was used after the new boat had been sent away.

"Last week the crew rowed a fast half course, and also a good two-minute burst, in which the watch showed 40 strokes in the first minute and 38 in the second. On Friday 13 August, Horsfall developed a slight chill and was advised to take two or three days' rest. In his absence the spare man H. O. C. Boret, who rowed bow for Cambridge this year and stroked Third Trinity at Henley, was called upon to take the position. On Saturday with Boret at stroke, the crew rowed the Henley Regatta course. The conditions were fairly favorable, but there was more stream than is usual in July, three of the big sluice gates at Hambledon Weir being open. There was a slight wind drawing up the course at the start. Boret rowed 18 and 34 in the first 3:29. Opposite the Remenham Club the rate was 30, but the crew quickened along the Lion Meadow and reached the Regatta finishing point in 7:12. This was a promising performance at the relatively slow rate of striking, for with Horsfall at stroke the oarsmen have proved themselves quite capable of rowing at 35 without losing their length or uniformity. The crew rowed with fine precision and dash, and if they train on should make a very fast eight. At present the coach is devoting his attention to securing a sharper catch of the water at the beginning of the stroke."[9]

In passing conversation when asked about conditions, Nickall's response was stoic.

On our arrival at Vilvoorde Canal near Brussels, where the Olympic Regatta was to take place, we found the American Navy crew from Annapolis comfortably ensconced in a house alongside the course. They had been brought over by an American cruiser, together with a second crew to act as pacemakers. They had brought their own cooks, servants, masseurs, and a doctor, and naturally enough appeared perfectly at home in their new surroundings. In the intervening years we have come to take for granted this superb and lavish American organization. In those days it was new, and we regarded it with astonishment and envy.

Perhaps the excellence of their organization made the

arrangements of the British authorities appear even more sickeningly inadequate than they were. Not until our arrival at Antwerp were we informed that the Regatta was to take place near Brussels. The only accommodation to be found in Brussels was a rather dreary Station hotel where the food was, to say the least of it, unsuitable for athletes. To add to our troubles, the only means of getting to the course was by an eight-mile journey in a dusty tramcar. The first few days we tried returning to the hotel for lunch, but thirty-two miles a day in a tramcar was too much, so we arranged to have our midday meal at an inn adjacent to the course.

Our boat was late in arriving, and when we finally got news of it, we were told it was waiting on a railway siding two miles from the course. Off we went, unpacked it, and marched with it two miles through the Belgian countryside to the boat-house bordering the canal. The American crew were kind enough to send their lorry to fetch our oars and riggers.[10]

Victor Jacomini, the young, wide-eyed—like a deer in the headlights—exuberant bowman for Navy, wrote home:

We arrived here last Friday afternoon but as yet we have not put the shells in the water. The weather here the first day was exceptionally cold but since then it has been alright with the exception of the rain.

This surely is a quaint old town and is amusing at first but I am sure that the novelty shall soon wear off. We get 12 1/2 francs for an American dollar so in terms of our money most things are comparatively cheap. Our rowing course is a few miles outside of Brussels, so it was necessary for us to find a place to live and to keep our shells. This was not such an easy job in this country as everything seems to be a thousand years old. We finally managed to locate a Tavern near the course in which we could all be quartered. It was necessary however for us to provide everything from the cooking utensils on up, so this morning we had a canal boat come alongside, and we loaded everything aboard, including our shells. From all outward appearances it looked as if we were outfitting a landing party. . . . [11]

We came here to Vilvoorde, Belgium, this morning and this afternoon we took the shells out for their first dip in the canal. This tavern which we have taken over is surely an awful place. During the war a large munitions plant blew up near here so all the window glass was broken and has never been replaced. The inside of the Tavern is absolutely bare so we had to bring our cots and bedding. However we have a good cook and the food is really good so we make the best of it and figure that we are here to win the race and not to have a good time.

It seems now that the Swiss crew is considered the best but I really don't know as we are the first to arrive. We created quite a sensation this afternoon when we went out on the river. They all thought that our shells were awfully large but when they saw us they realized that we had to have a large shell as we are quite large ourselves. [12]

Jacomini finished scribbling just as Clark entered the boat tent and called for "hands on." Victor shoved the letter toward the side pocket of Chandler's overalls with a plea in his eye of, "Would you be sure this makes today's mail?"

"Yeah, sure, sure," was the reply and, "Hey now, don't you be breaking any more of them blades!"[13]

Finally, their last practice before the Olympic Games. A veritable "League of Nations" followed the U.S. crew; and every time the crew left the boat shed, "awestruck silence prevailed."[14] Glendon chuckled as he caught glimpses of the Norwegian coaches peeking from the bushes to look at his "awkward crew" fly by.

THE CREW LEAN INTO THEIR OARS. GLENDON barks orders. Blades skip over the water surface, careful not to touch and raise a telltale splash. Ten meters, twenty meters, "Don't sit back, Gallagher. Up! Up! Come on together. Lower your shoulder, Eddie. Keep your legs down!" Sixty, seventy meters, "That's it, work it, work it. Don't let up. Now! Row *through* the finish line. *Through* the finish line. Good! Good!" With the launch engine putt-putting a tight semi-circle around the rowers in the launch, Glendon makes mental notes on his stopwatch before readying the crew for another effort. Two more passes are made down the course to familiarize the cox with needed landmarks to distinguish the length away and the length to go until the finish; the clouds are breaking. On the third run Glendon sees breaking points on human faces. Strangely young again himself, Glendon feels his hands strain on the oars with them. His mind momentarily finds memories of the self-same limits of endurance, that never-neverland of haze and exhaustion, oxygen depletion, pounding chest, and of wondering, "Where is the air? *Where is the air?*" Eight mouths gasp as their faces strain on the stroke, flushed, yet pulling on. Clark corrects, snaps orders; oars cut in and out, the launch drones, and for a moment crew and coach are one.

The last buoy passed, the cockswain signals "way 'nuf!"(stop) and the crew strews itself backward or forward like so many Raggedy Andy dolls propped precariously against gunnels.

All sounds are quiet now. The hour passes. The borrowed surface is given back to the canal traffic and fishermen stalking its depths. Three hundred-yard-long incisions are already healing without a trace. The crew head back to the boat tent. Glendon speaks only occasionally to a lone rower or two-man shell as the great Jack Kelly and Paul Costello row by.

On the water and off Glendon's intensity gives away his thoughts that are constantly about this sport, this canal, this crew, his dreams never far from launching the contending World and Olympic champion. He ponders how will the members of this young team fare as *men* in the years to come? They're not from the banks of the Schuylkill or Charles River, up East, where the powerhouses of the sport berth their shells. They're from unlikely midwestern cities like Grinnell, Iowa, and remote Pittsylvania County, Virginia; yet here to toss their hats in with the prestigious—those traditionally from Oxford and Cambridge and Royal boat clubs from Norway and Belgium with bluer-than-sky-blue blood—these athletes of the Naval Academy don their sweats and row their "hearts out" hoping, always hoping that, with enough focus, energy, concentration, and effort, they can overcome almost anything.

Glendon smiles wryly as he drives the launch up to the wooden floating dock and cameras from newspapermen click open and shut. His job for today is done. Filing up the path to the boat tent through a maze of oarsmen from other nations, of shoes, shirts, towels, and

200-pound boats, Glendon is saddened to leave their pulsing, single-minded pursuit. Most are silent, and the trees on each side of the boat path mutes what little conversation there is. Their minds are already on tomorrow's efforts . . . the Olympic races, at last.[15]

15. OPENING CEREMONY

Soon you will be crowned with laurels, which will wither, because you have fought and conquered, but fight above all the human beast within yourself and conquer it, to be crowned with the laurels of immortality.

—Désiré-Joseph Cardinal Mercier's blessing to the 1920 Olympic athletes

———————

WHY ANTWERP? WHY BELGIUM? AFTER STOCKHOLM in 1912, Berlin was to be the site of the next Olympic Games, but due to the war, no Olympics were held in 1916. And in 1920, due to the war, those held responsible for the war were "not invited" to participate in the Olympics, namely Austria, Germany, Hungary, Bulgaria, and Turkey, by the IOC and predominantly by Pierre de Coubertin and Henri de Baillet-Latour, head of the Belgian organizing committee.[1] This noninvitation was a tricky maneuver within the chapter of the IOC, which did not really allow "exclusion"—it was considered a detriment to the overall separation in Olympism of politics and sport. However, because Belgium was so seriously devastated in the war and the damage emotionally and physically that had scarred the nation was so recent, a motion was framed by the IOC that only members of the IOC could participate in the games—and thus, the separation of politics and sport was preserved and the disallowance of these nations seen to be a fundamentally critical link to the survival of the fledgling Games.

For the first time since the beginning of the Modern Olympics' rejuvenation in Athens in 1896, doves of peace were released in memory of those who had lost their lives in the Great War. Antwerp also marked the start of other traditions, such as the white Olympic flag with its interlocking five rings of black, green, yellow, red, and blue, denoting all the nations. Also, the Olympic Oath was taken for the first time. It was Belgian fencer Victor Boin who stepped up to a small white platform while holding the Belgian flag and flanked by two military escorts, who pledged, "We swear that we are taking part in the Olympic Games as loyal competitors, observing the rules governing the Games, and anxious to show a spirit of chivalry for the honor of our countries and for the glory of the sport in the true spirit of sportsmanship."[2]

The war had taken a huge economic toll on Belgium and, indeed, on all of the Allied powers in both lives and potential competitors lost, as well as on the means and public spirit to support what might seem a frivolous display of the outpouring of money and attention to play, when devastation surrounded the Olympic walls themselves and spread to the families and the psyches of every nation of Europe. This was touched upon by the young Winston Churchill, who said, "Despite these scars and impacts perhaps human hope and a primordial need to express themselves in play and friendly competition . . ." England must urge the Olympic spirit on.

The Games of the VII Olympiad were bigger in Antwerp than they had ever been before, with 2,669 competitors. Surprisingly, in a shift toward modernity, there were almost 80 women from 29 nations taking part in 154 events. And while there were many firsts in Antwerp, including the debut of the winter sport of ice hockey, these games and the ever-changing Olympic program saw the last of certain athletics events such as: tug-of-war, the 3,000-meter walking race, and weight throwing. The 400-meter breaststroke was eliminated after Antwerp, as were several sailing races.[3]

At 10 A.M. on Saturday, 14 August, the Games of the VII Olympiad were consecrated with solemn worship in the Onze Lieve Vrouwekerk (Notre Dame Cathedral). In the morning there had been a Solemn Mass and Te Deum in the Cathedral, where Cardinal Mercier delivered an oration in memory of the athletes who fell in the Great War. All the nations were represented by military delegations.

Amid the great Gothic columns and soaring heights of the cathedral, candles flickered by the dozens. Wooden pews held families, children rich and poor, athletes, the military, coaches, the Navy crew. Coughs echoed in the waiting silence of the sacred Mass. Children asked questions of fathers and mothers who tried to answer, to turn down the inquisitive pointing finger, and to silence their "too loud for the occasion" questions. Morning sunlight streamed in through stained glass marking the air with its captured presence, held for a moment as if wishing to sanctify the place with the external blessing of the universe, as well. All stood proud and hopeful. Feet echoed on medieval granite; and as altar bells chimed, and bells pealed, somewhere in the ethereal heights a choir sang as pages turned in hymnals to catch up and join in while priests, bishops, and altar boys shuffled into place, and standing and soon-to-kneel worshipers bowed heads to receive a blessing sanctifying their engagement in competition.

As the ancient Greeks had done in Olympia from 800 BCE to 300 CE under the watchful eyes of their gods and their gods' emissaries on Earth (Demeter, the high priests, and Zeus), these gatherers, worshipers of the sacred and the sacred as they interpreted it, sought to please their God and to celebrate the value of performance and excellence. Here was truly the *arêté* moment, the mystical transformation of the body and blood mingling with spirit. Catholic or not, all attending understood, having pursued this ethereal goal and transformation in their training for months and years, that this moment, this day in time, to be seated here, was their destiny. They sang and worshiped and celebrated the ideals of sport reflecting humanity's need to excel.

DÉSIRÉ-JOSEPH CARDINAL MERCIER, THE PRELATE of Belgium, began the Mass by speaking to the many sports officials and participants of the Games, including the youngest competitor of the Games, fourteen-year-old American swimmer Aileen Riggin; the oldest competitor of the games, the seventy-two-year-old marksman Oscar Swahn from Sweden; Finnish epic runner Paavo Nuri; the Hawaiian King and Olympic swimmer Duke Kahanamoku; and Jack Kelly, whose daughter Grace would one day be the Princess Grace of Monaco.[4]

"You, Ladies and Gentlemen, before the opening of the Olympic Games, have wished to commemorate those who belonged to you and who did not return from the terrible war. . . . It should be reminded that, for you, the stadium events are not vain, idle games. They represent an education. Before 1914, they were used as a preparation for war and the war demonstrated the wisdom of their founder; today, they are a preparation for peace . . . and for the dreadful eventualities which have not yet disappeared over the horizon." The Cardinal finished his speech with, "Soon you will be crowned with laurels, which will wither, because you have fought and conquered, but fight above all the human beast within yourself and conquer it, to be crowned with the laurels of immortality."

Glendon and his Navy men stood quiet and proud. Then the "Te Deum" by Benoist was sung. Shortly after eleven, the Cardinal departed from the church and was cheered by a large crowd outside the church.[5] The crew was shuffled into a large open-backed car and whisked away from the onlookers and distractions to eat, rest, and gather for the first time with their competitors on the field of play in the opening ceremonies.

THE OPENING CEREMONY STARTED AT 2:30 P.M. under beautiful sunny skies. King Albert and the young royal family journeyed to the stadium by rail and after arriving at the newly constructed station, walked the last few hundred yards amidst a sea of well-wishers.[6]

Friends and relatives at home, seeking newspapers and telegrams, would read, "After having inspected a body of Belgian troops and the foreign military representatives, their Majesties had presented to them the members of the International Olympic Committee and the Belgian Executive Committee, to whom King Albert expressed his hope that the meeting would be a great success.

"Their majesties were next conducted to the Royal Box, where they were greeted by the sounding of a military call and great cheering. The singing of the National anthem by a Swedish Choir aroused a further outburst of enthusiasm, and after a resounding salvo of artillery, the great march past of the athletes began. Each group was preceded by official delegates and their national flag. The spectators, too, included almost every nation. The Swedes especially are extraordinarily numerous, for many have made the journey in order to help sustain the spirit of their compatriots who are taking part in the Games. The procession trooped by to the strains of the Royal march, and each group saluted as they passed the Royal Box, and themselves received a great welcome. They then ranged themselves in the center of the Stadium to be inspected by the International Committee, who afterwards crossed over to the presidential stand, where the Comte de Baillet Latour delivered an address ending with the words: 'I ask your Majesty to declare open the Olympic Games of Antwerp.'

"The formal opening by the King followed, and at the conclusion of His Majesty's words there was a further salute by cannons. Then came a surprise, for, at a given signal hundreds of pigeons were let loose to carry the news to all the countries concerned that the Seventh Olympiad, as it is called here, was indeed open. . . ."7

Papers worldwide extolled "the official inauguration of the Seventh Olympiad which took place this afternoon in beautiful weather and amid great scenes of pomp and splendor in the presence of the King and Queen of the Belgians and their young family.

"Australia had the pride of place owing to the accident of alphabetical precedence. The costumes were as varied as were the numbers that followed the different banners. Canada made a brave show in white shorts trimmed with crimson. Egypt wore somber black coats with red fezzes. France was tastefully attired in uniforms of blue and white, with red Gallic cocks embroidered on their breasts. British India showed muscular shoulders in their sleeveless jerseys. Perhaps the most engaging feature in the procession were two blue bands of fair-haired maidens in close-fitting, bright blue garments marching under the flags of Denmark and Sweden. The numbers ranged from an immense cavalcade of Belgians and a healthy crowd of Americans down to two representatives apiece from Chile and

New Zealand, and not many more from Portugal, Luxembourg, and Monaco. Among the new Olympic flags were seen those of Estonia and Checho-slovakia.

"Beautiful day as it was, there were a number of empty seats in the stadium. After a group of black-coated officials had marched up to the Royal Box and been presented, the nations filed past once again in the same order and the ceremony was over."[8]

The newspaper stories were quick off the racks back in places like Annapolis, California, New York, Illinois, Iowa, and the likes where family, friends, lovers, and neighbors waited and read excitedly the news—any news—of what was happening over there.

16. HEATS AND SEMIS

As a friend put it to me between watercress sandwiches and champagne, "you've started a tradition."
—Bill Engemen of Harry Graves, organizers of the 1988
Olympic Rowing Trials, Cincinnati

———————————

REGATTA WAS NOT A WORD THAT IS INDIGENOUS to most Belgians. They tended to associate it with gatherings held on manicured banks of yacht clubs in England or on the North Sea. Rivaling the curious onlookers and folks with picnic baskets, those in the know were decked to the hilt with "official" regatta accoutrements abounding. On shore starched, white, double-breasted suits were de rigueur for the ladies. For the men, modest university jackets, pocketed with three-tiered, gold-embossed emblems of past collegiate honors won; plated buttons with school insignias and simulated nautical rope piping on the seams were set off with a crew tie of crossed oars or club colors.

As has been done for hundreds of years surrounding the sport of rowing, a fairlike atmosphere prevailed along the banks with tents, food cooking, children playing, dogs running about, and pennants of rowing clubs and countries flying as if atop medieval castles.

Old-timers would gather in welcoming meetings at the various boat clubs and talk about the great races of past days and the great races soon to be rowed. Champagne and watercress sandwiches brought a touch of Old England class to the whole affair. Pimms and lemonade, hot coffee, Danishes, and brioche were in abundance. On this Friday, 27 August, even the overcast, somewhat somber mood of the dingy, industrial canal couldn't help but be cheered by the celebratory mood.

UP UNTIL THIS TIME THE AMERICAN CREW HAD been in almost constant training for seven months—seven long months of hard work in the biting winds of March on the Severn and under the hot sun of August and July; months of self-denial and sacrifice. The long siege of coaching, training, and anxiety under which all had labored to be prepared for this moment was nearly over.

On the water and in the crew area, dress was at a minimum. Sleek, close-fitting togs and tank tops gave unrestricted movement for the competitors racing hundredths of seconds apart trying to gain every advantage of "walking through" an opponent like a giant, eight-legged centipede. Racing equipment was scrupulously watched, assembled, checked, and rechecked. Oarlocks were set for "pitch" to adjust the plane of the oar's strike into the water. Oars were inspected for nicks or cracks that might allow infinitesimal traces of sluggish water into the hollow, balanced blades. Slides which secure the tiny seats that look like a nightmare for the sacroiliac were rolled carefully forward and back on their 12-inch track for any trace of rubbing or resistance.[1]

The boats, those poetic lines of strength and stealth, sat ready to be lifted, carried, shouldered, cradled, and pampered as much as any baby there. Coxswains, the short people with crew jackets on, were fiddling with rudder cables, and megaphone straps that carry their orders or threats and encouragement to their shellmates. Rowers, the tall nervous people with the enviable physiques, were stretching out, pacing, going to the toilet, sipping some water, stretching out in more extreme contortions, and generally trying to look tough and cool in an attempt to psyche out their opponent. Coaches, identified with the clipboards in their hands and stopwatches around their necks. After analyzing all the conditions they think they can predict, tactics will be slyly communicated to an entourage of assistants, coxswains, and stroke oars who are the last oarsman in the stern of the shell who set the pace for the crew. The pomp and regalia, crews limbering up, shells getting a last inspection, and on the side away from others, three or four huddled forms, boatmen like Chandler discussing conditions of the water and the boat. They cared for every nuance of the shells to keep them in tip-top condition and at the ready. Surely by virtue of the time spent lovingly caring for their charges, the boatmen were instilled with much the same pride, fear, anticipation as felt by the crew themselves. Lose and they would feel the same disappointment. Win and they would feel the same pride, though not the same accolades (as the crew).[2]

Wooden boats needed to be sanded and varnished every season. All the metal riggers and oarlocks needed to be lubricated and kept in order to withstand the tremendous forces exerted against and through them when the crew was rowing full tilt. Every seat, every slide, every foot stretcher and bolt, top screw, and oar was inspected, repaired, or replaced as needed, and then cleaned and rubbed until it shined in the light. "A clean boat is a fast boat!" was heard in the boat tent at every race. And the rowers: Each of them could be seen before the race lovingly going over their seat station one last time, with Chandler waiting if needed with his box and assortment of wrenches, bolts, and tricks to keep the boat toned to the ready. Anticipation was as thick in the air as a heavy fog.

Outside of the boathouse and away from the crew area, the athletes and crowd mingle. They hear all of the different languages and see the styles of different countries' sport drawing the world together here where war had driven them apart. Yet the differences separating them are not as many as the similarities bonding them together forever. These athletes are bonded in an amalgamation of emotion, achievement, and glory. Children, lovers, laughter, smiles, hugs, cheers, families, the customs of humanness bind them. Natural animosities? Natural camaraderie? When the officials call the crews to order for the first time as the official rowing members of the VII Olympiad to hear the regatta rules and regulations at the coaches and coxswains meeting—don't they wonder? Don't they just wonder how the world and they have changed?

All the Olympic crews were gathered at a meeting to hear the starting commands of Mr. V. De Visschop. The honor of being Olympic starter was given to De Visschop, who was a member of the King's Royal Nautique Boat Club. The commands and regulations for a false start were explained to all competitors. The French international start of "Etes vous prets? Partez!" would be used, which means, "Are you ready? Go!" A red flag would be held upright throughout the commands and dropped on the "P" of *Partez*. The crews would be permitted to engage on the "P" of *Partez*. They would race 2,000 meters down the calm waters of a canal turned Olympic racecourse.[3]

In the crew area, where the boat sheds and tents became the temporary home of the crews, French, Swiss, Americans, athletes all, posed for photographs twenty-four abreast, linked arm in arm. They vowed to meet again after the games "some day," exchanged addresses, and vowed "to write to one another"—language was a barrier to some of the Americans, but not to others willing to try out their freshly learned French and German from the Academic Building along the Severn at Annapolis, so far distant, yet still with them. They were becoming the journey and the dream—aware and alive with more than just making a wooden boat win—that the reward was already theirs, and they loved every minute of it.

Friday afternoon's heats consisted of the singles, doubles, and eights. Saturday's semifinals would see the fours, singles, and eights. On Sunday all of the aforementioned events, with the inclusion of the pairs, would be rowed as the last events of the Olympic Games.

A touch of glamour was added to the dingy working canal of Antwerp when the good-looking Jack Kelly rowed and won in the singles and turned around entering the doubles with his cousin Paul Costello and won again. Kelly, a prominent Philadelphia businessman, had come out of the depths of bricklaying and Philadelphia's Schuylkill and had been the central point in a furious transatlantic British cyclonic flurry over his qualifications as an amateur. He beat England's single sculler, J. Beresford, in a time of 7:35, England, Italy, Belgium, Holland, Sweden, New Zealand, USA, Switzerland, and

Checho-slovakia having been represented. In the final, Beresford secured a slight lead in the first minute, and from that point to within 100 yards of the finish the relative positions of the scullers remained unaltered. It was not, as sometimes happens in sculling, a case of one man waiting on the other. Both men were sculling "all out" from start to finish, but in the last few strokes Kelly proved the better stayer, and won by one second. In the double sculls Kelly and Costello won over Italy and France in 7:09 — 10 seconds clear of Italy.[4]

In the eights, the first race of the Friday heats, Norway defeated Checho-slovakia in a time of 6:35. Then Britain's Leander crew defeated Switzerland in 6:19, the United States defeated Belgium in 6:26, and in the final heat France defeated Holland in 6:33. Leander's race with the Swiss proved to be a tight, fast heat for the British. The American draw against Belgium did not push the American crew, and so their speed and potential threat remained unseen by the confident Leander eight.[5]

The Navy eight was finally ready to be placed on the starting line, 3,000 miles from home in a foreign country, and no one could detect by their calm exteriors the nervous strain under which each man in the boat labored.

Papers around the world, including the *Mirror* in Flemish, that were circulating around the venue publicized every moment of the beginning of the racing: Olympic Regatta at Vilvoorde, 27, 28, 29 August 1920. 2000 Meters. First heat—Norway, 1; Checho-slovakia, 0. The Norwegians, who had been coached by Wingate, of Battersea, rowed in a style modeled on America's. The Checho-slovaks hurried forward and only half-covered their blades. Norway led at once and won easily. Time 6:32: 1/5th. Second heat—England (Leander

Club), 1; Switzerland, 0. Leander were unprepared for the promptitude of the starter and got off very badly, rowing 38 in the first minute. In spite of this they led by one third of a length at the 500 meters, and were just clear at the halfway mark. At the 1,500 meters the Swiss made a gallant effort, and closed up to half a length, but Horsfall did not raise the stroke above 36, and Leander won, without being unduly pressed, by three-quarters of a length. Time 6:20. The Swiss, who had won the "Championship of Europe" in France, rowed with a tremendous leg thrust at the finish, and with much dash and determination. Third heat—USA (Navy crew), 1; Belgium 0. The Americans made short work of the Belgians. Belgian rowing suffered more than that of any other country from the war. The Germans pillaged their boathouses and wantonly destroyed nearly all their boats. The crew that represented the Belgians were lacking in experience and were badly boated. They suffered defeat in a time of, 6:26. Fourth heat—France, 1; Holland, 0. Holland, a well-coached and rather attractive crew, made a muddle of the start, and never seemed to recover themselves.[4] It was a moment Glendon took advantage of and reiterated to his watching crew, "You can't win a race at the start but you sure can lose one." Clark and King exchanged understanding in raised eyebrow glances of "Got it."

The French rowed in a smooth, easy style, and won a desperate race over Holland by 1 second. Time 6:32. Fifth heat—England (Leander club), 1; Norway, 0. Leander rowed 42 in the first minute and soon drew clear of the Norwegians, who rowed 33. After two minutes Leander drew right away, and slowing down to a long swinging 32, won as they liked. Time, 6:26. Sixth heat—USA (Navy), 1; France, 0. The Americans led at once, and slowed up at the 1,000-meters post, winning easily. Time 6:24.[5]

When the water lay flat on the canal at the end of the day and the boats were back on the rack, it was down to two. Leander and Navy were now the only ones remaining for the Sunday's final Olympic race for the gold medal. For the Americans, all that was left to do was—beat Leander tomorrow.

17. THE OLYMPIC RACE

I met a solid rowing friend and asked about the Race.
"How fared it with the wind," I said, "When stroke increased
   the pace?
You swung it forward mightily, you heaved it greatly back.
"Your muscles rose in knotted lumps, I almost heard the crack.
"And while we roared and rattled too, your eyes were fixed like glue.
"What thought went flying through your mind, how fared it, Five,
   with you?"
But Five made answer solemnly, "I heard them fire a gun,
"No other mortal thing I heard until the Race was done."

—R. C. Lehmann

———◦———

RACE DAY. A TIME FOR ATHLETES TO STAY OFF their legs, to mentally prepare and get their minds occupied and focused; a time to relax as much as possible before the race; a time to write some last notes in a journal or a letter home. Some boys went off and walked around the beautiful Three Fountains estate and did their best to pray or think of memories that gave them strength and comfort. Some stayed at the Tavern and slept or talked quietly. All of them gathered at the shell an hour before launch time and spent what time was needed communing with their seat and rowing station and getting their heads together. Reverently, diligently, each was making absolutely certain the foot stretchers were in the proper notch for leg length, that the top nut on the oarlock was tight, and that his seat rolled smoothly. Their hands felt for imperfections in the sliding of the seat and they were quick to pick up a towel and clean away any telltale dust or bit of dirt that was going to make the wheels bind or run slow. Chandler was at hand, if needed, checking the pitch on the oars and locks. And when the boys had finally finished their inspection of the shell and stepped away to take off their sweaters and stretch their muscles, only then did Glendon stride its length up and down each side, carefully eyeing the bottom of the hull, the tiller, making certain each oarlock swiveled just freely enough. He ran his hands over the decking to be certain it was watertight and the craft was sound. He nodded to Chandler, who had learned over the years to stand away at these moments and watch, but not to interject comment or suggestion. Glendon's nod said it all. Everything was in order. It was time.

AT LONG LAST, ON THE AFTERNOON OF 29 AUGUST, Glendon gathered his boys before him. "You all know what you have to do today. And I believe you shall do it. Let your hands rest lightly on your oars today, feel the water, feel the boat, enter into the experience, for we as a team will not pass this mark together again. I have every confidence that your training will carry you through. Now go out there and do what you love to do—do what you have trained to do—*row!*" And the crew, uncharacteristically, caught up in the moving speech from a man who rarely gave speeches to them, yelled back "Row!" and stood up confidently, nodding their heads and shaking hands as they headed for their oars.

This day in Olympic history was attended by the greatest crowd for any Olympic event up to that time.[1] At 4 P.M., with a flurry of oars and synchronized movement orchestrated as well as any ballet, two sets of rowers, coaches, coxswains, oars, boats, hopes, and dreams headed toward the water's edge.

"Lay hold!" Navy and Leander lifted the boats from their resting places on the shelves.

"Ready off the rack!" They moved the boats out of the racks.

"Shoulders, ready up!" The boats were lifted to the shoulder height of the rowers who were placed in staggered style right left, right left, down the gunnels.

"Walk it forward, ready, *walk* it!" Boats were walked toward the dock.

"Way 'nuf!" Boats were stopped.

"Toe the edge!" Oarsmen felt the edge of the dock, the last bit of solid ground before entering their watery world.

"Down and in, ready, down," and the boats were rolled and placed softly in the water.

"Bow and seven, hold the boat, the rest get the oars." And the crew went for their blades as Jacomini and Gallagher opened the oarlock gates.

Clark and Johnstone inspected their respective tillers on each of their shells and plucked the strung lines passing on each side of their cox seats for tautness and good steering as the rowers laid their blades into the oarlocks, pushed the spoons of the blades out, shut the gates to lock them in, and waited for the coxswains' commands.

They were loading portside-to, so Clark called, "Ports, hold the boat; starboards, run your blades out, one foot in and down." As Jacomini, Jordan, Sanborn, and Gallagher slid onto their seats, Glendon, Clark, the four ports, and Chandler all held the boat steady. "Portside, one foot in and down!" Clark commanded and finally, "Coxswain getting in" as he slid into his seat with a tiller line in each hand. The men adjusted foot clogs and rowing trousers and looked at the coach.

Glendon walked down the dock and murmured a few private words to each rower, clapping them on the shoulder, shaking a hand or two, rustling the hair on the heads of the seniors, saying, "Row the race we practiced. See you at the finish line."

And as he pushed out on Country's oar and Jacomini's bow edged out into the canal free to catch water, Clark called, "Bow and two arms only, take a stroke, more pressure portside," and with that, they were off.

"Three and four add-in in two. One, two! Arms only," and the bow four of the boat was sitting up legs out straight toward the coxswain, back erect, pulling, using only their arms paddling toward the start. "Add in legs and backs and go to half slide." The crew slid toward the stern, up to half slide to add in their legs and backs, and added some pressure to the stroke. They pulled farther away from the dock, leaving a wake for Leander to follow. Clark led them through the warm-up of arms, arms and back, half slide, three-quarters, full slide until bow and stern sections of the boat had done the drill. "All eight at half pressure in two, one two!" and the American hull jumped to life beneath them.

Paddling to the line for their Olympic debut, each man's thoughts swirled amid the small whirlpools left from the dipping oars and cutting track of their shell beneath them. English and American, at this moment they were men, human beings, bodies and souls churning up the depths of the canal bed, raising memories from the murky depths, calling on the water gods to aid them, to give them strength. Victor Jacomini thought of his dead brother Clem, Lt. Clement Jacomini, a flying instructor for the U.S. Army Air Corps. Theirs was a friendship as well as blood relationship, having written countless letters to each other when Clem was away during the war about fishing and "catching the limit" at Big Bear Lake, remembering cameras, and how they had submerged their roommates in the bathtub over the last weekend in their boyish shenanigans. Clem had died 2 August, only a year and a half earlier—never to see his brother row and become an Olympian. Vic was determined to make this boat today fly as his older brother's plane had, remembering his words, "I felt like a caged bird turned loose, made a perfect getaway and never did want to come back to earth . . . like a bat out of hell . . . [I'd] take it down—let the machine fall to the runway and straighten it out to glide in to the deck."[2] Victor, proud of his brother's life and death for his country in the war, was rowing to resurrect Clem today . . . like a phoenix.

He could hear occasional yells from the vast crowd lining the canal. His friend Charlie Paddock, the U.S. Olympic runner, was watching Vic, his former high school track squad captain, row. They had won a State Championship together, with Vic competing in shot, discus, high jump, and high hurdles, and now Charlie was cheering him on. . . .

Zeke Sanborn pulled his oar for his younger brother who had died at twelve of scarlet fever.

Country Moore tucked a letter from Daisy into his waistband and wondered if she had received his last letter.

"Ready all, half pressure now in two. One, two!" And the crews picked up the pace on the paddle toward the start.

"Three quarter pressure, three quarters now," the coxswain said, as they continued to row the 2,000 meters toward the hamlet of Marly and the starting line.

THE BRITS LAUNCHED AFTER THE AMERICANS rowed by. It was a tactic in rowing to show up to the line last, thereby making the crew that arrived first wait on you—in hope of causing them to get nervous. As they left the float and began to paddle in their warm-up, Swann thought of his father. Today, he wanted to be a gold medalist Olympian as his father had been, and he wanted to pull for his brother Alfred, who had not made the team—he uttered a prayer to God. . . .

"Clean up the blade work now, lads, let's look sharp," Johnstone, the English cox, asked of his crew when they were 500 meters toward the start. . . .

There was a light following wind drawing up the course as the crews paddled up from Vilvoorde to the start. The contrast between the two styles was remarkable. The Americans with their exaggerated swing-back, looked as if they had to take more out of themselves in paddling to produce the same pace as was produced by Leander. The latter, with their long steady swing, sharp beginning, and well-held-out finish, were perfectly together and looked the picture of what an English crew should be.[3]

Shove, captain of Leander and a past Cambridge Blue, made the Leander toast in the boat for the entire crew to mouth after him.[4]

Earl set his determined eyes on the Americans.

Horsfall rowed for the glory of Oxford, Madgalen College.

Nickalls remembered the wink in his father's eye and how proud of his father he had been, and knew his father would be waiting in Oxfordshire to receive a cable stating merely: "Gold." No other color would do. No other color was expected. Reminiscent of the famous America's Cup quote from Queen Victoria, "And who finished second?" With the race official's dry reply, "Your Majesty, there is no second."[5]

"Easy on!" and they glided to the line. Poised now, they waited, coiled like springs to unleash their youth and power to the world.

The American crew was not intimidated by the grandeur of the Olympics. More than anything, they were excited and sitting in anticipation. They didn't want their rowing to end. For some of them the end of this race was the end of their careers in the Navy, the end of their days at the Academy. They did their best to pinch themselves and remind themselves that they were so fortunate to be wearing the American "Olympic Crest" on their torso. They were very, very proud.[6] At 5 P.M. on Sunday afternoon, Navy's bow inched to the line first. The British came down on the line, the pride and flower of England.[7]

There was a hush over the crowd. The water lay perfectly flat. Before each of the boats the canal stretched straight ahead, its sides converging toward the finish line 2,000 meters away. Each cox whispered his final alignment commands to their bowmen. "Touch it, bow, touch it. Good! Hold. Hold. Sit ready, guys, sit ready." The coxswains lowered their hands to let the starters know that they and their 64-foot-long shells were straight and ready. Swann blessed himself. Jacomini clasped and unclasped his hands. Sixteen rowers buried the spoons of their blades into the black water, hands resting lightly; their boats ready to leap.

"When both crews were lined up, the starter said in French: 'Are you ready, America?' 'Are you ready England?' Every heart stopped beating. 'Are you ready all?' (*Etes vous prets?*) — 'Row!' (*Partez!*) The starting cannon boomed, the flag dropped, the oars dug in, and the men in both boats started to row the race of their lives."[8]

Blaring over the loudspeaker with just the starter's commands and then contrasted to the rush of slides, water, and flashing blades, was the excited commentary from the announcer, "There is huge noise here when these eights go off, very different from singles or doubles, with all the blades and coxswains shouting."

Clark and Johnstone braced themselves. Their fingers pinched the steering cables to the gunnels to keep the shells moving out perfectly straight from the start against the rowers' thrusts. With each catch the coxswains felt the pressure of the hard wooden shells in the small of their backs. Their heads jerked as the behemoth beneath them began to accelerate. Each coxswain shouted into the guts of the boat, his voice carrying up the length of the hull to the bow. *"Half, half, three-quarters, full, FULL! And TEN!"* *"Gimme One! Two! Three! Four away, six to go! Five! Six! Seven! Eight! Nine! TEN and SETTLE!"* Ten hard exhilarating power strokes are hammered out as the shells lurched forward, wood trembling with unleashed energy.

"Britain is off with a six-seat cushion." Announcer.

"Both crews settling into an exciting rhythm." Announcer.

"We got a capital start, rowing 41 in the first minute to the Americans' 38, and lead from the first stroke. Both crews rowing at top pressure,"[9] shouted Pitman to his British entourage.

"United States two seconds shy of Britain." Announcer.

"And Horsfall stroking Leander, relying on his experience from the Boat Race, leads by a canvas." Announcer.

Rowers punched out the rhythm that each cox called and racing strategies began to unfold.

"Foot by foot, we are going ahead!" yelled Pitman.

LEANDER CREPT UP UNTIL TWO-THIRDS OF A length ahead at 500 meters and were still two-thirds of a length ahead at 1,000 meters. Each of the sixteen men appeared to be rowing every single stroke as if it was the supreme effort of his life.[10]

Down at the finish line the great mob roared, and every neck was craned to watch the crews. "Here they come!" shouted Glendon.

Leander was out by six seats right off the start. Eddie Graves glanced over his left shoulder, surprised to see Lucas and James stealing looks at him, too. *Were they surprised we are so close? Am I surprised we are so close?* Neither crew had much time to think as backs strained and hands deftly swung the blades in and out at the catches and finishes of the strokes. The boats rose slightly as the tempo of the striking caused a slight hydroplaning effect. Water rushed down the gunnels. . . .

"FULL ON, LADS, FULL ON!" SHOUTED JOHNSTONE to the Leander crew.

Each rower strained feet against the foot stretcher and hands against the oar handles, exerting as much power and force as humanly possible. It felt like they were doing max squats and cleans in a door jam—and the boats were flying.

"At the halfway mark England is ahead by half a length. Rowing like demons; but we've kept our heads; one slip though, and it'll all be lost." Glendon practically spit the words out to Chandler.

Leander jumped from a 40 to a 42 strokes-per-minute pace to try and draw away for a safer lead. Navy answered by jumping from a 37 to a 39 strokes-per-minute and at this terrific pace the two crews tore down the course.[11]

From the bank, "Well rowed, Leander!" was heard loud and clear in the American shell. Clyde King dug in harder.[12]

But Navy was hard to shake. What was unperceived by the crowd was becoming a nightmare for Leander. The Americans were inching up. They weren't making a bold showy move—they were doing something worse—*outpowering them stroke by stroke.*

That kind of power this late in the race?

Shove could barely believe his eyes. They had closed the gap!

The Americans were walking through them! "Come on!" he yelled to his shellmates. Horsfall saw it, too, and shot a telling glance at Johnstone: *It was time to sprint!*

"RUNNING TRUE TO FORM. THE GAP BETWEEN United States and England closing, though Leander still marginally out in front." Announcer.

"The Americans are beginning to close up, and inch by inch they've reduced our lead." Pitman worried.

"A fantastic row!" Announcer.

The Americans kept coming. They had patiently waited, wisely never letting the Brits get too far ahead and now *they* were going to be the ones cutting down.

"Great Britain have just their bow ball ahead now." Announcer.

The bows of the two great eights seesawed back and forth, bow ball to bow ball. At each catch the boats would pause for a split second, their bows lowering and cutting into the water before the drive of the crew thrust them back up and out to the lead again. Chests heaved. Legs burned.

"At 1,700 meters away and 300 to go, America behind by a coat of varnish!" shouted the announcer.

"Here they come! Look at those two big crews!" Chandler.

"Three hundred yards from the finish!" Glendon.

"England is just barely at the head of the field. Reigning Henley Royal Regatta Champions." Announcer.

It began to look like England's race, but Clark yelled, "Forty in two. *One, TWO!*" and the stroke went up.

"Clark's put the rate right up to 40, which is just what was needed." Announcer.

"King will make his move now, Clark's got them. We're beginning to gain!" Up they came foot by foot. "They're even!" said Glendon.

"Absolute level pegging now for the lead!" the announcer gasped. "Both crews have keen anticipation of the finish line."

Horsfall and Swann dug in for more, but *where was the line?* Clark could see it. It was theirs, he knew it was theirs.

In the last yards of the race, King and the others were "shooting ahead of their opponents at a rate of about four feet every stroke."[13]

"Ten more strokes!" Glendon yelled. And with that, the Navy shell slid across the line half a length ahead of the fastest crew England ever turned out.

"AND THE WINNER OF THE GOLD MEDAL AND Olympic Champion is the United States of America!"

The words hung in the air. Resonating, captured in time. A great roar exploded from the crowd as many leapt to their feet, screaming and tossing programs and hats into the air.

WAS IT OVER? IT CAN'T BE, THOUGHT NICKALLS. Yet as they glided across the finish, Horsfall stopped rowing and held his blade in the air just above the water's surface to acquiesce, even before Johnstone shouted, "Easy on." And with that the Leander rowers slumped on their oars before the full 64 feet of their shell crossed the line. Some lay flat, exhausted, heaving, their chests gasping for air as their legs burned with lactic acid.

The Americans let the oar handles fall, splashed their hands on the water, and released hot feet from the laced stretchers and stuck them over the sides in glee. They had done it! They could hardly

believe it was finally over—done. They shouted and slapped one another, thanked God, and mainly beamed smiles that could be felt in
California.

A mob of people began to crush in on Glendon, who began to
make his way to the float-dock amid slaps on the back and cheers of
"Way to go!" "Good show!" "Congratulations, you did it!"

IN THE AMERICAN BOAT TEARS AND SMILES WERE
all around as they turned and splashed water on one another up and
down the boat. Clark stood up in the boat and tossed his hat to the
canal banks in glee. For a moment both great eights just glided
slowly.

Horsfall, James, and Campbell slumped on their oars. Swann was
studying the Americans in shock and admiration. Nickalls stared
into the depths of the canal; he couldn't believe it. Was it over? He
didn't want it to be over—not because he missed a medal but because it had been so good! *That* was a boat race!

Time blared over the loudspeaker, "six minutes, two and three-
fifths seconds, an Olympic and World record!" Another shout went
up from the crowd. And both the Americans and Leander knew at
that moment that they had shaved off *seven seconds* from the World
record of 6:10 set by Leander in Stockholm in the 1912 Olympics.[14]
They were that great.

In the eights, composure and reality began to take hold. Characteristic of the champions they were, within and without, Navy paddled over to congratulate Leander. Moore, in four seat, from "freshly
plowed fields with his boyish grin and enthusiasm that had him
swinging an oar in much the same manner as one of his father's hoes,
congratulated his British counterpart in four seat on a 'mighty fine

race.' His genial soul was genuinely hurt by the failure of Campbell to appreciate his well-intended remark while they were regaining their respective breaths just the other side of the finish line."[15]

Leander was stunned. In disbelief, they kept replaying the last minute in their minds: In the last 300 yards Navy had gradually, steadily pulled even, and with just yards from the finish Navy had still been behind, but in what seemed like a blur of a few strokes, Navy's sheer physical strength carried them to the front. The British had been beaten and America had won by about 10 feet in the truly wonderful time of 6.2 and 3/5 seconds, to England's 6.5.

This winning time, accomplished in the dead water of a canal, was significantly faster than the World record of 2,000 meters, which was made on much livelier water at Stockholm. It is not easy to make the correct allowance for the stream and the extra distance at Henley Royal Regatta, but there cannot be the slightest doubt that boats traveling at such a speed would cover the Henley course some seven seconds or more inside the existing record for that course of 6:51. The weights of the Americans on race day were not published but they were an evenly weighted crew, averaging four pounds per man heavier than Leander.[16] Shove eyed the young Americans and felt proud. Earl did, too. That admiration was spreading through Swann and the others—the Leander boat was overcoming any sense of failure. There was no failure on the course this day. Both crews were the best there ever were.

AT VILVOORDE WHEN THE CROWDS LEFT AND THE water's surface lay flat again, only the flags waved in the gentle breeze, identifying who and what happened there. But around Belgium and around the world, a buzz was spreading. . . .

Camera shutters snapped when, following the tradition in rowing, the winning coxswain, Clark, was vigorously tossed off the dock by all hands. Applause deafened the crowd when Glendon stepped up to receive the stack of gold medals for his men—boys no more. A jubilant Moore and Graves were photographed running with oars overhead in a scene that could only be dubbed "joy in the streets" past baffled, demure, reserved Europeans watching with wide-eyed amusement at the unabashed exuberance of the American youth. American newspaper reporters circulated the record time so quickly and so widely that even the members of the Navy crew were astonished and doubtful that they had accomplished such a feat.[17]

What a moment it must have been as they laid hands on the hull and at the coxswain S. R. Clark's bark, lifted it, "Overhead, ready up!" And the Olympic shell rose even higher than its watery glory into the air, droplets streaming off, and then dropping down to the shoulders of the Olympians to be walked off into the world away from Olympic records and cheering crowds. Their battle won, their point proven, the Naval Academy crew strode off the dock with Dick Glendon beaming with pride and clapping backs, shoulders, and the backs of heads in unabashed glee as his boys walked by. They had done it—beaten the unbeatable British—and they had done it together: a power ten, ten power strokes called by a coxswain to win a race.

NO ONE CLEARLY REMEMBERS THE ORDER OF events after that. The Englishmen proved to be good sports by coming around in the evening to congratulate the Americans. One of the Navy crew fell off a barstool and broke a rib as he and Navy rightfully celebrated. The midshipmen dispersed, most went to Paris, some to Switzerland, some to Germany, and some to England for two weeks of sightseeing.[18] On the way home Glendon visited Charbourg, France, then spent a day in London, visited Westminister Abbey, and other points of interest, and left England on the Cunard Liner *Aquitania* from Southampton; and five and a half days later he and some of the crew arrived in New York to a ticker-tape parade before he headed to the Cape—home sweet home.[19]

And what of the fundamental question? "How did the crew look?" They looked grand.

18. A RADICAL TURN OF EVENTS

"Superiority on the water is something on which an Englishmen prides himself in. . . . He might go a little shy in paddling a canoe off the Marquesas, or outrigging with the Hawaiians, but he will not take a back seat, if he can avoid it, in anything which has to do with pulling a shell."

—The Glendon Collection

THE 1920 OLYMPIC ROWING COVERAGE IN *THE Times* reflected the British surprise and inability to cope with the American breakthrough. In the article entitled "Defeat of Britain in the Eights," the readers could see Glendon's race strategy of under stroking the British unfold. "Great Britain started at 41 strokes a minute to 39," reported *The Times* observer. By letting the British crew play themselves out, near the end of the race (always the critical time to sprint if a crew can), the Americans rowed through the British from being down "half a length" (roughly 30 feet), to winning by "a few feet," all in the "last 30 yards."[1]

To put this in perspective, being rowed through is the most embarrassing insult one crew can bestow on another—in crew races it is still seen as a failure of the leading crew's manliness. In front of all the cheering fans, racing for the Olympic gold medal, the British could not hold off the Navy crew. The Navy cadets wisely held position until they broke the spirit and physical limits of the British crew. At the critical moment, the U.S. crew decisively accelerated the pace to gain 32 feet in only 30 yards. A winning distance of "a few feet" in rowing is considered a sound thrashing; and a crew that has been coached to keep a cool head, pace itself, and know when and how to unleash its ability to deliver such a blistering fast pace while at the edge of exhaustion, is indeed exhibiting effort of Olympic proportion.

The American press coverage of the event underscored the prowess of the American team. News of the Admirals' defeat of the British made newspapers coast to coast. *The Washington Post* reported that the Americans sat upright at the finish while the British were bent over while crossing the line—a telltale indication that the U.S. Navy crew was superior.[2] Glendon himself reported that the British were so impressed that they "came by the American quarters that night" in respect for their conquerors.[3]

Newspapers coast to coast covered the win in the United States. *The Washington Post*, the newspaper nearest to the Academy, proudly boasted "Navy Eight Oared Crew Win at Brussels."[4] The *New York Tribune* reported the King of Belgium himself would hang gold medals on the Olympians' necks.[5] From the *Atlanta Constitution* and the *Los Angeles Times*, the Navy Admirals had secured a glorious Olympic niche.[6]

PERHAPS THE STRONGEST EVIDENCE OF THE thrill and significance of the Navy crew lies in the fact that this rowing event—this day in Olympic history—was attended by the greatest crowd for any Olympic event to that time.[7] U.S. Navy documents reported, "The president of the American Olympic Committee pronounced it was probably the best performance by Americans in any department of the Olympic Games"; the report also stated that, "it was particularly gratifying that this distinction was won in a characteristic Navy sport."[8] Secretary of the Navy Daniels cabled his congratulations to the crew saying, "This crew's record will serve forever as an inspiration to the young men of the Navy to strive for excellence in rowing, in which the Navy should always lead the world."[9]

At last the Anglo-American rowing "debate" was resolved. The reality of the United States beating the British—not just defeating them, as had been done previously by mimicking their form—but by punishing them by setting a world record in 1920 was an unprecedented feat performed by the United States.

English tabloids and dinner conversation went round and round on what went wrong. "At the Olympic Regatta at the last weekend, England failed to maintain the supremacy established at the regattas held at Henley in 1908 and Stockholm in 1912. At the former we won the eights, fours, pairs, and sculls. At Stockholm we won the eights and sculls, but lost the four-with coxswain. Leander disposed of Switzerland and Norway before meeting the United States Navy in the final. A better race could not have been wished for. Leander rowed a great race, and Mr. C. M. Pitman puts them down as one of the finest English crews that ever sat a boat. The Americans deserve every credit for their victory.

"Both eights and sculls showed very fast times in the final. Mr. Pitman estimates that Leander's time was faster than anything ever done at Henley.

"Fortunately, the rowing events were carried through without any of the unpleasantness that marked some of the other sports at Antwerp, and the best of feeling prevailed between the competitors.

It is doubtful however, if England will again take part in any regatta organized in connection with the Olympic Games."[10]

One British correspondent says, "Nothing can detract from the honour due to the American crew themselves for the truly magnificent race which they rowed, and nothing, not even the 4/5 sec. by which they lost, can prevent the Leander Olympic crew of 1920 from going down to history as one of the finest and fastest that ever rowed."[11]

WEST POINT SENT A WARM CONGRATULATIONS TO Navy, "West Point sends its heartiest congratulations on your magnificent victory in the Olympiads which clearly entitles you to a world championship on the water."[12] And Navy gratefully acknowledged, ". . . Midshipmen keenly appreciate the Cadets' loyalty to the sister service and prize their approval more than that from any other source."[13] Coach Glendon received personal honors at the Annapolitan Club as guest of honor at a dinner for the Navy Oarsmen.[14]

It was the first time that America had sent athletes from the Navy as part of its Olympic All-American team.[15] J. G. Ware, Lieutenant Commander, writing the American Olympic Committee Report on what all the Navy athletes in all events did at Antwerp, emphasized that Navy's rowing win was the "best performance by Americans in any department of the Olympic Games" and that it was "particularly gratifying to the service that this distinction was won in a characteristic Navy sport."[16] Ware proudly stated, "Participation in the Olympic Games and the winning of the world's rowing championship by the Naval Academy crew has had an inspiring influence on the service in general, as well as attracting recruits." He heralded the crew as leaders who would return to their shipmates and stations and "inspire those around them with a greater zeal for physical education."[17]

The broad-sweeping energy that this win gave can be gleaned in several letters: The President of the National Association of Amateur Oarsmen, James D. Denegre, wrote, "My dear Mr. Glendon: . . . It was the greatest triumph that any American crew has ever won anywhere and everyone interested on this side of the water in rowing felt that it was a distinctive victory of his own crew, for the Navy boys were representing us all . . . I feel that this victory has done much for rowing in America."[18]

The English, on the other hand, were stunned. A sarcastic article after the defeat expressed English opinions as to what happened:

> Oarsmen in England haven't had a very easy time of it since that famous little race at Antwerp during the Olympiad in which certain midshipmen from a charming little Maryland town on the river Severn, a stream that leads up from the Chesapeake Bay, defeated Leander crew. English oarsmen have a habit of sitting forward and looking out of the car window when a Leander crew pulls second to a crew of any other nation.
>
> Superiority on the water is something on which an Englishman prides himself. . . . He might go a little shy in paddling a canoe off the Marquesas, or outrigging with the Hawaiians, but he will not take a back seat, if he can avoid it, in anything which has to do with pulling a shell.[19]

The article examined heavier crews, rigging, swivel oarlocks to replace the British thole pins, and Glendon's larger oar blades, saying, "Much has been made of the large oars which were used by the Annapolis crew at Antwerp." The article, after examining a broad sweep of English cultural pride, ended on an interesting national note, listing crew as a means available to anyone who wanted "his share of American athletic prowess."[20]

There were some additional sour grapes in reports by the English coach Pitman, who makes a lopsided analysis of the event that one of his own rowers, Gully Nickalls, later refutes in his own rendition of the events:

According to Pitman:

The arrangements for the regatta and for the comfort of the crews were wonderfully good, considering that the committee had no previous experience of conducting a regatta of that size, and the Belgian authorities were throughout most kind and hospitable to all competitors. The rowing of the eight-oared race although it resulted in an American victory thoroughly vindicated the superiority of English style and English oar and rig. The result of the race was a triumph for American organization and for the business spirit in which the American people undertake amateur sport. English amateur rowing has always been a form of sport which can be indulged in without any interfering with a man's ordinary school, university, or business career. The Leander crew consisted of six university men, a barrister, and a clergyman, who devoted five weeks of their holiday to training. In form and in pace they were as fine a crew as ever sat in a boat. The officials of the Olympic Organization did not even know until a week before the crew started that the regatta was to be held at Vilvoorde and not at Antwerp. When they made this discovery they housed the crew at a station hotel in the middle of Brussels no less than seven miles by dusty road to the course. They were most generous and active for making provision for the crew, but it was too late. The long daily drive took a lot out of the men and it was impossible to provide them with suitable food. Their boat was sent from Antwerp by rail instead of by canal, and the crew themselves had actually to carry their own boat two miles from the station to the boat tents, the Americans kindly lending their lorry for the transport of the oars and riggers. The American Navy on the other hand selected twenty-five rowing men as long ago as January last and employed them in the exclusive business of preparing for this regatta. From the beginning of February the crew were ground into one uniform whole by long steady rows of upwards of twelve miles. During the summer they rowed more than thirty races. They came over in a cruiser fitted with rowing machines, and arrived at Vilvoorde three weeks before the race with a complete second crew to act as pacemakers, four spare men, the ship's doctor to look after their health, men to rub them down, cooks to prepare their special food, a trainer and a staff of servants. They were quartered on the banks of the course, and had continual practice in racing against their second crew. It was in circumstances such as these that we suffered defeat.[21]

But Gully Nickalls, who later went on to be the British Olympic Rowing Chairman and an esteemed sportsman in Britain for the next forty years, reminiscing in *With the Skin of Their Teeth* about the 1920 race, says,

Early in my association with rowing I came to the conclusion that if I ever allowed myself to become disappointed or embittered by failure, I should rob myself of so much enjoyment that the game would soon cease to be worth the candle. No post-mortems, no regrets, was to be my motto, and as an oarsman and as a coach I have tried to live up to that principle. There is, however, one race I cannot look back upon without certain wistful meditations, because its result robbed me of victory in the Olympics—a gold medal denoting first place, an honor I was never destined to achieve.

In the preliminary heats we beat first the Swiss and then the Norwegians with comparative ease. Our great test was to come against the Americans in the final. We got away to a perfect start, striking 41 to their 38 in the first minute. Almost immediately we began to draw away. We were moving perfectly, the boat responding in a most heartening fashion. It felt almost as though we were flying along, so perfect was the cohesion. At 500 metres we had gained a third of a length, and all was going well; at the 1,000 metres we had increased this lead to two-thirds of a length. Never dropping our stroke below 37, we maintained this lead to the 1,800 metres. With 200 metres left we were still moving beautifully, and it didn't seem possible they could catch us now. Yet gradually, inexorably, they started to reduce the gap. In spite of all our endeavours they crept up inch by inch. One hundred metres to go, and we were still in the lead. Surely the winning post couldn't be far away now. Sixty-metres, and our bows still showed ahead. Why couldn't they drop the flag? But no! In the last few strokes the Americans with a last despairing spurt punched their bows ahead. There was no comeback; no answering spurt. Horsfall had timed his race to perfection, and there was nothing left. The Americans had won by four-fifths of a second. One of the Belgian papers summed it up in these words: '*On jugera de la valeur des deux equipes par le temps veritablement sensationnel qu'elles ont realize. Temps 6.05 and 6.05 4/5th*'.[22]

Loosely translated to read, "The truth and the valor of these two crews is to be judged on their sensational times."

This race haunted British Olympian Gully Nickalls for the rest of his life, as with Sidney Swann, who would tell his children that it was so *great* a race that he didn't want to see it end—it was so magnificent to be amidst the greatness that *both* crews were exhibiting and mythically, briefly, were inside of for a moment—they were living history in the making. They had raced their hardest and their best; to be part of such a great moment of human endeavor—there was no shame, no dishonor, no excuses made. The Americans were one of the greatest crews ever—the greatest of the day and so were they. They had *both* shattered the Olympic and World records, and had done in still water with no wind, no current to assist them. They had competed as true athletes and loved every minute of it.[23]

And while it is a romantic notion today that the Brits excuse this loss as due to the war decimating their great crews, in the words of one of their greatest rowers and coaches and writers on the sport at the time, Nickalls, or in the memories of Swann and Pitman and Lehmann, there is no mention whatsoever of the fact or remorse that the war took out the best of their rowers. Therefore, to honor these great crews—both truly great crews—setting a world record pace on flat water, this race, with the fervor it created in its day surely was one of the greatest boat races of all times . . . and sentimental excuses cheapen the valor with which both crews competed. British rowers and American rowers celebrated amicably and in respect and admiration for one another before and after the event. They were heroes, Olympians.

A TICKER-TAPE PARADE IN NEW YORK WELCOMED the American Olympians home. Six of the nine Navy Admirals walked in the parade to the roar of thunderous crowds "cheering for the men and women who won glory for their native land."[24] That night, during the dinner for the Olympians at the Waldorf Hotel, nationalistic rhetoric of addresses from members of the dais, Father Duffy and Commissioner Whalen, reminded the crowd that, "what they accomplished was no more than what America expected of them. It is an American's duty to win and to win always."[25]

The U.S. success story continued for forty years with American eight-oared shells winning every Olympic gold from 1920 until 1960.[26] This is the longest winning streak by any one nation in any single event, and it still stands. British style and tradition gave way to American scientific oarsmanship, and because of it rowing on all continents changed. Later, at a New York City dinner interview for the coaching job at Yale, Glendon was tight-lipped about his coaching secrets and spoke only about "resistance on the hull skin and fluid dynamics."[27] But Glendon's standard American style was forever out of the bag. The United States now led the world in rowing. Epitomizing the words of Mahan on what it takes to affect the sea power of the nation, Glendon's leadership, will, and energy achieved its destiny and fulfilled cadet Churchill's dream.[28]

Navy went on to win consecutive National Poughkeepsie Regattas in 1921 and 1922. The Navy Admirals, as they were now affectionately called, accomplished what no other American crew had done before.[29] Coach Dick Glendon, Olympic gold to his credit, considered retiring from the Naval Academy in 1921 after beating Harvard, Yale, Penn, Cornell, and Washington at Poughkeepsie. Glendon's American style, though, had captured the imagination of even the most resolute Anglophiles among the nation's crews. In 1921, and again in 1922, both Harvard and Yale tried to lure him to take over their crews. Harvard and Yale had been steeped in British rowing orthodoxy since the 1850s.

So deeply was Yale ensconced in the British tradition that in 1919, Yale acquired a Leander Boat Club hull from England and brought it to America.[30] But after the Admirals' defeat of the British, the alumni associations of Harvard and Yale pressured their teams and coaches to win—even if it meant breaking with the English tradition.[31] Glendon was a proven winner. He touted his total American system and methods—boats, oars, and stroke style—as scientific oarsmanship. He proclaimed that his innovations were, "acknowledged as *the* standard American style—the salient points already being adopted by progressive American coaches."[32]

This was a radical turn of events: The American stroke style was being copied by the defeated British and even by the Anglophiles at Harvard and Yale who were seeking to alter their seventy-year lineage in the English orthodoxy in favor of the standard American style.[33] Navy's victory with the new American system represented a takeover, a coup of the highest order. In a telltale news article, reflecting the shift of power, Harvard—long noted for its club officers running the crew with coaches as little more than figureheads doing their bidding or getting ousted—made an offer to Glendon of "large expense" and promised a "free hand" in the way the Crimson crew would be run. "A few live ones are ready to forget the Mayflower ancestry and the imitation Oxford accents," the author noted including mixing Jewish athletes in with the Puritan Groton blood.[34]

THE AMERICAN WIN WAS COMPLETE—THE BRITISH would not win another Men's Olympic Eight race in the twentieth century. Navy's Olympic win was akin to when a performance barrier, sometimes of mythic proportions, is finally overcome, thereby leading to philosophic musings. They are akin to what philosopher

Michael Novak describes as the power of athletic achievement in revealing moments of perfect form. Historian C. L. R. James, in *Beyond a Boundary,* muses about this phenomenon but does not define his intuition concretely when he states that Roger Bannister broke a mental barrier by running a mile in four minutes. Once broken, once the collective unconscious manifested itself through the conscious act, such as surpassing the four-minute mark, the barrier was broken and the mark became easier and easier to surpass.[35]

Sport has been the medium of such barriers—Bannister's sub-four-minute mile, Babe Ruth's sixty home runs, the summiting of Everest without oxygen. As years passed and individual after individual fell short of these goals, the barriers became in some ways larger than life. "Out of reach," "Can't ever be broken," "Beyond human capability," "Never seen in our lifetime," are descriptions often given to such mythic barriers. But strangely, when someone finally does surpass the mark, as with ice skating's quadruple jump, Ty Cobb's base hits, a sub-10 second 100-meter dash, the barrier quickly loses its aura. The hero soon has company.

As old myths fall, of course, new myths take their place. Athletes are forever looking for the next great feat, the performance that resides just beyond what is humanly reasonable to expect—a perfect 10 in each event of All-Round gymnastics competition, a lifetime .400 baseball batting average, a field goal kicker in football who places 80-yard kicks through the uprights every time, the archer who splits every arrow in a match. And when these speculative moments are someday reached, such as Dick Fosbury's flop in high jumping, they, too, may be recognized instantly as the new mark, the better way of doing things.

These breakthrough feats, though possibly couched in invention or innovation, will advance the sport from that moment forward toward the next mythical realm. Differing from setting or surpassing a sport record as described and defined by noted historians Allen Guttmann and Richard Mandell, "breakthrough kinesis" represents a new—intangible—component added to a skill or event that thrusts the level of performance and aesthetics of the contest beyond the previously unattainable, beyond the scientific.[36] The idea of such an event as a breakthrough kinesis can be intuited from the following passage in James: "The achievements of athletes in recent years which have so astonished the world are not as great as so many people imagine that they are. None of them is anywhere near the ultimate limits. By far the most important part of a great performance is played by the mind." He continues, "Long hours of training are not at all necessary." And, "the greatest performances will be produced by the 'poet, the artist, the philosopher.'"[37] Such a perception by the great cricketeer, James, turned social spokesman and philosopher, is intriguing. His claims lead one to ponder other writings regarding the phenomenon of mind and performance, including Carl Jung and his theories of the collective unconscious. Is there a deeper "well" feeding the spring waters of great performances?

It seems that some philosophers imply that there must be something more than just aspects of athletic ability that can be attributed to hard work. Even those who explore the realms of the "inner athlete," are still looking primarily to the mind-body conscious abilities, in present time, to synthesize and execute. But what if time takes on a different role? What if the present is also heavily influenced by the past? What if the past is not lost back there, but is with us, and the collective memories in that past consciousness are with us too? What if there is a collective body wisdom, inherited from all the past body movements of the human race and beyond, from the moment we learned to walk upright until now that is stored and transmitted in the collective unconscious as described by Jung? This would represent a

collective kinetic intelligence in each one of us that is in the unconscious, that is passed from generation to generation and is greater
than the single self-embodiment knowledge of any one individual. It is
as if humankind rises up and passes through, in Jungian terms, a collective unconscious of sport, which advances us all.

This moment of "breakthrough kinesis" challenges those like
me who muse over the deeper meaning of Bannister's seconds and
laps, pint-size horses like Seabiscuit running down monstrous four-
legged speed demons, upstart American naval cadets rowing
through a veritable pantheon of British and Olympic gods, to try
and draw tenuous—though necessary for human comfort—lines between the mortal and the mythical to inspire us and carry us on.

When empirical knowledge fails where else can we go but there?

AND MEANWHILE, ON THE PURELY HUMAN LEVEL,
everything returns to the mundane business of a slight, blue-collar,
workingman's coach who rocked the elitist world of Leander and Harvard and Yale and, worse, had not accepted their lucrative job offers.
Glendon closes the white frame door of the second-story hallway at
the Annapolitan Club, and walks down the stairs one last time. His
leadership, will, and energy having achieved its destiny and come
around full circle—fulfilling cadet Churchill's dream, the dreams of a
nation, his boys, and his own—he is as content with himself now as he
was when he arrived seventeen years earlier. He sets his bag on the
floor, gathers his oiled canvas coat from the hall coatrack, and pauses a
moment to muse at the new, large, oil painting of him and his boys
standing on the dock in Antwerp, gold medals on their chests, which
now hangs over the fireplace in the Annapolitan Club. It has answered
quite well the fundamental question of "How did the crew look?" And

as he turns to leave, he shakes hands with the aging attendant, thanks him, wishes him well, and nods in the direction of the painting saying, "Doesn't that just warm your feet?" and with characteristic New England aplomb, goes home to the Cape to raise cranberries.[38]

19. THE LONGEST STREAK

It's a great art is rowing
It's the finest art there is
It's a symphony of motion.
And when you're rowing well
Why it's nearing perfection.
And when you reach perfection
You're touching the divine.
It touches the you of you's
Which is your soul.

—George Yeoman Pocock, quoted in *Ready All!: George Yeoman Pocock and Crew Racing,* by Gordon Newell

———————————

LIKE LEXINGTON'S "SHOT HEARD ROUND THE world," the Olympic race of 1920 began a revolution. In the decades of the twentieth century following the 1920 Olympic Games, the British never won the Olympic gold medal in the men's eight-oared shell again. Scientific approach and study had succeeded. A new world order, highlighted by the age of American stroke style, technology, and invention, had won. Breaking through English orthodox tradition in the 1920s with a new American orthodoxy exemplified the best of American know-how and ingenuity. The forty-year U.S. Olympic winning streak from 1920 until 1960 held many points of

interest, notably, that with the 1920 Olympic win, Navy crew unwittingly spurred an East versus West rivalry in the United States that
shaped American rowing during the Golden Age of Sport.

Glendon's Navy crew was not from New England boarding
schools or the Ivy League colleges. His was a crew from across the
nation, thereby diminishing the notion that the best U.S. rowers
were solely from up East. Inspired by Navy's Olympic win over the
British, West Coast crews, coming into their own, believed they had
a chance now also to threaten the dominance of long-established
East Coast crews that were steeped in tradition and wealth. The development of West Coast rowing, mainly at Stanford, the University
of California, and the University of Washington, coupled with the
boat-building talent of Seattle's George Pocock, soon rivaled the
eastern powerhouses of Harvard, Yale, Syracuse, Penn, Cornell, Columbia, and Navy.[1]

The surprising threat of West Coast "bumpkins" using native
red cedar to build boats that could beat well-heeled Eastern crews is
a memorable story in the U.S. intercollegiate rowing dynasty that
dominated the Olympic scene for forty years between 1920 and
1960. The rivalry sparked controversies in several areas, including
biases in journalistic coverage, treatment of athletes, coaches, and
equipment, and racing. The Intercollegiate Rowing Championships
held at Poughkeepsie, New York, the American Olympic trials, and
Olympic Eights' finals from 1920 to 1939, produced intense media
hyperbole and showcased the controversies and the regional rowing
rivalries. Charles W. Paddock, U.S. Olympic sprint champion, wrote
an article dedicated to this rivalry whose caption read, "East vs.
West at Poughkeepsie: It will be a Battle of Stamina and Grit, a Fight
to the Finish, When California's World Champion Sweep Swingers
Meet Columbia's Crew Tomorrow in the Poughkeepsie Regatta, for

There Is an Old Score of Trans-Continental Rivalry to Be Settled There."[2]

Popular writers and sportswriters in the twenties focused on the rough pioneer Western image versus the sophisticated well-bred Easterner and mused over its origins and possible deeper meaning.[3] Gertrude Stein, Ernest Hemingway, and F. Scott Fitzgerald wrote about the nostalgia of the past and the loss of the predictable Victorian mind-set.[4] Frederick Jackson Turner wrote on the loss of the frontier and the impact and struggle with modernity that faced America at this time.[5] For example, in the *North American Review* for October 1929, A. A. Brill, a leading American Freudian analyst, wrote on the meaning of American athletics.[6] Brill concluded that sports stem from the hunting impulse of primitive societies and that the primary motivation for play is the "mastery impulse"—an inherent aggressiveness in human nature. Moderns had largely transcended direct physical challenge with the advent of machines and the Industrial Age, but the need for it remained in the human psyche. The theme, coupled with coastal polarities and rivalry, became a popular venue for expression across American society at large, with sportswriting being a dominant and popular outlet.

Rowing was not the only sport shaped by geographical conflicts during this era. Regional rivalries, hyped by the media, successfully took center stage in other sports of this era, namely football, horse racing, and boxing. Historian Bruce Evensen's *When Dempsey Fought Tunney* describes boxing in the 1920s as a media contrast created between Westerner Jack Dempsey and Easterner Gene Tunney to "personify a certain anxiety about living in the 1920s."[7] The mass media took a down-on-his-luck Westerner, Dempsey, and found it could sell newspapers by hyping the Western boxing rivalry of Dempsey against Eastern shipping clerk and ex-Marine Gene Tunney; Dempsey's image was created by his handlers and media promoters, Jack Kearns and Tex Rickard.[8] One New York jazz-age journalist quipped, "The fundamental principle of metropolitan journalism is to buy white paper at three cents a pound and sell it at ten cents a pound."[9] A similar Western country bumpkin versus Eastern supremacy was hyped in the rivalry of Seabiscuit against War Admiral.

Regional differences, and the way the media depicted these differences, were extremely influential in shaping the perception of teams and players. Crowd size evidenced the growing popularity of other media-driven sports in this era. Historian Michael Oriard in *King Football,* states "football teams became pubic symbols of universities, communities, and entire regions in a hugely publicized national drama, intersectional games and post-season bowl games proliferated in the 1920s and 1930s. For example, the Rose Bowl served in the 1920s as the unofficial East-West championship."[10] Further, the power of images in art, newspapers, radio, and by the late 1920s, newsreels, painted the sounds and sights of American culture.[11] As sport historian Ronald Smith notes, in these decades sports grew within the emerging national culture, "taking on many of the features of the larger America."[12]

One such image is rowing. It is typically perceived as solely an Eastern sport. Thomas Eakins's late-nineteenth-century paintings of languid waters, the Schuylkill River's leafy banks, and dedicated oarsmen, immortalized Philadelphia's Boathouse Row and etched images of Eastern rowing in the mind of a nation.[13] The perception of East Coast colleges—leaves turning in the fall, sculls gliding on the Charles, football bowls packed with fans, snowy columns at Harvard—invited the association of academic and athletic greatness with the East. Whether these associations were factual or contrived, they existed nonetheless.

Evensen reveals that the media in the 1920s moved from factual presentation to playing up perceptions and associations to fuel, and, to even create the "slant" and drama it was selling. He states, "Dempseymania was a struggle between competing visions of journalism's future."[14] In rowing, not unlike boxing (Dempseymania) or horse racing (Seabiscuit), it was Eastern brains against Western brawn. In short, regional rivalries manipulated by media hype became formulaic in selling newspapers—making millions and making empires. The power of images in art, newspapers, radio, and by the late 1920s, newsreels shown weekly in 85–90 percent of the 18,000 movie houses in the United States, reached weekly attendance of 108 million people. In short, regional rivalries manipulated by media hype became formulaic to sell newspapers, surging from 28 million papers sold in 1920, to 34 million in 1925.[15]

Furthering the media hype, newspaper newsreels are seen by Oriard as a powerful driving force in sports.[16] The media frenzy created around East Coast versus West Coast rowing drew attention and crowds to the sport. Olympic attendance records indicate that rowing was second only to track and field in overall attendance at the era's games.[17] As stated earlier, the 1920 Olympic Eights final won by Navy in Antwerp recorded the largest crowd at any one Olympic event to that date.[18] Collegiate rivalries of the day at the Poughkeepsie National Regatta drew record crowds of as many as 100,000 who lined the race course, flotilla style.[19] These numbers testify to the popularity and importance of rowing in the United States in these decades.

Adding to the thrill was the ability of aerial photographers to present a bird's-eye view that provided a treat for newsreel viewers in contrast to the text and still pictures of the press. The visual appeal of this added dimension of viewing a race, and the sixty-foot-long boats striking paddles rhythmically along the entire 2,000-meter length of the course, as in the film footage of the 1933 National Sprint Championships, adds a beauty and grace to the contests not seen in newspapers or magazines.[20] While not live, the Universal Newsreel's thrilling footage of the short-lived Intercollegiate Sprint championship, viewed from the Goodyear Blimp's camera, shapes and completes an image for the fan.[21]

Biases in coverage also existed. First and foremost, the press in all its forms favored the East. The predominant Eastern crews, Navy, Harvard, Yale, Penn, and Cornell, were covered in the media as a matter of course. The newsreels covered even their lesser cup races, such as the Carnegie Cup in Derby Connecticut—an early season race between Yale, Princeton, and Cornell—and billed them as "gala" events.[22] Newsreels showed the East Coast crews more frequently than the West Coast crews.[23] Of the twenty-four newsreel citations in the 1930s, twenty of them refer to Eastern school dual meets (Harvard and Yale as an example), or to a nationally interesting event beyond the races themselves, such as President Franklin Delano Roosevelt coming to see his son row for Harvard against Yale or Navy.[24]

The public perception of the East and West Coast Crews showed differences as well. The stock image of the Eastern rower is typically that of a tall, muscled man holding an oar straight up on a dock.[25] But the media portrayed West Coast rowers as sun-drenched men engaged in battles of courage and blood, and often photographed them clumped in front of the boathouse or even bare-chested.[26] One photograph had a shirted Columbia on top, with a dock full of bare-chested California Golden Bears beneath.[27]

Such flamboyant behavior seemed too outlandish for the Ivy Leaguers. Capitalizing on this mystique and perhaps upping the ante on their boats' ability to win, in 1923 the Washington Huskies, after soundly beating Navy, Cornell, and Syracuse to win the Poughkeepsie Regatta, handed out totem poles to the fans who were heard asking, "Where on earth is Seattle?"[28]

The decades of the 1920s and 1930s saw Yale win the 1924 Paris Olympics, the University of California win the Olympic Gold medal in the eights in 1928 and 1932, and the University of Washington win the Olympic eights in 1936.[29] Yet, even the Olympic prestige did not seem to affect the coverage of the crews as one might think, the extensive coverage of rowing continued to stem mainly from the four-mile International Collegiate Poughkeepsie Regatta, held in June on the Hudson.[30] Interestingly, the snobbishness of the Big Three extended from the gridiron to the rowing waters, and Harvard, Yale, and Princeton did not compete at Poughkeepsie, yet the site loomed large in the rowing coverage.[31]

Why might this be? This course is a picturesque setting, flowing past the foot of West Point, a living American landscape from the Hudson River School of American painters.[32] The visual backdrop in Poughkeepsie is dramatic, and the proximity of the Metropolitan East Coast areas, particularly New York City, the communication center of America, might certainly affect the coverage. President Roosevelt's son was a rower at Harvard, so it is easy to understand the draw of the press coverage also to any Harvard races at this time.[33] The Roosevelt estate is on the banks of the Hudson in Hyde Park, New York, near Poughkeepsie. The national and international draw of a U.S. president in the crowd watching his son compete in an athletic contest was noteworthy to American people; their president was "just a regular dad."

In contrast to the picturesque and old-money milieu of the East Coast, the West Coast held its Rowing Championships at the Oakland

Estuary or Long Beach Marine Stadium, the latter the site of the 1932 Olympic regatta course.[34] Here the visual backdrop of the rotted wharfs and hundreds of oil derricks raking the sky behind the spectators gathered for the race is a notable contrast—in descriptive print or newsreels—to the forested cliffs of the Hudson.[35]

The spectators in Long Beach stood along the sunbaked bank, whereas the spectators in Poughkeepsie formed a flotilla line on the river and thereby, became an integral part of the actual rowing course.[36] For the viewer of a newsreel, Poughkeepsie is more visually appealing. And since the newsreels especially were a visual medium, appeal meant money. Newspapers tried to induce this with photos of spectators picnicking along the tree-lined banks, watching the crews streak by, and with descriptions of "Prospects for the race beneath the wooded highlands of the sweeping river are for fast and close finishes."[37]

Other Eastern regatta sites, such as the home course of Yale on the Thames River in New London, Connecticut, were quaint and portrayed in the June 1938 newsreel as "colorful background." It is not difficult to close one's eyes and envision a New England river, flanked with pleasure craft bobbing in the tidal basin with Harvard and Yale eights streaking by.[38] Eastern schools' regattas carried a more social atmosphere that was covered by the press like a society page with a veritable who's who in the crowd, further diminishing the rightful respect given to western successes.

Perceptions and biases influenced the treatment of crews. This matter is presented in two parts: first, in physical housing and reception of crews at regattas, and secondly, in the treatment of crews in the press. One example of Westerners ungraciously accommodated on the East Coast took place in 1923 at Poughkeepsie. Yankee hospitality failed when it housed the University of Washington Huskie "frosh eight" in the boat-shed region along the Hudson River. There was no inside plumbing; it was infested with bedbugs, and illuminated by antiquated oil lights instead of electric.[39] The University of Washington varsity was properly housed but the team remembers being tagged as "rugged" and with the implication that they therefore should not mind the challenging accommodations.[40]

Lifestyles—real or perceived—of the students in the East versus West universities were also different. One popularized perception of the two thousand students of the University of Washington, in the 1920s, was that of a pioneer lifestyle.[41] However, the traditional Eastern schools were close to New York jazz clubs and speakeasies that lent an air of sophistication to the Eastern crews—at least in their own perception. They could draw on nearby prep schools for athletes, while the West Coast had no preparatory or high schools that supported rowing in this era.[42] Robert Harron wrote about the University of Washington Huskie crews using lumberjack saw to keep in shape for rowing.[43] The combination of good material—athletes, lots of them, and good water from January on—related Harron in the article, was why Washington and California crews had won nine of the seventeen postwar races at Poughkeepsie.

In actuality, East Coast crews cultivated a traditional conservative heritage. The Western crews brandished a "man's man" ruggedness that added to their mystique; when the Cal men's eight beat Washington in the first race of their 1928 season, their hands—bloodied and blistered—stained their crew shirts red. The Cal eight, superstitious and wanting to keep the winning streak going, wore the same "lucky" shirts for every race in their season.[44] At the time, the winner of the college championship became the Olympic boat; so for luck, they wore the same rumpled and dirty racing shirts on which, after they won, they hung their Olympic gold medals on.[45]

Washington crews were featured in a photograph in one paper as using lumberjack saws to keep in shape.[46] The rowers were paired off down the length of a log several feet in diameter. The crews lunged back and forth, driving the saw through the log with the caption reading, "Don't rush your slides boys! Huskies at Play."

The article poked fun at the Washington training program, with rowers wielding saws instead of oars and in a faux advertisement indicates where "prime fir lumber can be obtained."[47]

Wythe Williams, a *New York Times* reporter for the trip, gives a classic example of the ballyhoo technique used by the press to manipulate and entice the public, in the 1928 Olympic final between the British and California in Amsterdam. He described the Cal "Golden Bear" coxswain Donald Blessing by saying, "Blessing's lungs are magnificent and for the entire 2,000 meters he gave what by unanimous accord was one of the greatest performances of demonical howling heard on a terrestrial Planet."[48]

The form of media, too, particularly with the addition of motion through newsreels, contributes to the popularization of sports in these decades in the United States. In the Olympic year of 1932, while newsreels focused on the events in Los Angeles, newspapers gave an interesting look at the continuing prejudice toward the West.[49] For example, the Olympic trials were held in the East, on Lake Quinsigamond in Worcester, Massachusetts.[50] The headlines and hackneyed stories of the trials repeatedly portray Eastern crews of Yale, Harvard, Syracuse, and Columbia in front of 40,000 fans. Ten-inch square pictures of the Columbia Lions and full-page columns of text covered the Eastern crew defeats at the trials, while California, noted as being the favorite, is given but one paragraph.[51] Harvard's Crimson got an equally large picture and headline just by showing up to practice![52] But on 10 July California made believers out of the East when the collegiate champions beat the national champion Penn AC boat (heralded as the very best boat of the modern age, though it had not won an Olympic medal as California had in 1928) to win the Olympic trials and to gain the right to represent the United States in the Los Angeles Games.[53]

One might think that West Coast papers would cover their own with top billing. However, while Cal was in the East training for the Olympic Trials, one *Los Angeles Times* headline reads, "Penn Crews Make Grand Slam," referring to the Penn AC boat club in Philadelphia.[54] Buried in the article on page two is a small box which states that Cal is a popular favorite to win, but "Yale looked particularly impressive, as did California and Syracuse"—Cal is thrown in as just part of the lot.[55] On 9 July, nearing the end of the trials, the *Los Angeles Times* highlighted that, "Bears Reach Finals of Crew Trials" and the subtitle reads, "Penn Oarsmen Oppose Californians Today."[56] An interesting choice of words appears on 10 July. When the trials are over, the *Los Angeles Times,* typically having identified the University of California crew as the "Bears" or "Cal," now embraced these men as people who have had to earn the respect of their own state, which endears them only in victory with, "[fellow] Californians qualify for Olympic Battles."[57]

In front of 100,000 fans, oil derricks, and a stiff crosswind from the Pacific, California, in its home state, went against the Italians on 13 August 1932, in the culminating event of the Olympic Summer Games.[58] "California's Crew for a California Olympics" was the rallying cry for the Golden Bears all season long, and they did not disappoint.[59] In tough international-style racing the Bears won, with only half a length (roughly 30 feet) separating first through fourth.[60]

The rivalry continued in 1935 when the University of Pennsylvania set its sights on the collegiate national championship race. *The Literary Digest* quipped that Penn's eight, "with Navy, Constitutes

East's Chief Bulwark Against West Coast Threat at Poughkeepsie."[61] The University of California, after winning, was portrayed the same month in *The Literary Digest* as a team lacking in form and technique—relying on brawn.[62]

The newsreels of the 1936 Olympics focus on the departing ceremonies from American docks and the opening and closing ceremonies overseas.[63] In like manner, when the University of Washington beat Italy and Germany in the eights final in 1936 at the Berlin Olympic Regatta, *The New York Times* reported, "Courage boiled high and gray, cold waters were churned into white-flecked foam by the fury of their efforts."[64] The word choices used to describe Washington seem more colorful and more dramatic, again conjuring up images of the courageous, rugged, frontier West in contrast to the sophisticated, well-bred East. The romance and nostalgia—accurate or not—was fodder for the press to magnify the popularized West Coast images.

The West Coast crews were heralded as sunburned giants, and the man-against-man, man-against-nature image was a pleasant anomaly, but it did not readily overcome the mind-set of America that the Ivy League and Philadelphia clubs were the real competitors.

If there was one clear prejudice, it is that for over thirty years, the roads and rails in national collegiate rowing competition ran East. Beginning that decade, the Olympic Trials for the 1932 Los Angeles Olympics were held in the East at Quinsigamond, even though Cal won the 1928 Olympics gold.[65] There are no accounts in the newsreels or the texts of the Eastern colleges traveling West to race until 1933.[66] In this sole example, the Long Beach Marine Stadium, built for the 1932 Olympics, was fenced in to act as a gated facility following the football stadium trend and was utilized in 1933–1935 to host international-style rowing sprint races of 2,000 meters. Eastern schools were invited for the trip West. The event got little attention and died after only three years in favor of the Poughkeepsie course.[67]

Interestingly, one of the rowing powers of the nation was Wisconsin and yet, in these decades there is no mention of an East-Midwest-West rivalry. The press divided rowing into the East and West Coasts. They played up this regional competition on a bi-coastal stage. For example, in 1938, when Harvard beat Navy on the Severn River, the newsreels hyped it as an "end to the Navy's supremacy in the East."[68] In like manner, in June 1938, when Navy went on to beat California at Poughkeepsie, the middie oarsmen are portrayed as bringing the "country's rowing supremacy back East."[69] The news service seems to be trumping up the rivalry to engage the largest population base—the entire country—to sell its product. And the choice of words "bringing it back East" leaves one to believe that the East is rightly where the supremacy belongs.

The press did not give the West Coast crews their due until the end of the 1930s. In 1939, after winning the Poughkeepsie Regatta four times each, and after winning the Olympics three times, California and Washington heard words like "thrilling," "brilliant," and "famous" now attributed to their West Coast rowing.[70]

Olympic rowing struggled during World War II and briefly afterwards as athlete ranks were decimated and war damage wreaked havoc on the financing and staging of Olympic games. The 1936 Berlin Olympics was bannered in Adolf Hitler's swastika and military image. The 1940 and 1944 games were cancelled due to the world war. It led to an uneasy feeling about whether the Olympic movement would survive at all. In 1948, 1952, and 1956, however, the U.S. crews did not disappoint. They picked up the reins of the pre-war record breakers and carried on the tradition of winning every Olympic gold in the Men's Heavy Eights.[71]

In Rome, Italy, on 3 September 1960, the Navy men's eight made history again. In 1920, Navy began the unprecedented forty-year winning streak by one country in one event. It still stands today. However, in 1960 Navy had a hand in tarnishing the record streak. The vaunted Navy eight came in fifth, losing to Germany in the finals.[72] It is an intriguing and perhaps fitting culmination for Navy—to have the honor to begin and end the Olympic gold medal streak of such magnitude. It is a credit to the depth of their program over the years and a contributing factor adding to the mystique of the great Navy crews of old.

Echoing bygone Olympic days in Antwerp, Navy beat Britain, and proceeded to the Olympic finals.[73] Once in the finals the Germans outclassed the midshipmen, leaving them behind by three lengths of open water.[74] The midshipmen managed to beat only the host team Italy at the Olympic regatta held on Lake Albano, where nearby, Pope John the XXIII was summering at the papal palace of Castel Gandolfo. The 1960 Navy crew, unpolished and uncharacteristic of the great Navy style of the past, was more a lucky than a talented entry to the Olympic finals.

This medal was the first Olympic gold for Germany, which had a composite crew from nearby villages of Kiel and Ratzeburger. Rhetoric in the *New York Tribune* drew heavily on nationalism depicting the Germans "storming" Uncle Sam's American rowing "citadel." The fighting words were not enough to see the U.S. boat across the line first, but seem a fitting end for the much-heralded military crew. This unusual beginning and end saga of the Navy crew is but one more piece in the puzzle of their *opus*. Their young rookie coach, Lou Lindsay, had no reason to hang his head—he failed while trying to fill the large shoes of the venerable Dick Glendon and the 1920 Navy crew.

In the end, the East versus West rivalry spurned by the 1920 Navy crew undoubtedly strengthened U.S. rowing and pushed America's best oarsmen to the front of the world rowing community. Newsreels captured the glory and excitement of the Olympics, as evidenced by the teams of 1932 and 1936 readying for world competition.[75] The newsreels gave added life to Glendon's shipboard efforts to keep the athletes in training to inform and to pique the national interest of viewers.[76] To an audience in the midwest, for example, scenes from the Navy deck in newspapers and newsreels could conceivably have been the first time some landlocked viewers glimpsed the challenges of sea travel as well as heightening an interest in the Academy at large.[77] To fans who only heard or read of these great regattas as one of the nation's most popular sports, the jumpy, fast-whirling newsreels of the late twenties and thirties captured and indulged the senses to the elegance, grace in strength, and seemingly effortless flight of a shell being hurled along the waters that previously only those privileged enough to be at the regatta site would have witnessed.

How much these pictures and images added to the media "hype" of newspapers and radio affected participation of athletes and fans from the 1930s on is not clear, but we know these formulaic techniques influenced the rise of interest in sports in this time across the United States. Newsreels and visual arts, such as the photographs in the Glendon Collection, enhanced the silent stealth of rowing shells. U.S. rowing, due in large part to Richard Glendon and the 1920 Navy crew, boasted images of cheering fans, Adonis-like physiques, and froth-filled oar puddles diminishing into the temporarily etched water surface, capturing and unifying the support of a nation. Without a doubt, Richard J. Glendon and the 1920 Navy crew thrust rowing to the forefront of the international athletic stage, making it one of the most widely watched intercollegiate and Olympic medal events of its time, and in doing so, contributed in no small part to elevating the United States to the highest rank of international naval supremacy.[78]

EPILOGUE

I have been and will always remain a believer in the true Olympian's ability to roar across the sky with a meteor's one time blinding flash rather than be that dull more steady recorded glow for eternity on the faded memory of humankind. My greatest pleasure as a coach is to see my athletes reach the podium and know that I helped create the opportunity for them to be the best.

—Coaching motto of Ted Nash, U.S. Olympic rowing gold medalist and Olympic coach

SITTING IN A WHEELCHAIR, LEGLESS, GLENDON exhaled his cigar as Admiral Chester Nimitz's staff car left the driveway of his son Hubert's home. Admirals King, Moore, and Clark were out there beyond the crushed rock of his drive—leading the nation, leaving pools of still water at the end of their oars that vanished into the lives of thousands of young men and women that laid hands on their shells after them.

From bow to stern, first and foremost, he had seen each of the nine men of his 1920 eight graduate from the Naval Academy. Victor Jacomini went on to found an engineering firm in Texas; Cutie Clark, after coxing the Navy eight in Antwerp to gold, substituted into the four-with for Penn Barge Club at Antwerp and won silver, the only coxswain in the history of the Olympics to win two medals at the same Olympiad.[1] He became a rear admiral. King, a noted California football official and founder of the Lake Merritt Rowing Club, retired from the Navy in 1958 as a rear admiral; Gallagher retired as a commander after a lifelong service to the Navy; Jordan became president of Curtiss Wright Aircraft in Columbus, Ohio, and president and general manager of Hughes Aircraft; Johnston retired as an Air Force captain; Country Moore, a lifetime officer in the Navy, winning the Legion of Merit and two Presidential Unit citations during his term as chief of staff to the Commander of the Pacific Task Force in World War II, retired as a rear admiral; Graves retired from the Navy in 1950 as a captain; Sanborn retired from the Navy as a captain and worked with his shellmate Jordan at Wright Aeronautical. They all retained a close friendship with one another throughout their lives, held reunions, and as a boat were inducted into the Helms Rowing Hall of Fame.

AS FOR DICK GLENDON, HIS WIFE MARY HAD passed away and their seven children—Mary Marguerite, Richard John, Alice Theresa, Thomas Alfred, Hubert, Charles Francis, and Kathleen "Rose"—as a family stayed near Harwich in Chatham, Massachusetts, and lived a life of summer cottages, Olympic glory, and personal tragedy in the seemingly idyllic Cape Cod village. Two sons followed in his footsteps as rowing coaches. Hubert coached at Columbia and Richard "Rich" John coached at Navy. Dick Glendon and his two sons, Rich and Hubert, dominated rowing news at Columbia and Navy for the next decade in a series of decisions and tragedies that would see Richard A. "Old Dick" Glendon come out of retirement three times to carry on the family pride.

In 1920, 1921, and 1922, Rich assisted his father at Navy, until he retired the first time. He gave the crew to Rich, who then resigned in 1925 over a dispute with Navy. Rich left Navy for Columbia University while his father stuck to his cranberry farming in Cape Cod and would not enter into the politics of the dispute between Navy and his son. In 1925–1927, however, with the Columbia crew gaining stature, the great Richard Glendon came out of retirement the first time and assisted his son Rich with the "Lions."

Hubert joined Rich at Columbia in 1927, coaching the lightweight crews. Hubert was the most successful coach in that division with two champion lightweight eights and two runners-up. Richard Glendon was persuaded back to Navy in 1928. Rich's varsity won the Poughkeepsie Regatta in 1927 and 1929, with a second in 1928 to his father's first place.[2]

IN JUNE 1931, NAVY WAS THE SURPRISE WINNER AT Poughkeepsie again, where the Glendons were portrayed megaphone to megaphone with the respective eights in between father (Navy) and son (Columbia) in the *Boston Globe*.[3] Perhaps thinking he had won and had done all there was to do, and wanting to "go out on top," in a surprise announcement on 22 September 1931, at age sixty-seven, Glendon made another resignation from Navy. He was succeeded by C. A. "Buck" Walsh, his assistant of the previous four years.

The Glendons as a coaching trio had thrilled athletes and fans alike well into the 1930s, with the legacy looking to continue with Rich and Hubert, but fate would deal a cruel hand. Urged out of retirement by necessity in May 1932, Glendon came to the aid of young Rich at Columbia by proudly and yet humbly coaching the 150-pound crew, when Hubert, the lightweight coach, became ill of scarlet fever.[4]

Once Hubert recovered, their father returned home again for three years.

After coaching both the Naval Academy's plebe crews and the varsity, and helping his father write *Rowing*, Rich Glendon was tragically killed in a hunting accident in Chatham in 1937 at Christmas. Rich and his wife Mary had three children: Richard John, Jr., Thomas Alfred "Tommy," and Mary Elizabeth. Then, in a hauntingly similar manner, at the same time of year and under similar circumstances, Tommy was also killed in a hunting accident near Chatham, with a school chum, during Christmas vacation in 1938. The chilling story tells of the two boys, when duck hunting, set adrift by a strong tide and offshore winds. With temperatures near freezing and darkness upon them, the boys drifted past the anchored lightship, *Stone Horse*. Their location was sent via shortwave to a coast guard surfboat that launched an all-night search but only an upturned duck boat was ever found—spotted by a low-flying search plane.[5]

So for the third and final time, as Hubert took over his brother's varsity job at Columbia, Pop Glendon came again out of retirement at nearly age seventy to help get the Lions going.[6]

When Richard Glendon left Columbia for the final time and returned to the white clapboard house on Main Street, it was a huge honor for tiny Harwichport to have the world-renowned figure back in its midst. He spent the rest of his days here in his son Hubert's home—who built an addition on the back of the first floor of the house near the backyard with its shade trees and fishpond.

Many celebrities came to visit Richard Glendon in his twilight years. The illustrious names included Cap. Noble E. Erwin, the first athletic officer at the Naval Academy who allowed Navy crew to row in the 1920 Olympics. Also visiting were Admiral King, the 1920 Olympic stroke, Wallis Simpson (the future Duchess of Windsor),

Admiral Bull Halsey, and Charles Francis Adams III, Secretary of the Navy, whom Old Dick simply called "Charlie," and who was a schoolboy rower in the Boston coaching days of Dick Glendon.[7]

Family members remember many dignitaries visiting him over the years, and the family house was littered with memorabilia, including photographs of the signing of the Japanese Surrender on deck of the USS *Missouri,* Tokyo Bay, September 2, 1945, from Admiral Chester Nimitz inscribed, "To Dick Glendon with best wishes and warmest regards," signed, "Nimitz—Fleet Admiral, stroke 1905."[8]

Telltale of their friendship, another photo from Nimitz is inscribed, "To Dick Glendon old friend of long standing—the best crew coach the Navy ever had—best wishes and warmest regards, C. W. Nimitz, Fleet Admiral." Nimitz also said, "Dick Glendon, by what he put into successive generations of Navy midshipmen, undoubtedly helped us win the naval battles of World War I and World War II."[9]

It isn't surprising that many of his rowers felt a lifelong bond to Glendon, who was referred to affectionately as Old Dick, the Old Man, and Pop Glendon. Unlike many of his contemporaries who wielded megaphones of criticism instead of praise, Glendon was known for saying almost nothing while on the water, and then speaking to the men one at a time. His son Richard, trained by his father, reportedly would ask men to "think about not rushing the slide" and, if they could "just concentrate on that, what great oarsmen they would be."[10]

IN AN INSIGHTFUL ARTICLE BY GEORGE CARENS written two years before Glendon's death, Old Dick is described as sitting serenely in his shady backyard on Lower County Road, today's

Main Street, his house a veritable rowing museum, himself a living and lively monument to American rowing and:

> To the current generation of sports enthusiasts the name means little. Among rowing cognoscenti, he is a legend. For his has been a great career as a coach. He taught oarsmen what he called the dory-style of rowing, taken he said from the way Cape Codders row their dories . . . . the great names of the nation are just old friends to him. As he talks of the old days, such as in 1920, when his Navy Crew won the Olympic championship, his eyes light up.
>
> Something new has been added at the Glendons' residence—a miniature rowing Hall of Fame. There's a gaudy array of silver trophies. There's a picture gallery that includes fleet Admirals of World War II who were winning strokes under Old Dick. And of course there are the heroes of 1920 who manned the oars, at the express command of Boston's late Charles Francis Adams, then Secretary of the Navy.
>
> Chester Nimitz and Jonas Ingram are centerpieces in the pictorial display. Also framed is the Tip Goes Trophy, which perpetuates the names and fame of Cornell's Charley Courtney, Syracuse's Jim Ten Eyck, and Navy's Glendon, for the annual triangular regatta involving the modern eights of these old rivals. Add the diplomas and Olympic doodads, and you can understand how Old Dick's memories remain sharp. His forty-two-year coaching span ended decades ago, but he recalls them as though they were yesterday.[11]

The aging process was not kind to Dick Glendon. Having lost both legs in later life to circulatory problems, the venerable Dick Glendon died in 1956 in a Cape Cod hospital at the age of eighty-six.[12] But his legacy did not die with him. In the Golden Age of Sport, Glendon and his crew opened a door and began a streak that approaches the mythical. Glendon and his boys were portrayed in newspapers as being among the greatest sports heroes of the century—listed as equal to such household greats as Babe Ruth and Man-O-War.[13]

Is it any wonder that Olympic attendance records indicate that rowing was second only to track and field in overall attendance at the era's games? Or that the 1920 Olympic Eights final win by Navy in Antwerp recorded the largest crowd at any one Olympic event to that date? These numbers testify to the popularity and significance of rowing in the United States in these decades and the lasting impact Richard Glendon and the 1920 Navy crew made on the sporting tradition and social consciousness of our nation. Through the unprecedented American accomplishments of the 1920 Naval Academy crew, this group of nine midshipmen, known thereafter as the "Navy Admirals," were elevated above the event itself to immortality.[14]

NOTES

Introduction

1. "Navy Oarsmen Win by Half a Length," *New York Times,* 30 August 1920, sec. Sports, p. 10.
2. Olympic times recorded in Richard A. Glendon and Richard J. Glendon, *Rowing* (Philadelphia and London: J. P. Lippincott, 1923), 207. See also the *American Olympic Committee Report, Seventh Olympic Games* (New York: American Olympic Committee, 1920), 344.
3. Ibid., 97–109. While Richard A. "Dick" Glendon coined the term "American Scientific Oarsmanship," others, including rowing historian Thomas Mendenhall, cite the importance of this concept under the name of the American Orthodox style. See also Thomas Mendenhall, *A Short History of American Rowing* (Boston: Charles River Books, 1980), 34.
4. Glendon, *Rowing,* 179.
5. From the private collection of Barbara Luscomb, South Carolina.
6. From a personal interview with Sister Mary of the Pure Heart, O.P. and photographs of the Glendon Collection.

1. The Old Man

1. Family genealogy information given by Wayne Geehan, husband of Susan Glendon, who is a granddaughter of Richard A. Glendon. Geehan was at his home during a phone conversation of 30 October 2003.

2. From a phone conversation 5 November 2003 with Wayne Geehan at his home in Massachusetts.

3. Ibid.

4. "Richard Glendon, Crew Coach, Dead," *New York Times*, 10 July 1956, sec. Obituaries, p. 31.

5. From a personal interview and notes in the Glendon Collection.

6. Available on the Internet, http://en.wikipedia.org/wiki/Boston _Athletic_Association, accessed 2007.

7. "Noble and Greenough Academy Bulletin: The History of Noble's Rowing," no. 3, vol. V (June 1932). The Glendon Collection is part of the private collection of Duncan Glendon (hereafter referred to as the Glendon Collection), processed by Susan Saint Sing. It is important to note that many items in the collection are personal clippings or writings with no date, page, or source reference, and these will be listed as the Glendon Collection. If any identifying marks are present, these will be noted in the reference. The collection is located in Massachusetts.

8. The Glendon Collection.

9. "The Sporting Pulse," the Glendon Collection.

10. "Schoolboy Oarsmen," the Glendon Collection.

11. "Trainer of Oarsmen," the Glendon Collection. Though most of the source information of the clippings in the scrapbook have been cut off, this page has two dates from newspapers, the *Boston Daily Globe*, 21 September 1892 and *Boston Evening Record*, 22 April 1893, pasted next to the stories. The pictures of Glendon in the articles substantiate his youth and correlation in time to the article dates.

12. "Active on River," the Glendon Collection.

13. "Trainer of Oarsmen," the Glendon Collection.

14. The January blizzards of 1904 were known to kill hundreds of people and livestock from Minnesota to Manhattan. These reports can be found in numerous city newspapers of the midwest and eastern coastal cities of the United States.

2. A Corpse, an Olympics, and a Midshipman Named Nimitz

1. Mame Warren and Marion E. Warren, *Everybody Works But John Paul Jones: A Portrait of the U.S. Naval Academy, 1845–1915* (Annapolis: Naval Institute Press, 1981).

2. The photograph of Nimitz and the 1904 Naval Academy Crew is cited with permission of the Department of the Navy, Special Collections and Archives Division of the Nimitz Library, Annapolis, Maryland. See photo catalogue number #2702. See also *Lucky Bag: The Annual of the Regiment of Midshipmen,* by P. E. Pihl, W. D. Johnson Jr. (Annapolis, Maryland: The United States Naval Academy, 1904 and 1905).

3. From a personal interview with Barbara Luscomb, daughter of Vincent Gallagher on 12 May 2007, with her husband Bill, at their home in South Carolina.

4. Available on the Internet, http://www.nimitz-museum.org/nimitzbio .htm, accessed 2006.

5. The Glendon Collection.

6. "Two Admirals were Crewmen," by Malcom Ray, the Glendon Collection.

7. "Eastern Crews Come Fast As Season Grows: The Glendons Ignore Megaphone," by Joe Williams, the Glendon Collection.

8. The name of the boatman is unclear, however, it is reported to have been Chandler by most of the descendants. It has also been reported to be Cantler.

9. "From Another Angle," the Glendon Collection.

10. Christopher Dodd, *The Story of World Rowing* (London: Random Century Group, 1992).

11. Ibid., 396.

12. Mendenhall, *A Short History of American Rowing*, 120.

13. Stephen Kiesling, *The Complete Recreational Rower and Racer* (New York: Crown, 1990), 138.

14. Bill Mallon, *The 1900 Olympic Games: Results for All Competitors in All Events* (Jefferson, N.C. and London: McFarland and Company Inc. Publishers, 1998), 155.

15. John A. Lucas and Ronald A. Smith, *Saga of American Sport* (Philadelphia: Lea & Febiger, 1978), 403.

16. Glendon, *Rowing*, 199.

17. Ibid., 28.

18. Available on the Internet at http://www.timesolympics.co.uk/historyheroes/historylon1908.html. Accessed in 2006.

19. Ibid.

3. Navy's Love Affair with Crew

1. Glendon, *Rowing*, plate inside front cover.

2. Ibid., 179.

3. Vice Admiral William Ledyard Rodgers, *Naval Warfare Under Oars, Fourth to Sixteenth Centuries* (Annapolis: U.S. Naval Institute, 1940), fig. 26.

4. Ibid.

5. Thomas J. Cutler, *The Bluejacket's Manual, 22nd Edition* (Annapolis: U.S. Naval Institute, 1998, orig. 1902), 1.

6. Glendon, *Rowing*, 234–35.

7. Ibid., 549.

8. *Illustrated Catalogue and Oarsman's Manual for 1871* (Troy, N.Y.: Walters, Balch & Co., Patent Paper Boat Builders, 1871).

9. Commander W. E. May, *The Boats of Men-of-War* (Annapolis: U.S. Naval Institute, 1999), 77.

10. J. R. Hill, *The Oxford Illustrated History of the Royal Navy* (Oxford: Oxford University Press, 1995), 266.

11. *The American Sportsman's Library "Rowing and Track Athletics,"* edited by Caspar Whitney, Samuel Crowther, and Arthur Ruhl. (London and New York: Macmillan Co., 1905 p 3–4), 147.

12. Walter Camp, *Walter Camp's Book of College Sports* (New York: The Century Co., 1893), 50.

13. William G. Durick, "The Gentlemen's Race: An Examination of the Harvard-Oxford Boat Race." *Journal of Sport History* 15 (Spring 1988): 1, 42.

14. Joseph Mathews, "The First Harvard-Oxford Boat Race" *New England Quarterly* 3 (March 1960): 74–82.

15. Ibid., 173.

16. The Navy boathouse was destroyed in a hurricane in 1870. Churchill's letter to the editor of the 1892 *Army and Navy Register* is in the narrative of the Alumni History on the Academy site. Available on the Internet, http://pusna.com/History/Churchill/1.htm. Accessed 2006.

17. Glendon, *Rowing,* 179.

18. A. T. Mahan, D. C. L., LL. D., *The Influence of Sea Power Upon History, 1660–1783* (Boston: Little Brown, 1890), 57.

19. Mahan, "The United States Looking Outward," *Atlantic Monthly* 66 (December 1890), 816–24.

20. Ibid.

21. Glendon, *Rowing,* 173–74.

22. Ibid.

23. Helen A. Cooper, *Thomas Eakins: The Rowing Pictures* (Yale University Press, 1996), 27.

24. Ibid.

25. Glendon, *Rowing,* 178–80.

4. The War Years: 1914–1918

1. Bruce J. Evenson, *When Dempsey Fought Tunney: Heroes, Hokum and Storytelling in the Jazz Age* (Knoxville: University of Tennessee Press, 1996), 60. See also Ronald A. Smith, *Play by Play: Radio, Television, and Big-Time College Sport* (Baltimore and London: The Johns Hopkins University Press, 2001).

2. Nan E. Woodruff, *American Congo: The African American Freedom Struggle in the Delta* (Cambridge, Mass. and London: Harvard University Press, 2003).

3. Frederick Jackson Turner, *Rereading Frederick Jackson Turner* (New Haven: Yale University Press, 1998, originally published by Henry Holt in 1994). Roderick Nash wrote about the hero image and the vanishing American frontier in terms of the loss of manliness and a need for displaced aggression; see Roderick Nash, *The Nervous Generation: American Thought, 1917–1930* (Chicago: Rand McNally, 1970).

4. Lucas and Smith, *Saga of American Sport,* 305.

5. Mendenhall, *The Harvard-Yale Boat Race,* 306.

6. Ibid., 304–305.

7. *Lucky Bag 1922,* 449.

8. Glendon, *Rowing,* 145–54.

9. "Navy Oarsmen Chosen to Meet World's Best Crews Abroad," *The Literary Digest* 66 (21 August 1920): 98.

10. Glendon, *Rowing,* 53–54.

11. Ibid., 137.

12. Major George Wythe, Capt. Joseph Mills Hanson, and Capt. V. Burger, eds., *The Inter-Allied Games* (New York: The Games Committee, 1919), 11. The first three chapters of this text contain the organizational documents for the games at large. See pages 270–280 for the rowing events. See also Colonal James A. Donovan, *Militarism, U.S.A.* (New York: Charles Scribner's and Sons, 1970).

13. Ibid., 17–18.

14. Ibid., 17.

15. Ibid., 35.

16. Ibid., 270.

17. "Fix Events For Henley," *New York Times*, 10 June 1919, sec. S, p. 16.

18. "Henley Again: 'All the fun of the Fair'" *Times* (London), 3 July 1919, p 15.

19. Roland Renson, *The Games Reborn: The VIIth Olympiade Antwerp 1920* (Antwerp: Pandora, 1996), 8–9.

20. World War I poster of rowing acquired on the Internet. The poster was billed as being authentic to the era.

21. Renson, *The Games Reborn*, 8–9.

22. "Commander Clyde King," *Grinnell Herald Register*, 27 and 30 December 1943.

23. *Lucky Bag 1922*, 56.

24. Charles Dickens, *The River*, "Sketches by Boz" p. 65. Original publication date 1836.

25. This story of Sherman Clark related by Barbara Luscomb in a private interview.

26. "In the Limelight: Clyde King Gets Publicity for Athletic Prowess in Navy," *Poweshiek County Palladium*, 7 September 1920.

27. *Lucky Bag 1922*, 426.

5. British Rowing Roots

1. J. A. Mangan, *Europe, Sport, World: Shaping Global Societies* (London: Frank Cass, 2001), 9.

2. Ibid.

3. From its military roots rowing evolved to the practical purpose of moving cargo along rivers where watermen toiled in England and the continent. Rowing progressed in England from the watermen plying oars of trade to a betting contest for "Doggett's Prize"; see Daryl Adair, "Two Dots in the Distance: Professional Sculling as a Mass Spectacle in New South Wales, 1876–1907." *Sporting Traditions,* 9 (November 1992): 52–82. Professional rowing evolved not unlike professional boxing and cricket. It was a hugely popular affair of racing for purses around stakes and racing long river courses of four-mile distances, often tidal, with currents and wind requiring the skills of a sailor's knowledge of watermanship and a horse jockey's sense of when to cut in; see William G. Durick, "The Gentlemen's Race: An Examination of the 1869 Harvard-Oxford Boat Race." *Journal of Sport History,* 15 (Spring, 1988), 59. Regattas for pleasure were held on the Thames as early as 1800. Sharing in the quagmire of the English tradition of amateurism and professionalism, rowing was also a gentlemen's sport with the first organized rowing at Eton and later at Leander in 1818 or 1819, from Joseph Strutt's book, *Sports and Pastimes of the People of England from the Earliest Period* (London: Methuen and Co., 1801; reprint, by J. Charles Cox, 1903), 77–78 (page references are to reprint edition). Like soccer and cricket, crew expanded as a passion of the sporting traditions of England; see also Eric Halladay, *Rowing In England: A Social History* (Manchester, England: Manchester University Press, 1990), 2–3.

4. Richard Holt, *Sport and the British* (Oxford: Clarendon Press, 1989), 23.

5. Archibald MacLaren, *Training in Theory and Practice* (London: MacMillan and Co., 1874), 2.

6. Christopher Dodd, *Small Oxford Books: Boating* (Oxford and New York: Oxford University Press, 1983), 1. This quote is from Kenneth Grahame, "*The Wind in the Willows*," 1908.

7. R. P. P. Rowe and C. M. Pitman, *Rowing* (London and Bombay: Longmans, Green and Co., 1898), 163.

8. Available on the Internet, http://www.magd.ox.ac.uk/history/ww .shtlml. Accessed 2006.

9. Available on the Internet, http://www.trinhall.cam.ac.uk/about/ history.asp. Accessed 2006.

10. Personal interview with David Swann at Langdon House in Cambridge England, Tuesday 1 P.M. on 28 August 2006.

11. Available on the Internet, http://www.magd.ox.ac.uk/history/gardens .shtml. Accessed 2006.

12. Available on the Internet, http://www.ox.ac.uk/aboutoxford/boatrace .shtml. Accessed 2006.

13. Halladay, *Rowing In England,* 108–111.

14. The anonymous correspondent's quote is from *The Field*, 2 May 1896.

15. Ibid., Halladay, 124.

16. Allen Guttmann, *Games and Empires: Modern Sports and Cultural Imperialism* (New York: Columbia University Press, 1994). Guttmann, throughout this text, discusses the struggle of various colonies throughout the British Empire to at first imitate, and then try to surpass, the imperial power's culture. See page 179 for imitative behavior; the introduction for the general overview of colonial sport under British influence, 1–11; and trends in cricket, 16–40.

Sport historians David Lane and Ian Jobling discuss and outline a similar process in Australia. Amateur intercolony eight-oar races had been held annually since 1878 between New South Wales and Victoria. In the 1890s, Queensland, Tasmania, Western Australia, and South Australia began racing against one another, too; by 1905, all states were competing on a regular basis. A look at sculling and eight- and four-oared racing and World champion victories in 1876 by Edward Trickett led to "the growing attitude that they (colonials) should think of themselves as Australians first, and inhabitants of separate colonies second." Much of the research in Australian sports in the nineteenth century has shown that it contributed "in no small way" to the development of an Australian National Identity. Nor was this limited to rowing—the eloquent C. L. R. James relates his saga of the similar struggle through cricket to surpass the West Indian British Administrators in order to beat them at their own game.

6. Henley vs. the Olympic Games

1. Halladay, *Rowing in England: A Social History*, 117–22.
2. Ibid.
3. Ibid., 118.
4. G. O. Nickalls, *A Rainbow in the Sky* (London: Chatto and Windus 1974), 170.
5. *The British Rowing Almanac*, 1912, 226. Additionally, Halladay explained that this ARA statement was in reaction to a *Times* article where the BOA suggested raising £100,000 for the 1916 Berlin Games (not held due to the Great War) that gained the support of Sir Arthur Conan Doyle and T. A. Cook, who was the only British oarsman on the International Olympic Committee (IOC) at the time. See also Halladay, *Rowing in England: A Social History*, 117–22. See also *Times (London)* 27 August 1913 and 1 December 1913.
6. For a general overview of this concept, in particular the German gymnastic school, see Turnerbund and its influence on American

physical education; see Henry Metzner, *A Brief History of the American Turnerbund* (Pittsburgh, Penn., 1924).

7. Halladay, *Rowing in England: A Social History*, 117–22.

8. Ibid.

9. Ibid. Additionally, the ARA, in its patent refusal to join pace in 1920 with the trend of the NARA and the BOA to reach a harmonious resolution, set a precedent for itself of being outside the ever-increasing larger international community; this continued throughout the interwar years, even after 1945. For example, the ARA controlled the Henley Royal Regatta and refused to permit professional coaches to coach the amateur college rowers while racing at Henley.

   See also "Dick Glendon Sends Crews Through Last Hard Workout for MIT Race Tomorrow" and also, "Columbia Oarsmen Sail for England," the Glendon Collection. These articles describe Hugh Glendon having to give up his coaching of the Columbia *Lion*'s Henley crew for 6 weeks prior to racing in order for his crew to be coached by an "amateur coach," Don Farley. Hugh did see the crew off and joined them later, "as a spectator" in England.

10. Halladay, *Rowing in England: A Social History*, 117–22.

11. Ibid. Fearing international embarrassment by this provincial attitude, the secretary of the Henley Stewards sent "an artful letter" to the *Field* praising the virtue of the stewards for allowing the race and thereby causing them to lose face if they did refuse. As a result, they were trapped by the very highbrow attitudes that they preached.

12. Glendon, *Rowing*, dedication page.

13. "The Olympic Games, British Rowing Success," *Times* (London) 28 August 1920, p 6. On the opening day of Olympic heats Great Britain had a fast heat with the Swiss with an impressive time of 6 min 18.1 sec. The U.S. crew was not mentioned in the article.

14. Rowing, "The Leander Crew at Henley," *Times* (London), 16 August 1920, p. 5.

15. "Henley Regatta: The First Day's Racing," *Times* (London), 1 July 1920, p. 7.

16. Bill Mallon and Ture Widlund, *The 1912 Olympic Games Results for All Competitors in All Events, with Commentary* (Jefferson, N.C. and London: McFarland, 2002), 250–55.

17. Glendon, *Rowing*, 207.

18. Mallon and Widlund, *The 1912 Olympic Games Results for All Competitors in All Events*, 250–55.

19. "Annapolis Eight Won American Title Clearly," the Glendon Collection.

7. American Scientific Oarsmanship and the Crew

1. The story of the coaching launch's nickname "the watchful Dart" was related by Barbara Luscomb.

2. Mendenhall, *The Harvard-Yale Boat Race*, 271.

3. Camp, *Walter Camp's Book of College Sports*, 69.

4. Halladay, *Rowing In England: A Social History*, 127.

5. Mendenhall, *The Harvard-Yale Boat Race*, 329.

6. Ibid., 136. See also Gordon R. Newell, *Ready All!* (Seattle: University of Washington Press, 1987), 42, who states that the University of Washington's stroke of 1913 had "overtones of the traditional Thames Waterman Stroke." See also Thomas C. Mendenhall, *The Harvard-Yale Boat Race, 1852–1924* (Mystic, Conn.: Mystic Seaport Museum, 1993), 274–75 describes that in 1912, the Yale coach, boats and style indicated that "Yale seemed determined to recover the very best of the English Orthodox style." For a description of the distinctions between American and English boats and oars, see Glendon, *Rowing*, 146–53. Additionally according to Durant, "It was

not uncommon for American coaches to do internships in England."
John Durant, *Yesterday in Sports* (New York: A. S. Barnes and Co.,
1956), 66.

There were a few occasions previous to the 1920 Olympic victory when the U.S. and British crews faced off, particularly at Henley,
with the American club victorious. But these victories were by
Harvard—who rowed a distinct American hybrid of the English
style—and once by Cornell, coached by the professional, Charles
Courtney, whose victory was considered questionable due to starting procedures, and who were soundly beaten the following day by
an unheralded Trinity Hall boat; see Halladay, *Rowing in England*,
110–11. These American wins therefore, are not seen to diminish the
luster of Glendon's "standard American style," Glendon, *Rowing*, 138.

7. "Navy Oarsmen chosen to Meet World's Best Crews Abroad," *Literary Digest* 66 (21 August 1920): 98.

8. "America's First Triumph," *New York Times*, 5 July 1914, sec. S, p. 1.

9. "America's First Triumph," *New York Times*, p. 1.

10. "Eastern Crews Come Fast as Season Grows," by Joe Williams, the
Glendon Collection.

11. Mendenhall, *A Short History of American Rowing*, 33.

12. Charles Van Patton Young, *Courtney and Cornell Rowing* (Ithaca,
N.Y.: Cornell Publication Printing, 1923), 31–32.

13. Mendenhall, *A Short History of American Rowing*, 30.

14. Mendenhall, *The Harvard-Yale Boat Race, 1852–1924*, 241.

15. Mendenhall, *A Short History of American Rowing*, 34.

16. Glendon, *Rowing*, 106.

17. Guy Nickalls, *Life's A Pudding: An Autobiography by Guy Nickalls
1866–1935*. (London: Faber and Faber, 1939), 229. The idea that the
British were warned of the 1920 Americans' speed was also supported by David Swann.

18. Susan Saint Sing, *The Complete Indoor Rowing Guide* (Stuart, Fl.: Arete Press, 2000) 13–28.

19. Glendon, *Rowing*, 97–109.

20. Ibid.

21. Ibid.

22. "Vincent Treanor Looks Them Over," *New York Evening World,* 14 June 1929, the Glendon Collection.

23. Glendon, *Rowing*, 122–25.

24. Ibid., 115.

25. The Glendon Collection.

26. Glendon, *Rowing,* 148–49.

27. This scalloped rim at the top of the gunnels was ingenious. It can be observed on close-up photographs of the Navy eight of 1920. "Navy Oarsmen Chosen to Meet World's Best Crews Abroad," *Literary Digest.*

8. The American Seasons of 1919–1920

1. "Navy Crew Fit For Race," *New York Times,* 5 April 1919, p. 30.

2. *Lucky Bag 1921: The Annual of the Regiment of Midshipmen,* by P. E. Phil, W. D. Johnson Jr. (Annapolis, Md.: The United States Naval Academy, 1921), 528.

3. The Glendon Collection.

4. "Navy Crew Fit for Race," *New York Times,* 5 April 1919, p. 30.

5. Ibid.

6. *Lucky Bag 1920,* 448.

7. "Navy's Crack Crew Beats Penn Easily," *New York Times,* 13 April 1919, p. 21.

8. "Varsity Oarsmen Fit for Hard Test," *New York Times,* 17 May 1919, p. 11.

9. Glendon, *Rowing,* 193.

10. "Navy Ready for Henley," *New York Times,* 30 May 1919, p. 15. This pertains to the American Henley, not the more famous English Henley.

11. "Navy Here with $65,000 to Bet on Crew; $13,000 Covered by Penn." The Glendon Collection.

12. Ibid.

13. Ibid.

14. This information was found in the *Race Program of the Fifteenth Annual Regatta of the American Rowing Association* in Box 2, "Regatta Programs 1914–1916, 1919–1925," Schuylkill Navy Archives, Independence Seaport Museum, Philadelphia.

15. Ibid., See also Glendon, *Rowing,* 193.

16. "Navy Crew Shows Heels to Quakers," *New York Times,* 1 June 1919, p. 21.

17. Dr. Walter Peet, "Annapolis Crew Declared to be by far the Best College Eight of the Season," *New York Times*, 8 June 1919, p. 28.

18. "Navy Oarsmen Chosen to Meet World's Best Crews Abroad," *Literary Digest* 66.

19. "Change in Navy Schedule," *New York Times,* 2 February 1920, p. 16.

20. *Lucky Bag 1921,* 532.

21. Ibid., 528.

22. "Navy Crews Quit Tank," *New York Times,* 13 March 1920, 21. Litchfield's name was omitted in the original article of 13 March, the name found in the *New York Times,* 27 April 1920, p. 7.

23. *Lucky Bag 1921,* 529.

24. Ibid., 530.

25. "Navy Oarsmen Easily Outrow Harvard Crews in Three Races on the Severn," *New York Times*, 27 April 1920, p. 11.

26. "Columbia Oarsmen At Work On Severn," *New York Times,* 7 May 1920, p. 13.

27. *Lucky Bag 1921,* 531.

28. Ibid., 531–32.

29. Ibid., 532.

30. *1920 Sixteenth Annual Regatta of the American Rowing Association* Box 2, Schuylkill Navy Archives.

31. Glendon, *Rowing,* 194.

9. The British Season of 1920

1. "Good Full Course Row by Cambridge," *Times* (London), 24 March 1920, p. 7, col. D.

2. "The Boat Race: Fast Row by Oxford," *Times* (London), 25 March 1920 p. 7, col. F.

3. "The Boat Race: Cambridge Row the Mile," *Times* (London), 26 March 1920, p. 5, col. D.

4. "Boat Race. Revival of a Great Event," *Times* (London), 27 March 1920, p. 15, col. G.

5. Ibid.

6. Ibid.

7. Ibid.

8. "Battles of the Blues: Cambridge First on the River," *Times* (London), 29 March 1920, p. 7, col. A.

9. Ibid.

10. Ibid.

11. The Glendon Collection.

10. The U.S. Olympic Trials

1. "Navy Crew Getting Ready," *New York Times*, 6 June 1920, p. 96.

2. "Comment on Current Events in Sport," *New York Times*, 26 July 1920, p. 16.

3. Glendon, *Rowing*, 194.

4. Ibid., 200.

5. Gustavus T. Kirby, "U.S. Government Supports U.S. Olympics," Walter Camp Papers, Box 50 "1908–1920." Yale University, Sterling Library; *New York Times*, 23 May 1920, p. 4, sec 8; *New York Tribune*, 5 June 1920 p.13; *New York Times*, 5 June 1920, p. 21.

6. Congressional Record, 59, part 5, 66th Congress, 2nd Session, p. 7511, 24 May 1920; 3 June 1920, p. 8303.

7. Ibid.

8. "Navy Will Retain Most of Its Crew," *New York Times*, 15 August 1920, p. 22.

9. "Lads from 7 States Compose Navy's Crew." This clipping from an unknown newspaper was inside the back cover of the "Official Program of the National Association of Amateur Oarsmen Forty-sixth Annual Regatta, Lake Quinsigamond, Worcester, Mass." This program is located in Box 2, Schuylkill Navy Archives.

10. Report of the Cruise of the USS *Frederick* to the Antwerp Olympics by W. Pitt Scott, to the Chief of Naval Operations 18 October 1920, State Dept. Records Division, Record Group 59, Foreign Relations Microfilm Files, National Archives and Record Administration II, College Park, Md.

11. Reports from the files (855.4063/5) of the Secretary of the Navy, 16 June 1920, indicate that the U.S. Ambassador and ministers of the Belgium government worked on special behalf of the Navy men onboard the USS *Frederick*, relative to other athletes being transported on Army vessels.

12. John Lucas. "American Preparations for the First Post War Olympic Games, 1919–1920." *Journal of Sport History*, Vol. 10 Number 2, 1983, p. 30–44.

13. Reports from the files (855.4063/5) of the Secretary of the Navy, 16 June 1920, indicate that the U.S. Ambassador and ministers of the Belgium government worked on special behalf of the Navy rowers

onboard the USS *Frederick*. Numerous correspondences from the Department of the Navy and the State Department in the weeks proceeding the Navy crew departure indicate the special handling and nature of their transport relative to other athletes being transported on Army vessels. See also *New York Herald Tribune* on 7 August 1920, "U.S. Olympic Athletes Threaten to Go on Strike: Dissatisfied with accommodations . . ." and "Navy Olympic Team Arrives in Antwerp in Good Condition."

14. Edward R. Bushnell, "Clubmen May Get Places on the Olympic Team," *Pittsburgh Press,* 6 June 1920, sec. sports, p. 6.

15. "Olympiad to Start Soon," under the Ralph Davis column. *Pittsburgh Press,* 8 July 1920, p. 20.

11 The Crossing

1. USS *Frederick* Log, National Archives, Washington, D.C. See also the Glendon Collection.

2. The America's Cup history of naval design and architecture is intertwined with the U.S. Navy as well as American pride. There are many references but please see online: http://en.wikipedia.org/wiki/America's_Cup. Accessed 2006.

3. Newspaper photograph of Muriel Vanderbilt at the Army-Navy Game in both the Sanborn and Jacomini Collections.

4. From the chapbook *USS* Frederick *Olympic Cruise: August–September 1920*. Two descendants of the 1920 crew mentioned in their interviews that their relatives met with and dined with the Vanderbilts. This is possible since the Vanderbilts lived in Newport and were noted yachtsmen and equestrians.

5. USS *Frederick* Log, p. 59.

6. Navy Dept., letter, 5 May 1920. National Archives file 28550–1319:11. Also page 56–57 USS *Frederick* Log.

7. USS *Frederick* Log, p. 61.
8. Ironically, Glendon's grandson Tommy and a school chum, years after the 1920 Olympics, would be lost at sea, unable to row against an outgoing tide and an offshore breeze. They were last seen by the Lightship *Stone Horse*.
9. The name "Daisy" from a personal phone interview with Country Moore's daughter Barbara Finch, Winter Park, Florida, October 4, 2006.
10. From a personal correspondence of Victor Jacomini, "Atlantic Ocean, 1 August, 1920." The Jacomini Collection.
11. Ibid.
12. From a personal interview with Beverly Jacomini.
13. In the interviews with the various families and the articles of the Glendon Collection and the Ship's Log, a one hundred-piece band was on board to keep the athletes at ease. In this unique circumstance the Navy Olympians were passengers onboard, not part of the crew.
14. From the chapbook *USS* Frederick *Olympic Cruise: August– September 1920.*
15. Coach Glendon eliminated as many variables as he could from training. He controlled the training table diet and the overall welfare of his rowers—emotionally and physically—as much as he could. This quotation on routine was not uttered by Dick Glendon in 1920 but in 1993 by a U.S. rowing coach at the World Rowing Championships in the Czech Republic.
16. USS *Frederick* Log and the Glendon Collection.
17. From a personal interview with Oz Sanborn.
18. From personal correspondence of Victor Jacomini. The Jacomini Collection.
19. From personal interviews with the Moore and Johnston families.
20. From personal interviews with Duncan and Eileen Glendon.

21. USS *Frederick* Log, p. 61.

22. USS *Frederick* Log, p. 74.

23. According to the USS *Frederick* Log and personal correspondence from Victor Jacomini, the crossing was relatively calm, with more placid days than rough. They encountered one storm and rough weather nearing England.

24. Ibid.

25. From personal interviews with the families of the U.S. 1920 crew. After the Olympic games this crew kept close contact and correspondence, more like a family than schoolmates, until their deaths.

26. From Glendon's post-Olympic speech. The Glendon Collection.

27. From Glendon's post-Olympic speech. The Glendon Collection.

28. The Glendon Collection.

29. From a personal interview with Steve Woodall.

30. From a personal interview with Terese Glendon, Sister Mary of the Pure Heart.

31. The Jacomini Collection.

32. From personal correspondence of Victor Jacomini.

33. The Leander crew stayed and practiced at Henley for weeks longer while the Americans were at sea. Leander Crew log, Leander Rowing Club Archives, Henley-on-Thames.

34. Newspaper accounts verify that there was much interest in the whereabouts of the American crew during the crossing. See "Naval and Military Intelligence" *Times,* 17 June 1920, p. 16.

35. Though the actual words of the Captain to the crew and Olympians is lost, this speech is a collection of pre-rowing talks between a nationally ranked coach and her crews.

36. Richard Woodman and Jane Wilson, *The Lighthouses of Trinity House* (United Kingdom: Thomas Reed Publications, 2002).

37. The Glendon Collection.

38. Available from the Internet, http://www.trinityhouse.co.uk/
    interactive/gallery/dungeness.html. Accessed 2006. See also Richard
    Woodman and Jane Wilson, *The Lighthouses of Trinity House* (United
    Kingdom: Thomas Reed Publications, 2002).
39. USS *Frederick* Log, p. 82.
40. From the Glendon Collection.
41. From the Glendon Collection. Note: To fit the text, the tense of
    this has been modified but not the context.

12. 1920 Henley and Leander

1. *Punch,* 26 June 1907.
2. "Naval and Military Intelligence," *Times* (London), 17 June 1920, p 16.
3. Available from the Internet, http://www.arlingtoncemetery.net/
   flanders.htm. Accessed 2006.
4. "The Olympic Games. Royal Appeal to Sportsmen, Funds for
   British" *Times* (London), 25 June 1920, p. 18.
5. Ibid.
6. Ibid.
7. Ibid.
8. Richard Burnell and Geoffrey Page, *The Brilliants: A History of the
   Leander Club* (Great Britain: Leander Club and Bath, 1997), 98.

13. Cutting Down

1. Rowing, "The Leander Crew at Henley," 16 Aug 1920, *Times* (London), p. 5.
2. Ibid.
3. Ibid.
4. Information about the Swan Marker, the Swan Warden and the
   Coxswain during Swan Upping Days is available on the Internet,
   http://www.thamesweb.co.uk/windsor/windsor1999/upping.html.
   Accessed 2007.

5. Burnell, *The Brilliants*, 201.

6. Ian Buchanan, *British Olympians* (Middlesex: Guinness Publications 1991), 63.

7. Ibid.

8. G. O. Nickalls, *A Rainbow in the Sky* (London: Chatto and Windus, 1974), 9.

9. Ibid.

10. Henry Bond, *A History of the Trinity Hall Boat Club* (Cambridge: Heffer and Sons, 1930).

11. Personal interview with David Swann and telephone interview with Sue Swann.

12. Buchanan, *British Olympic Champions*, 9.

13. The Jacomini Collection; see also the Glendon Collection and Buchanan, *British Olympians*.

14. "Battles of the Blues: Cambridge First on the River" *The Times*, 29 March 1920, p. 7, col. A.

15. G. O. Nickalls and P. C. Mallam, *Rowing* (London: Pitman, 2nd Edition 1952), 168.

16. Ibid., 166.

17. Ibid.

18. Ibid., 167. Quoted to reflect conversation.

19. From the Cambridge University Boat Club log, Archives, Cambridge University, England.

20. This information was related by David Swann about his father. It was not uncommon for students of Cambridge or Oxford to go to America to coach as an assistant to Yale or Harvard crews while carrying on their studies. Interviews indicate that Nickalls and Swann most likely both had done this.

21. From the coaching notes of S. M. Bruce in the private collection of David Swann.

22. P. Haig-Thomas and M. A. Nicholson, *The English Style of Rowing* (London: Faber and Faber), 126.
23. Ibid.

14. Vilvoorde

1. The Glendon Collection.
2. Ibid.
3. Ibid., "Notes on the Olympic Trip."
4. Eric J. Hobsawn, *Nations and Nationalism since 1780: Programme, Myth, Reality.* Second Edition, (Cambridge: Cambridge University Press, 1990), 143. Hobsbawn discusses the idea of the imagined community where sport events in particular bond groups through a spirit of nationalism.
5. "American Scullers Win in Antwerp," *Atlanta Constitution,* 30 August 1920, Sports p. 7.
6. "Navy Eight-Oared Crew Win at Brussels," *Washington Post,* August 30, 1920, p. 8. See also, "U.S. Navy Crew Sets Record in Olympic Victory" *New York Herald Tribune,* 30 August, 1920 p. 1 and 11.
7. From the *Field* as cited in Mallon, *The 1920 Olympic Games,* 223.
8. Renson, *The Games Reborn,* 21–22.
9. From a clipping "Rowing: the Leander Crew at Henley" in the scrapbook of S. Earl at The River and Rowing Museum, Henley-on-Thames.
10. *With the Skin of Their Teeth: Memories of Great Sporting Finishes.* Contributors: Bernard Darwin, Hernert Sutcliffe, C. Gadney, Bernard Joy, John Olliff, Barrington Dalby, Harold Abrahams, G. O. Nickalls, Geoffrey Gilbey (London: Country Life Limited, 1951). Additional information about the English crew having to pick up their boat from the railroad siding two miles away and the United States going to help them with their lorry is from a personal

interview with David Swann, at his home in Cambridge, England, 28 August 2006.

11. The Jacomini Collection, 10 August 1920.

12. The Jacomini Collection, personal correspondence from Victor Jacomini to his parents, 11 August 1920.

13. From the *Lucky Bag 1922* account of the Olympic Trip and boatman Chandler.

14. Ibid.

15. Susan Saint Sing, "Crewing the Limits of Endurance," *Cincinnati Magazine*, 18, no. 12, p. 19. September 1985.

15. Opening Ceremony

1. Bill Mallon and Anthony Th. Bijkerk, *The 1920 Olympic Games: Results for All Competitors In All Events, With Commentary* (Jefferson, N.C.: McFarland, 2003), 5.

2. Renson, *The Games Reborn,* 33. See also, Mallon, *The 1920 Olympic Games*, 8.

3. Available on the Internet, http://www.timesolympics.co.uk/historyheroes/historyant1920.html. Accessed 2006.

4. There are many references to the participants of the Antwerp Olympics including Renson, *The Games Reborn,* and Mallon, *The 1920 Olympics.*

5. Mallon, *The 1920 Olympic Games,* 6–7.

6. "The Olympic Games of Antwerp: Formal Opening by King Albert," *Times* (London), 16 August 1920 p. 9 Col. F.

7. Ibid. See also Mallon, *The 1920 Olympic Games.*

8. Ibid.

16. Heats and Semis

1. "These Guys Have Both Oars in the Water," *Tristate Magazine,* 8 June 1986, 4–11. Some images from the Cincinnati regatta

were added to this article to augment the ambience of the 1920 racing.

2. Ibid.

3. Glendon, *Rowing,* 202.

4. *The Rowing Almanack and Oarsman's Companion,* Leander Club Archives, 1921, p. 120. Similar information can be found in Glendon, *Rowing,* Mallon, *The 1920 Olympics,* and *The Report of the American Olympic Committee.*

5. "The Olympic Games: British Rowing Success" *Times* (London), 28 August 1920, sec. Sporting News, p. 6.

6. *The Rowing Almanack and Oarsman's Companion,* Leander Club Archives, 1921, p. 119–20.

7. Ibid.

17. The Olympic Race

1. "Annapolis Men set Record in Olympic Victory." *New York Tribune,* 30 August 1920, p. 11.

2. The Jacomini Collection. Personal letter from Lt. Clement Jacomini to Victor, 12 May 1918.

3. *The Rowing Almanack and Oarsman's Companion,* Leander Club Archives, 1921, p. 118–120.

4. From research by Lucy Lomas, photograph of a painted oar in possession of Robin Swann, grandson of S. E. Swann, with list of Cambridge U. Crew, including R. S. Shove, at six seat, dated 1913.

5. This quote from the 1850s is widely cited. It refers to the defeat of the Royal Yacht Squadron by the *America,* whose sail was seen coming first, to win the race from the British. The sailing competition, the America's Cup, is named after this sailboat.

6. From the personal reflection of Dwight Phillips, coxswain of a four-with in the 1970 World Games in St. Catherines, Ontario,

Canada; The USA Men's Heavyweight Eight for the 1971 Pan Am Games in Cali, Columbia, and Men's Pair-with in the 1973 World Games in Moscow, Russia.

7. The Glendon Collection.
8. Ibid.
9. Burnell, *The Brilliants*, 101.
10. The Glendon Collection.
11. Glendon, *Rowing*, 209.
12. *Lucky Bag 1921,* 325
13. *The Report of the American Olympic Committee*, 164.
14. Ibid.
15. The Glendon Collection.
16. *The Rowing Almanack and Oarsman's Companion,* Leander Club, 1921. p. 18–20.
17. *The Report of the American Olympic Committee,* 164
18. *Lucky Bag 1921,* 322.
19. The Glendon Collection.

18. A Radical Turn of Events

1. "Defeat of Britain in the Eights," *Times* (London), 30 August 1920, sec. Sporting News, p. 5.
2. "Navy Eight-Oared Crew Win at Brussels," *Washington Post*, 30 August 1920, p. 8. Interestingly, the press coverage of the exact distances in the race were seemingly played up by the Americans and played down by the British coverage—the Americans won by more in the U.S. press and the British lost by less in the British press, reflecting nationalistic pride issues on both sides.
3. Glendon, *Rowing,* 207.
4. "Navy Eight-Oared Crew Win at Brussels," *Washington Post*, 30 August 1920, p. 8.

5. "Belgian King to Present Olympic Medals To-Day," *New York Tribune,* 30 August 1920, p.11.

6. Many newspapers across the United States (other than the New York and Washington papers mentioned previously) covered Navy's win; for example, *Atlanta Constitution,* 30 August 1920, p. 7, and also the *Los Angeles Times,* 30 August 1920, p. 8.

7. "Annapolis Men Set Record in Olympic Victory," *New York Tribune,* 30 August 1920, p. 11. Note, there were discrepancies over the actual finish times of the two crews.

8. *Annual Reports of the Navy Department: For the Fiscal Year 1920* (Washington: Government Printing Office, 1921), 117–119.

9. "Secretary Daniels Cables his congratulations to Navy Crew," *New York Times,* 1 September 1920, p. 11.

10. From the scrapbook of Earl in an unknown clipping: "Rowing Notes: the Olympic Regatta. Our Two Defeats," River and Rowing Museum, Henley-on-Thames, England.

11. Ibid.

12. "Army Congratulates Navy," *New York Times,* 2 September 1920, p. 10.

13. Ibid.

14. "Crew Coach Is Honored," *New York Times,* 2 December 1920, p.18.

15. Ibid.

16. J. G. Ware, "What the Navy Did at Antwerp," *The American Olympic Committee Report, Seventh Olympic Games Antwerp, Belgium 1920* (Greenwich, Conn.: Conde Nast Press, 1920), 97–98.

17. Ibid.

18. Letter from the National Association of Amateur Oarsmen, the Glendon Collection.

19. "English to Adopt U.S. Crew Style," the Glendon Collection.

20. Ibid.

21. This description by Pitman of the race was found in a newspaper

clipping in Earl's Scrapbook at The River and Rowing Museum, Henley-on-Thames, England.

22. *With the Skin of Their Teeth: Memories of Great Sporting Finishes.* Bernard Darwin, Hernert Sutcliffe, C. Gadney, Bernard Joy, John Olliff, Barrington Dalby, Harold Abrahams, G. O. Nickalls, Geoffrey Gilbey (London: Country Life Limited, 1951).

23. Private interview with David Swann.

24. "Olympic Games Heroes Parade On 5th Avenue," *New York Herald Tribune,* 3 October 1920, p. 17.

25. Ibid.

26. Mendenhall, *A Short History of American Rowing,* 120–21.

27. Mendenhall, *The Harvard-Yale Boat Race*, 332. The vote to hire Glendon was eventually decided on personal issues. Yale snubbed Glendon and hired a young, personal friend of their crew's captain, coach Oscar Edward Leander, who had been beaten by lengths of open water by Navy.

28. Robert Seager II, *Alfred Thayer Mahan: The Man and His Letters* (Annapolis: Naval Institute Press, 1977), 207.

29. Glendon, *Rowing,* 193–94.

30. Mendenhall, *The Harvard-Yale Boat Race*, 271.

31. Ibid., 331.

32. Glendon, *Rowing,* 136–38.

33. Mendenhall, *The Harvard-Yale Boat Race,* 331.

34. "Harvard Crews Will Be Coached by Dick Glendon," the Glendon collection.

35. C. L. R. James, *Beyond a Boundary* (Durham: Duke University Press, 1993; orig. 1963), 220–21.

36. John Marshall Carter and Arnd Kruger, editors, *Ritual and Records: Sports Records and Quantification in Pre-Modern Societies* (Westport, Conn.: Greenwood Press, 1990), 3; Allen Guttmann, *From Ritual to*

Record: The Nature of Modern Sports (New York: Columbia University Press, 1978), 50; Richard D. Mandell, "The Invention of the Sports Record," *Stadion II*, (1976), 251.

37. James, *Beyond a Boundary*.
38. The Glendon Collection.

19. The Longest Streak

1. Gordon Newell, *Ready All!* (Seattle: University of Washington Press, 1987), 73.
2. Charles W. Paddock, *"East Vs. West at Poughkeepsie,"* 23 June 1929, the Glendon Collection.
3. Frederick Lewis Allen, *Only Yesterday* (New York: Harper and Row, 1946), 102.
4. Loren Barritz, *The Culture of the Twenties* (Indianapolis and New York: The Bobbs-Merrill Company, 1970), xvi–liii.
5. Turner, *Rereading Frederick Jackson Turner.* For further reading, Roderick Nash, writing in the 1970s in *The Nervous Generation: American Thought, 1917–1930* (Chicago: Rand McNally, 1970), states that while A. A. Brill did not openly say there was a relationship between the Turnerism loss of the frontier and the rise of American sports craze, Brill's arguments support this thesis.
6. A. A. Brill, "The Why of the Fan," *North American Review* 228, (October 1929): 429–34.
7. Bruce J. Evensen, *When Dempsey Fought Tunney*, xi.
8. Ibid., 48.
9. Ibid., 51.
10. Michael Oriard, *King Football: Sport and Spectacle in the Golden Age of Radio and Newsreels, Movies and Magazines, the Weekly and the Daily Press* (Chapel Hill: University of North Carolina Press, 2001), 7.

11. Robert Sklar, *Movie-Made America: A Cultural History of American Movies* (New York: Vintage Books, 1994), 121.

12. Ronald A. Smith, *Sports and Freedom: The Rise of Big-Time College Athletics* (New York: Oxford University Press, 1988), 4.

13. There are myriad sources on Thomas Eakins's rowing paintings. One example of his painting is "John Biglin in a Single Scull" at Yale University Art Gallery: Whitney Collections of Sporting Art, New Haven, CT. See also Darrell Sewell, *Thomas Eakins* (New Haven: Yale University Press, 2002).

14. Evensen, *When Dempsey Fought Tunney*, 51.

15. Ibid., 50.

16. Michael Oriard, *King Football* (Chapel Hill: University of North Carolina Press, 2001), 7.

17. Ellen Galford, *Olympic Century: The Official History of the Modern Olympic Movement*, vol. 10 (Los Angeles: World Sport and Research Pub., 1997), 34.

18. "U.S. Navy Sets Record in Olympic Victory," *New York Herald Tribune,* 30 Aug. 1920, p. 11.

19. Video Recording (Universal Newsreel Vol. II, No. 52); "Cornell Oarsmen Win Intercollegiate Championship Crown," 27 June 1930; Records of the U.S. Information Agency, Special Media Group; National Archives at College Park, Md. (hereafter NA II). As a special note regarding the Universal Newsreels, those viewed are in the National Archives in Washington, D.C. They are kept on VHS and 3/4-inch tape. It is recommended to use the index to locate the film, then follow the cities and subjects along through the footage to find the desired segment. While tedious, the minutes are not reliable due to film footage being damaged, miscalculated, etc.

See also, Richard A. and Richard J. Glendon, *Rowing*, insert front cover. The photograph sections riddle the text but are not numbered, showing the crowds along the banks and lining the course in canoes, steamships, platforms, etc.

20. Video Recording (Universal Newspaper Newsreel Vol. V, No. 161); "Washington Crew Wins Title," 10 July 1933; NA II.

21. Ibid. (Live radio broadcasts of rowing, such as Ted Husing's at the Olympic trials in 1932, were cumbersome at best when covering the 2,000-meter distance: they necessitated stationing a man at the start and another a half-mile away relaying the information to WABC. See "Harvard Crew's Arrival Completes Field of Nine for Olympic Trials Opening Today," *New York Times*, 7 July 1932, sec. Sports, p. 21.)

22. Video Recording (Universal Newspaper Newsreel Vol. IX, No. 565); "Yale 8 Takes Carnegie Cup," 24 May 1937; NA II.

23. Universal Newsreel, of the twenty-four news clips in the 1930s relating to crew, only four related directly to the West Coast Championships.

24. The newsreels covered FDR, Jr. both as a freshman rower, and as a senior against Navy. Video Recording (Universal Newspaper Newsreel Vol. VI, No. 261); "President Sees Yale Crews Defeat Harvard in Regatta," 25 June 1934, and Vol. X, No. 669, "Harvard wins Adams Claim," 23 May 1938. NA II.

25. In Glendon, *Rowing*, the book is riddled with photos in the classic portrait style of a rower holding an upright oar in his hand.

26. Jim Lemmon, *The Log of Rowing at the University of California. Berkeley 1870–1987* (Berkeley, CA: Western Heritage Press, 1987), 7, 15, 19.

27. "Favorites to Win Varsity Race in Poughkeepsie Regatta," the Glendon Collection.

28. Newell, *Ready All!*, 73.

29. American Olympic Committee. *American Olympic Committee Report, Ninth Olympic Games* (New York, 1928), 259.

30. The Poughkeepsie National Intercollegiate Regatta was always held the third weekend in June. For example, coverage of the event can be viewed in Video Recording (Universal Newspaper Newsreel); Vol. IV, No. 51; "California Oarsmen Sweep to Victory in Collegiate Regatta," 20 June 1932; and Vol. VI, No. 259; "California Crew Triumphs in Championship Regatta," 18 June 1934; and Vol. VII, No. 364; "California Crew Noses Out Cornell to Win Fast Race," 19 June 1935; and Vol. XI, No. 787; "Golden Bears Win Crew Race," 19 June 1939; NA II.

31. "Compton Cup and Connibear," *Time*, 3 May 1927, 41. See also, Lucas and Smith, *Saga of American Sports*, 243, for a brief look at the Big Three and football.

32. The Hudson River School of landscape painters was largely an eighteenth- and nineteenth-century trend and is considered America's first and exclusive school. See John Driscoll, *John Frederick Kensett, An American Master* (New York: Norton, 1985) and his *All That is Glorious Around the United States: Paintings of the Hudson River School* (Ithaca: Cornell University Press, 1997).

33. Video Recording (Universal Newspaper Newsreel Vol. X, No. 669); "Harvard Wins Adams Claim," 23 May 1938; NA II.

34. Galford, *Olympic Century*, 34.

35. Video Recording (Universal Newspaper Newsreel Vol. IV, No. 67); "World Athletes Hit Whirlwind Pace as Olympics Near End," 15 August 1932; NA II.

36. Ibid., and Glendon, *Rowing*, photograph insert front cover.

37. "Crews on the Hudson" 17 June 1939, the Glendon Collection. See also the *New York Times* Sunday Picture Section, 19 May 1929.

38. Video Recording (Universal Newspaper Newsreel Vol. X, No. 679); "Harvard Oarsmen Beat Yale," 27 June 1938; NA II.

39. Newell, *Ready All!*, 71. (Harvard, Yale, and Princeton did not compete at Poughkeepsie, as snobbishness of the Big Three extended from the gridiron to the river waters. See also *Saga of American Sports* by John A. Lucas and Ronald A. Smith (Philadelphia: Lea and Febriger, 1978), 243. These schools did not stop the West Coast's dominance as the West won both the 1932 and 1936 Olympic trials.

40. Newell, *Ready All!*, 71.

41. Thomas Mendenhall, *The Harvard-Yale Boat Race, 1852–1924* (Mystic, Connecticut: Mystic Seaport Press, 1993), 333.

42. "Unstarred Rowing Crew Champions," *Literary Digest* 122 (25 July 1936), 33.

43. Robert Harron, "Don't Rush Your Slides Boys, Huskies at Play," the Glendon Collection.

44. George Russell, *Olympic Century: The Official History of the Modern Olympic Movement,* vol. 9 (Los Angeles: World Sport and Research Pub. Inc., 1999), 34–36.

45. Ibid.

46. Harron, "'Don't Rush Your Slides Boys."

47. Ibid.

48. Russell, *Olympic Century*, vol. 9 (1999), 34–35.

49. Video Recording (Universal Newspaper Newsreel Vol. IV, No. 67); "World Athletes Hit Whirlwind Pace as Olympics Near End," 15 August 1932; NA II.

50. Robert Kelley, "Columbia, Cal, Penn AC and Yale Gain in Olympic Crew Tests," *New York Times,* 8 July 1932, sec. 3 Sports, p. 12.

51. Ibid.

52. "Harvard Crew's Arrival Completes Field of Nine for Olympic Trials Opening Today," *New York Times,* 7 July 1932, sec. S, p. 21.

53. Robert Kelley, "California Eight Defeats Penn AC: Sets Course Mark," *New York Times,* 10 July 1932, Sec. 3 Sports, p.1–3.

54. "Penn Crews Make Grand Slam," *Los Angeles Times*, 5 July 1932, Section II, p. 10.

55. Ibid, *Los Angeles Times*, p. 2.

56. Victor O. Jones, "Bears Reach Finals of Crew Tryouts," *Los Angeles Times*, 9 July 1932, sec. I, p. 5.

57. Victor O. Jones. "Californians Qualify for Olympic Battles," *Los Angeles Times,* 10 July 1932, sec. VI, p. 1.

58. Ralph Huston, "Bears Nose Out Close Crew Victory," *Los Angeles Times,* 14 Aug. 1932, part VI, p. 1.

59. Lemmon, *The Log of Rowing,* 26.

60. Ibid.

61. Stanley H. Howard, "Mr. Callow Takes on the West," *Literary Digest* 119 (15 June 1935), 32.

62. "Brawn Wins at Poughkeepsie," *Literary Digest* 119 (June 29, 1935), 35.

63. Video Recording (Universal Newspaper Newsreel Vol. VIII, No. 476); "Olympic Team Departs," July 15, 1936; NA II.

64. George Constable, *Olympic Century*, Vol. 11 (1996), 75.

65. Lemmon, *The Log of Rowing*, 25.

66. Ibid., 27.

67. Ibid., 27–29.

68. Video Recording (Universal Newsreel Vol. X, No. 669); "Harvard Wins Adams Claim," 23 May 1938; NA II.

69. Video Recording (Universal Newspaper Newsreel Vol. X, No.680); "Navy Crew Wins on Hudson," 29 June 1938; NA II.

70. Video Recording (Universal Newspaper Newsreel Vol. XI, No. 787); "Golden Bears Win Crew Race," 19 June 1939; NA II.

71. Lemmon, *The Log of Rowing*, 113.

72. Ted Smits, "Naiads Win but Trackmen and Crew Fail; Russia Near Title" *Philadelphia Inquirer*, 4 September 1960, p. 1.

73. "Navy Eight Gains Olympic Final As Five U.S. Crews Advance," *New York Times,* 3 September 1960, p. 11.

74. "Germany's Eight Wins; Navy Fifth," *New York Tribune,* 4 September 1960, sec. 3, p. 1.

75. Video Recording (Universal Newspaper Newsreel), Olympic coverage of 1932 can be found on Vol. IV No. 63; "Inspiring Rites Mark Colorful Opening of 10th Olympic Games," 1 August 1932; and Vol. IV, No. 66; "U.S. Athletes Add to Overwhelming Lead in Xth Olympic Games," 11 August 1932; and Vol. IV, No. 67; "World Athletes Hit Whirlwind Pace as Olympics Near End," 15 August 1932; and Vol. IV, No 68. "Final Curtain Falls in Blaze of Glory on Olympic Games of 1932," 18 August 1932. Olympic coverage for the 1936 preparations and return parade are found in Vol. VIII No. 476; "U.S. Olympic Team Departs," 15 July 1936 ; and 17 August 1936 Vol. VIII No. 485; "U.S. Athletes Eclipse All Rivals in Olympic Competition," 17 August 1936; and Vol. VIII, No. 484, "Americans Win Early Lead as 11th Olympic Games Open," 10 August 1936; NA II.

76. Video Recording (Universal Newspaper Newsreel Vol. VIII, No. 476); "U.S. Olympic Team Departs," 15 July 1936, NA II.

77. "Forth to War: America's Athletes Take Ship for Berlin Olympic Games," *Literary Digest* 122 (11 July 1936), 33.

78. Video Recording (Universal Newspaper Newsreel), Olympic coverage of 1932 can be found on Vol. IV No. 63; "Inspiring Rites Mark Colorful Opening of 10th Olympic Games," 1 August 1932; and Vol. IV, No. 66; "U.S. Athletes Add to Overwhelming Lead in Xth Olympic Games," 11 August 1932; and Vol. IV, No. 67; "World Athletes Hit Whirlwind Pace as Olympics Near End," 15 August 1932;

and Vol. IV, No 68. "Final Curtain Falls in Blaze of Glory on Olympic Games of 1932," 18 August 1932. Olympic coverage for the 1936 preparations and return parade are found in Vol. VIII No. 476; "U.S. Olympic Team Departs," 15 July 1936; and 17 August 1936 Vol. VIII No. 485; "U.S. Athletes Eclipse All Rivals in Olympic Competition," 17 August 1936; and Vol. VIII, No. 484, "Americans Win Early Lead as 11th Olympic Games Open," 10 August 1936; NA II.

Epilogue

1. Mallon, *The 1920 Olympic Games,* 228. See also Bill Mallon and Ian Buchanan, *Quest For Gold: The Encyclopedia of American Olympians* (New York: Leisure Press, 1984), 171–86.
2. "Glendons, Famous Rowing Coaches," *Harwich Independent,* 10 August 1932, the Glendon Collection.
3. "Surprise Victor in Four-Mile Varsity Race Big Feature of Regatta at Poughkeepsie," *Boston Globe,* 17 June 1931 and "Father and Son Rival Crew Coaches," the Glendon Collection.
4. "Giving his Son Some Counsel on Coaching a Winning Crew," the Glendon Collection. This article is of interest because it shows both Glendons side by side with a megaphone in the coaches' launch. See also, "Old Dick Glendon to Coach Columbia," the Glendon Collection.
5. "Tommy," the Glendon Collection.
6. "New Glendon Saga Starts," from the Glendon Collection.
7. The Glendon Collection.
8. Ibid.
9. Ibid.
10. Ibid.
11. Ibid., "Glendon Rowing Legend," by George Carens.

12. "Obituaries," *Time: The Weekly Magazine,* 23 July 1956, 82.

13. From the Gallagher Collection in a newspaper clipping from a personal scrapbook entitled "Three Maryland Heroes Reach World Perfection."

14. Mendenhall, *The Harvard-Yale Boat Race,* 343.